Trust to Talk

Wynford Vaughan-Thomas

HUTCHINSON

London Melbourne Sydney Auckland Johannesburg

To Charlotte

Hutchinson & Co. (Publishers) Ltd

An imprint of the Hutchinson Publishing Group

3 Fitzroy Square, London W1P 6JD

Hutchinson Group (Australia) Pty Ltd
30–32 Cremorne Street, Richmond South, Victoria 3121
P O Box 151, Broadway, New South Wales 2007

Hutchinson Group (N Z) Ltd
32–34 View Road, P O Box 40-086, Glenfield, Auckland 10

Hutchinson Group (SA) Pty Ltd
P O Box 337, Bergvlei 2012, South Africa

First Published 1980

© Wynford Vaughan-Thomas 1980

Set in VIP Sabon by D. P. Media Limited, Hitchin, Hertfordshire

Printed in Great Britain by The Anchor Press Ltd,
and bound by Wm Brendon & Son Ltd,
both of Tiptree, Essex

British Library Cataloguing in Publication Data

Vaughan-Thomas, Wynford
  Trust to Talk.
  1. Vaughan-Thomas, Wynford
  2. Broadcasters – Great Britain – Biography
  I. Title
  384.54′092′4   PN1990.72.V/

ISBN 0 09 143890 5

Contents

Illustrations   6

Prologue   7

1   Edwardian Childhood   9
2   Growing Up in Swansea   39
3   Oxford and the Hills   73
4   Struggling Through the Depression   93
5   Learning the Trade at the B B C   125
6   War Report   143
7   Ends of an Era   188
8   The Ones That Got Away   213

    Envoi: Back to the Beginnings   231

Illustrations

1 The author's father, Dr David Vaughan-Thomas
2 The author's mother, Morfydd Vaughan-Thomas
3 Aunty Bess in the Centre of the family group, 1919
4 The top form at Terrace Road School, 1919
5 A group of fellow students at Exeter College, 1927
6 As forward in the Exeter College hockey XI, 1929
7 Climbing on Glyder Fach, North Wales, 1930
8 The start of a commentator's career
9 W. V.-T. with Field Marshal Alexander at Montegufoni, 1944
10 A briefing on the Anzio beachhead, 1944
11 Broadcasting from Lord Haw-Haw's microphone, 1945
12 Wedding day, January 1946
13 David watching his father on the screen
14 The flat in Hampstead
15 At Buckingham Palace
16 Walking the Roof of Wales, 1958
17 Received into the Gorsedd at the National Eisteddfod, 1974

The line drawings which appear throughout the text are rough jottings taken from the author's own diaries and notebooks

Prologue

On a chill winter's day in January 1944, I found myself in wartime Naples, waiting to be sent off on a highly secret mission – a major landing to outflank the Germans in Italy – about which half the inhabitants of Naples seemed already to be better informed than I was. Hadn't I just left a bookshop where I had enquired for a good guide to the country of mid-Italy and Rome? The bookseller was more than helpful. He produced the perfect book and, putting his finger to the side of his nose in that gesture with which a Neapolitan indicates he is a man in the know, he said, 'You will find this most useful. I can thoroughly recommend the section on Anzio.' After that, I felt I needed something sensational to distract the mind.

I opened the book. It was written in that weird English which is a Neapolitan tourist speciality. My eye caught the entry, '*I Campi Flegrei*'. 'A zone eminently vulcanized,' said my guide. 'See the Solfatara, with its fumarole jetting the hot water and its mud where you can carelessly lose a leg. Guide provided. Marco Twain, American travel writer, tells us, "The Solfatara is a fore-casting of the Inferno." ' This seemed just the thing for me as I waited to join the assault at Anzio. I got a jeep and presented myself at the entrance gate to this 'temple of the Infernal Gods'.

The aged guide was delighted to see me. 'You are Inglese. All the Americans they go to Vesuvio, but here, in the Solfatara, you can see all vulcanismo in perfect safety, if you follow my footsteps implicity. The Solfatara shall be yours.'

The Solfatara is the shallow crater of a long extinct volcano, rather a small volcano by the look of it, and the cindery rim of the crater is not particularly high. The glimpse of Hell you are promised in the guide book doesn't seem so impressive when you enter the Inferno through a lane in a housing estate. The Solfatara, to me, bore a suspicious resemblance to the burning coal tip at Tondu in one of the mining valleys of South Wales. My guide led me enthusiastically forward. We peered into the smoking fumaroles. We admired the spouting hot water. We moved gingerly towards a seemingly innocuous level plain. My guide stopped me with a dramatic gesture. 'Do not move one small step onward, signor. Here the earth has turned into a traitor. How innocent is looks. Ah, how perilous it is. I, alone, know from long experience where to walk in safety.'

'I will follow your footstep implicitly,' I assured him.

'You are wise. Thus the great Dante came safely through Hell by following the steps of Virgilio! How foolish the American professore who says he knows better than me. Signor, he came here before the war. He is expert in vulcanismo, he says. I warn him, but he knows better. He tells me, "I can tell exactly if it is firm or not. I have visited a hundred volcanoes. I am expert." He step forward, and signor, his left leg slips in and he burns it half off.'

My guide paused impressively and drew the moral from this sad story of transatlantic pig-headedness. 'You are a young man. I give you this advice. Is not life itself like the Solfatara? How safe if you stay on the outside! How dangerous if you try to go to the centre! And if you must venture towards the centre' – and here he held his hand at a receptive angle – 'make certain you have a good guide.'

I gave the delightful old rascal a hundred lire in Amgot money and went off to my own private Inferno – the Anzio beachhead. Ever since then, he's had me puzzled. Perhaps he was right. Happiness may lie on the safety of the perimeter. And yet, what a lot you lose if you don't take a few risks. I sit down to write the story of my life, and I see very clearly the pattern it has taken: it's the story of how I wandered in happy ignorance over the Solfatara and, with no justice at all, came out safely on the other side. And if there's one thing that brought me to safety, it was Talk.

CHAPTER ONE

Edwardian Childhood

Talk, the Divine Amalgam that holds civilization together, the lovely whitewash of words poured over the asperities of life to make them bearable! The arrival of radio in the 1920s brought it back into fashion after a long Victorian and Edwardian eclipse by the printed word, and I was lucky enough to be on hand when the BBC nursed the new medium out of the swaddling clothes of scripts into the free speech of commentary. Luckier still to be born in a country, Wales, where talk is a national industry. In England the man who talks easily is under suspicion – 'Opens his mouth too much. Don't trust him.' In Wales, matters are reversed – 'Doesn't say much. Wonder what he's thinking behind our backs!'

I was born in 1908 in Swansea in South Wales; Dylan Thomas's 'ugly lovely town', where no one ever underestimated the power of talk. I was thus some years older than Dylan but the old town I knew seemed to spend its time rehearsing for his arrival. All his characters were already assembled. The heart of old Swansea was badly blitzed during the war and the new Swansea straightened itself out to acquire the graces of a city. In my early days the place was a deliciously friendly chaos of nondescript buildings. Old Swansea was never planned, it was doodled over the landscape. From the top-storey bedroom of our tall Victorian house on the lower slopes of Town Hill my brothers and I could look out over the wondrous architectural mix-up spread below. The builders of Swansea were masters of the art of surrealist juxtaposition. The enormous backside of the Plaza cinema flaunted itself in shameless splendour over the centre of the town. The Town Hall hid from the citizens among the docks. The local museum, a fine early Victorian dream of culture, was mingled with overhead railway arches. It contained a choice collection of dusty bones from the Gower caves, strange fossils from the local coal pits and, marvel of marvels, a stuffed elephant which filled the entrance hall.

Looming over Swansea, and dominating it as the Duomo dominates Florence, was the market. Under the great glass dome they sold everything, from herbal remedies to Welsh flannel shirts for colliers. The Penclawdd cockle women marched through the market crowd with their wooden pails balanced on their heads. Here you could buy the black treacly laverbread, made from seaweed, unkindly described by those not brought up on its delights as the only edible cowpat in the world.

The Art Gallery stood next to the Working Men's Club, Lucanias (the billiard saloons of the day) jostled the chapels and the pubs were sandwiched in between drapers' shops. Outside the centre of the town the streets shot up the hills at alarming angles. The primary school I attended was on a shelf carved out of the face of the rock like the temples of Abu Simbel. Untidy architectural chaos indeed but always dear to me, for its was full of the most wonderful escape hatches from convention. Swansea was the perfect place to grow up as the Happy, Unconforming Talking Man. My father decided to settle in Swansea in the year of my own arrival. This was certainly a providential decision for me but, looking back on it, I am not so certain if it was so providential a decision for him.

My father's family was a classic example of what the historians are pleased to call 'the uprooted peasantry'. I have never been able to take easily to those clinical-sounding terms that litter the pages of the economists. They make my great-grandparents on father's side seem like footnotes to a particularly stodgy treatise by Karl Marx. 'Uprooted peasantry' indeed! From all the family stories I heard as a small boy, they were an enterprising lot who wisely moved from the country because by the 1850s South Wales had become a boom area offering opportunity to people avid for education and improvement. They travelled about as opportunities developed, from the coal areas of Maesteg to the tin-plate works of Pontardulais. My father was born during a temporary pause in this Hegira at the top end of the Swansea valley. He was an exceedingly bright boy, an early Eisteddfod prize winner and pianist, who gained scholarships with enviable ease. They took him to Llandovery College and on to Exeter College, Oxford, as a mathematics scholar.

Oxford bowled him over. I still have a photograph of him in a college group taken on the steps of the oak-beamed Hall, as all Oxford groups seem to have been since Lewis Carroll first peered through his primitive lens from under a dark cloth. Father wears his college blazer, and his straw boater is set at a slightly rakish angle – a young Welshman looking with amazed and amused eyes at the strange, unfamiliar, highly stylized and exclusive world of late Victorian Oxford. As he entered Exeter in 1891 he saw an Oxford which seemed almost unchanged from Matthew Arnold's 'sweet city with its dreaming spires'. Father had come to Oxford with a fatal gift – he could play the piano. Inevitably he was drawn into the Oxford Musical Union. He played Chopin and Brahms and Schumann quartets when he should have been buried in the complexities of higher mathematics. Halfway through his Oxford career music claimed him completely, and he left the university, not as an accomplished mathematician, but clad in the rich scarlet and velvet gown of a Mus. Doc. (Oxon).

Those were heady days in the world of British music. The critics declared that a new English Renaissance was in progress. Vaughan Williams, Holst and Bantock were all at it full blast. Sir Thomas Beecham was busy promoting Delius. Rather unfairly faded figures like Cyril Scott distilled mysticism and hashish into sound. Father looked at this thrilling scene from his somewhat remote position as assistant music master at Harrow School.

I have a second picture of him, from the *Illustrated London News*, drawn by their artist during the visit of King Edward and Queen Alexandra to Harrow on Speech Day. Father sits at the organ high over the distinguished assembly. Below are the billowingly-dressed ladies, the bemedalled soldiers, the gowned masters and the immaculate royal party. I can imagine father looking down on this concentration of cash, position and social power and secretly admitting to himself that the organ loft at Harrow was no place for a musician who was dreaming of joining the musical Renaissance and proving that Welsh music, too, could be rejuvenated and startled out of its old-fashioned straitjacket of hymn tunes, anthems and eisteddfod test pieces.

He gave up his position and came back to Wales. He married and settled down in Swansea, in a principality which proudly called itself the land of song – with some justice for to the average Welshman at the turn of the century the voice was the supreme musical instrument. From every chapel, every public hall, at regular intervals came the sound of choral singing of mixed choirs, male voice choirs, children's choirs, all singing not with the polite competence of English choirs, but as if life depended on it.

How far away that musical scene appears today! No national orchestra, no national opera, no kindly Arts Council ready with happy hand-outs for a composer. Certainly not for one composer whose career we later charted in a slightly bibulous jingle, naturally sung far away from the teetotal fields of the National Eisteddfod.

When first in my cradle I started to yell
My howls were in tune and as true as a bell.
The nurses who heard me in chorus exclaimed;
'He's Eos Cwmllynfell so get his voice trained!
Chorus. Get his voice trained! Get his voice trained!
He's Eos Cwymllynfell so get his voice trained.'

At twelve my ambitions had started to soar.
I was asked to write hymns for the Cwmllynfell Côr.
The parts, it is true, all came right by a fluke,
So I called it an Anthem, entitled 'Saint Luke'.
Chorus. He's written 'St Luke'. He's written 'St Luke'.
That gem of an anthem, the glorious 'St Luke'.

But when I considered I found to my shame
I'd no row of letters stuck after my name,
So I wrote to New York for degrees going cheap.
I'm Mus. Bac. (Correspondence) – two dollars a week!

Chorus.	Two dollars a week! Two dollars a week!
	Mus. Bac. by instalments, two dollars a week.
	At local eisteddfods I'm in great demand.
	I lecture (plus ex's) all over the land.
	At chapèl Cymanfa's I show them my power,
	As I switch on the 'hwyl' at ten guineas an hour.
Chorus.	Ten guineas an hour! Ten guineas an hour!
	Damn, the hwyl's going cheap at ten guineas an hour!
	Now anthems, cantatas, they pour from my pen,
	All written four-parts with a lovely 'Amen'.
	Pizzicato, rubato and Con 'Sordinee'
	Beethoven and Bach have got nothing on me.
Chorus.	He's written a hymn! He's written a hymn!
	Beethoven and Bach have got nothing on him!

My earliest musical memories always seem to be of great waves of sound coming from packed chapels, with the conductor tossing back a mane of black hair as the pitch pine seats echoed to a thundering chorus from mysteriously named rituals called *Messiah* or *Elijah*. I remember father a little later in my life conducting himself, but he didn't waste his efforts on Handel. He boldly gave the first performance in Wales of Elgar's *Apostles*. The great man himself came to Swansea to hear it, and I was detailed to sit next to him at the rehearsals, ready to run any message for him and to relay any comment he might care to make. Sir Edward, I admit, didn't quite look like my idea of a composer. I had expected the brooding majesty of Beethoven, but got a sort of retired Indian colonel instead. I felt, however, that this was a historical moment for me. I was sitting next to acknowledged genius for the first time. I resolved to treasure forever his first words. At last Sir Edward leant over and handed me sixpence. 'I wonder would you be kind enough to get me the local paper. I want to see what won the 3.30 at Cheltenham.'

This was a shock. Was this the real *Dream of Gerontius*? Betting on the 3.30 while the choir was thundering out the *Apostles*? And his own composition, too! As a small boy in Wales, I took it for granted that Art was a serious affair, always to be taken with a capital A, especially when it was associated with Male Voice contests. Father was a much-sought-after adjudicator at the local eisteddfodau that were then the main excitements of vocal Wales. There was no cinema, no radio, no TV. The annual eisteddfod was the one event that everyone looked forward to, and, if there was a Male Voice Competition – as was nearly always the case – the local eisteddfod offered you the satisfaction of combining a feast of culture with the thrills of a hard-fought rugby match. My brothers and I were taken to a whole series of them. Father sat in power and glory in the centre of the pavilion; we wandered around outside. We boys didn't bother too much about the recitations, the poetry adjudications and the tenor solos. We waited breathlessly for the Battle of the Parties.

The Party, outside South Wales, conjures up pictures of grim-faced, padded-shouldered Iron Curtain mass-men, automatically obeying orders from above; but in the South Wales of my youth the Party was simply the local male voice choir. Like the local rugby team they symbolized pride of locality, a gesture of defiance against the terraces of slate-roofed houses, the unpaid-for Welfare Halls and the coal tips perched on rain-sodden mountains, which were the background of life in the mining valleys. The Party received a fierce loyalty from the community and a famous choir conductor received almost royal honours.

Just after the First World War, we were enlivened by the

visits of one well-known baton-wielder from the valleys who had done well out of meat contracting for the troops. He called in his car driven by Snow, the chauffeur, to take us for magical rides through the hills. The car was fitted with a horn that awoke musical echoes as we passed through the mining villages. When we approached the long lines of terrace houses the Great Conductor would change his headgear from his motoring cap to a grey topper. Then he gave the magical order 'Sound the Gabriel, Snow.' This musical last trump brought the inhabitants to the windows and Dan graciously lifted his hat. He turned to me, 'People like to know that I am passing through.'

Indeed they did. Under the Great Conductor's leadership they attacked all music as if exacting revenge at last for the defeat of Owain Glyn Dwr. In the battles that formed the male voice competitions there were no holds barred. All male voice *afficionados* relish the reply of defiance given by the conductor of the losing choir to his rival after a fierce eisteddfodic contest, 'All right, I admit you beat us hands down on "Lift up thy heads, ye Gates of Brass", but in "Love, Perfect Love", we gave you hell.'

The music sung by these choirs never seemed to exist outside Wales, but they were the lifeblood of the Party. Gather two or three singing South Walians together and whisper 'Martyrs' or 'Crossing the Plains' or 'Nidaros', and they will immediately go into a huddle, the leader will lift his hand with authority, hum the note – and 'They're off!'

The old European joke about 'one Englishman a bore, two Englishmen a club, three Englishmen the British Empire', can be changed in South Wales, with perfect truth into, 'one Welshmen a milk round, two Welshmen a committee, three Welshmen a male voice choir!' And ten to one that male voice choir will start singing 'Martyrs in the Arena'. The 'Martyrs' were always at their best when they entered the arena of a small country eisteddfod. I remember one such gathering – alas, it must be nearly seventy years ago – held in the unfrequented countryside on the borders of the old counties of Carmarthenshire and Cardiganshire, where the little hills have lost their ambition to become mountains and where the main features are still preachers, trout streams and little square prewar black cars driven by officials of the Milk Marketing Board.

I had come down to the eisteddfod in the chara, and the battle was due to be staged at two-thirty in a tent by the tumbling waters of the Cothi river. All around were the deep woods, secret and warm in the morning sun. We boys got into the tent by the simple trick of appointing one of our number to get the entrance stamp on the back of his hand. We slipped behind the hedge and transferred the impress of the stamp while it was still wet. The choirs set off to rehearse the test piece, 'Martyrs', in secret, well-guarded clearings in the woodland.

Our local choir was facing those formidable songsters, the Penybont Gleemen, and everyone realized that the battle was going to turn on that vital phrase just before the end, 'and when the lifeblood is pouring'. Should the choir pour out its lifeblood *mezzoforte* or *double forte*? The adjudicator was known to have strong views on this point. What were our rivals of Penybont doing? And how were we to find out, since they were rehearsing in their clearing surrounded by the defensive pickets of their supporters? Jack Rees, the secretary, approached us. 'Boys,' he said, 'are you patriots? Are you prepared to take a risk for the honour of the choir?'

'Of course, Mr Rees,' we hurried to declare.

'Then will you crawl through the undergrowth and find out what Penybont are doing about the *forte* in bar eight after the *tutti* before the end? Our fate depends on it.'

Like Red Indians we slipped from the tent. We crawled through the brambles, slid on our stomachs among the heather and became spies for the cause of art. We came back dirty but triumphant. 'Mr Rees, its a *double forte*.' Mr Rees raised his eyes to the hills in the mood of Cromwell before Dunbar. 'Pouring out their lifeblood *double forte*! The Lord hath delivered them into our hands!'

Indeed He had. Penybont were crushed and we returned home singing like satisfied angels in the chara.

The lurid delights of 'Martyrs', however, were rather frowned on at home. Father resolutely directed us to the musical classics. My two brothers and I eventually formed a trio, and scraped and hammered our way through the simpler works of Mozart, Haydn and Beethoven. I often wonder what our neighbours thought of it all, for we were not alone as noisemakers in our section of Walter Road, Swansea. Next door to us was Mr Miron the dentist and next to him, Mr Morgan Lloyd the distinguished Welsh violinist. Visitors to our home had to face a barrage of Celtic cacophony, which continued well into the small hours of the morning. For just after the First World War father finally began to give reality to the dream that had brought him back to Wales – the foundation of a truly Welsh style in music. And he did most of his composing at night.

It was now that I realized that my father was not as other fathers were, just the ever-present provider of holidays and the comforter in our childhood misfortunes. He was a scholar and an artist. He never made much money, but he made magnificent music and great happiness for his family. I can still hear the sound of the piano coming to me muted from his study as I lay half asleep upstairs as a small boy. Father was absorbed in the labour of setting to music the poems of the greatest poet of medieval Wales, Dafydd ap Gwilym. And labour it certainly was, for Dafydd and his contemporaries wrote in Cynghanedd – that wonderfully complex system of carefully arranged consonants and subtle internal rhyming which is the unique glory of Welsh poetry 'in the strict metres'. To write in Cynghanedd required years of disciplined study but the results, to an educated Welsh ear, are enchanting. The trouble is that there are not so many educated Welsh ears in the world. To be a great poet in a language spoken by a comparatively small number of people can be a passport to oblivion; but somehow Dafydd ap Gwilym refuses to go 'gentle into that good night' where most medieval poets, in any language, seem to end.

He wrote in the fourteenth century, influenced by the tradition of the troubadours of Provence, but with his own irresistible gusto for life and for beautiful women, all waiting to be lured to amorous adventure in the greenwood in high summer. How elegantly he sums up the Welshman's attitude to love.

Grant me, dear life, this lover's blessing –
A conquering kiss, a swift undressing,
A wild delight, a long caressing,
And all to end in Heart's Possessing.

Through the small hours my father strove to match music to
Cynghanedd and Dafydd. The sounds came to me and seemed
incredibly beautiful, remote, exotic – I could have wished that
all life would be like this dream world that father was building
at his fingertips on the piano. The songs are among the best
things he ever wrote. Every time I turn over a volume of Welsh
poetry I have a picture of my father, a cigarette at the corner of
his mouth, his manuscript on the piano before him, his sensitive hands touching the keys and his mind far away from such
matters as milkman's bills and school fees. Mother looked
after that side of life.

Some marriages are lucky from the moment the bride says
'yes'. Mother was father's perfect complement. He was a
dreamer, she was practical. He had no confidence in himself,
she had boundless confidence in him. He was a mathematician
who was a child when it came to counting cash. She was a
careful manager, to whom he wisely handed over every penny
he earned. They must have quarrelled sometimes, but we boys
never heard a cross word pass between them. Happy homes
are supposed to be dull homes, and all modern psychologists
and novelists assure us that a certain amount of aggro, born of
early conflict with unsympathetic parents, is essential for anyone anxious to get on in life; but I started life with the appal-
ling handicap of being surrounded by happiness, music and
long holidays in the nearby enchanting peninsula of Gower –
Gower of the golden sands and the glittering limestone cliffs.
In this general atmosphere of optimism and kindness to children, I grew up into a sort of Celtic Candide, a disciple of the
excellent Dr Pangloss who, you remember, maintained against
all evidence that 'all was for the best in this best of all possible
worlds'.

To encourage me in my assumption that life was meant to be
enjoyed, come what may, there was my Aunty Bess – short,
rosy-faced and a widow, who had returned in 1912 from wild
adventures in America to live near us in a small house

crammed with souvenirs of the west, from buffalo horns to gaudily-printed certificates for silver mines in Montana.

All families should have an Aunty Bess. She was our cinema, radio and television set all rolled into one. We didn't need a John Wayne or a James Bond or even a Kojak to give us a sense of thrilling adventure when we were around eight years old. All we had to do was to slip over to Aunty Bess's little terrace house for tea, buns and forbidden sweets. Sometimes she would take out bound volumes of the *Illustrated London News* of the 1850s and '60s and a strange world opened to our astonished eyes as she turned the pages and read out the titles; 'The Great Eastern caught in a storm while laying the Atlantic Cable'; 'The Emperor of the French receives the British Ambassador'; 'British tars man the rigging for the Royal Birthday at Spithead'; 'The New Railway opens at Brighton'. Very much later, I realized that this was the actual world of my Aunty Bess's youth. She was born in 1852, in the heyday of mid-Victorian confidence, when industry was slowly spreading through South Wales. Mother's family were sheep farmers on the high hills behind Pontardulais, and, according to Aunty Bess's account, lived a life of pastoral splendour, riding out to supervise their vast flocks as they wandered over the lonely moorlands. Llandremor, their headquarters up in the rich secret Dulais valley, was a manor house of epic proportions where the squires of Llandremor kept their packs of hounds and dispensed lavish hospitality at shearing time in a vast kitchen with hams clustered on hooks in the ceiling.

Years later I went to look at Llandremor. Somehow the place seemed to have unaccountably shrunk from the splendid manor house of my aunt's stories into a modest, even a rather delapidated, Welsh farmhouse. No matter, I shall always see it through my aunt's eyes. From Llandremor, my grandmother married my grandfather, Daniel Lewis – auctioneer, weaver, but above all romantic rebel and leader at Pontardulais of the once-famous Rebecca Riots.

When I started to learn history at school I was amazed to discover that hardly anyone had heard of these epoch-making events and that the most they rated in the schoolbooks of the time was an obscure footnote. To me at the age of eight they were as great a turning point in world history as the French Revolution. Aunty Bess made it seem so, for she had such pride in grandfather's great act of social defiance that she made me feel I was back a hundred years in the South Wales countryside, when the farmers were smouldering with fury at the spread of tollgates as Improvement Trusts took over the main roads, and grandfather was getting ready to lead his posse to smash the hated gates at midnight.

The whole thing started in 1839 at Efail Wen, a village on the borders of the old counties of Carmarthenshire and Pembrokeshire. This out-of-the-way part of the country had a particularly bad Turnpike Trust, and no one was surprised when the Efail Wen gate was smashed at night. This was Wales, and the rioters immediately sought justification for their action in the Bible. They found the perfect text in Genesis 24:60 'And they blessed Rebekah and said unto her, Thou art our sister, be thou the mother of thousands of millions and let thy seed possess the gate of those which hate them.' The rioters naturally did not look at the next verse in Genesis which said that 'they rode on camels'. They elected a leader as Rebecca, dressed themselves in women's clothes as her Daughters, blackened their faces and happily chopped up every tollgate in sight. By 1842 the movement had spread across Glamorgan to the village of Pontardulais, which was where my grandfather came in.

As related by Aunty Bess the subsequent riot grew into a great romantic saga. 'Your grandmother was in love with Daniel Lewis, but the squires of Llandremor disapproved of this reckless young man. He was a bit of everything – lawyer, poet, champion fisherman, weaver, a born leader, very handsome, but without much money. They had their eye on some-

near Llandremor, my grandmother's birthplace.

body better than this for their daughter – a smug young pillar of Goppa Chapel with cash. Your grandmother had heard rumours that Rebecca was going to attack the gate by the Fountain Inn on the Swansea road. She determined to be there.' Then Aunty Bess would pause and say impressively, 'I heard the whole story from your grandmother's own lips.'

On would go the vivid tale of how grandmother and a maid crept out secretly and came down to the Fountain Inn and looked out of the window. Away in the distance they heard grandfather's voice exhorting his followers, 'Come along, my little daughters, come along. There's good work to do tonight.'

'Then, down came the Daughters of Rebecca, led by your grandfather riding a white horse. They were all dressed in mob caps borrowed from their sweethearts and wives, and with women's dresses over their men's trousers to add to their disguise. The old soldier who took the tolls at the gate was easily persuaded to step into the bar and in no time the whole gate was reduced to matchwood. There was no opposition because they had persuaded the authorities that they were going to attack another gate that night, so the militia were all standing guard a mile away at the other end of the village.

'Ah, but there was a traitor in the camp, who went to the magistrates and revealed that your grandfather was Rebecca. The police arrived to arrest him, but he knew the law. He insisted that the carriage should be brought to the very door before he would step in. Away he went to Swansea jail – it was in the old castle, then – and the farmers all brought him their best fowls and butter and eggs and jugged hares. He always said that he never fed better than when he was in jail. And when the trial came – do you know what, Wynford? – he was triumphantly acquitted!'

'But, Aunty Bess, how was that possible when he was Rebecca?'

'Not a soul in the village would testify against him. They all swore he'd been at home writing a poem that night. The magistrates had to let him off, because the only hostile witness they had did not appear. The farmers had made certain of that – they kidnapped the traitor and held him in the mountains until the trial was over. Of course, it was perjury but it was for

a good cause on a heroic scale. Your grandfather came out of
court a free man. He escaped transportation to Australia, and
that is why you were not born at Wagga Wagga!'

'And what about grandmother?' I asked. 'Did they let her
marry Daniel Lewis, after all that?'

'They had to, Wynford, for the traitor in the camp was the
very man her family had in mind as her husband. After the
trial, the whole countryside sent him to Coventry and he fled
the village – perhaps it was he who went to Australia in the
long run. But Llandremor got their revenge on my mother.
When she married Daniel Lewis they didn't give her the best
timber from the farm to make her wedding dressers and her
chairs, which, after all, was their duty to do in those days for
their daughters – and that, you remember, led to the great
disaster.'

The great family disaster was the terrible morning – I was
very small at the time – when mother tugged at the drawer of
the dresser and brought the whole thing crashing down to the
stone-flagged floor of the kitchen. Into a thousand pieces went
the Swansea and Nantgarw china, and my chance of inheriting
a family fortune was swept into the dustbin! What would it
fetch today? I cannot read of the prices at Sotheby's and
Christie's without feeling ill. But the dresser is still there, and
the oak chairs from Llandremor are still set about my table,
and I never look at them without thinking of my grandmother
lovingly polishing them until the oak has the patina of rich
bronze, and of my Aunty Bess, sitting on them with her 'young
man' as she shyly introduced him to her parents. She showed
me the very chair. I'm sitting on it as I write these words.

'Your Uncle David,' began my Aunty Bess in the second
section of her version of the family saga, 'was a gambler. I
realized this on the first day I married him. It was in September
1870, and we were on our way to Tenby for our honeymoon.
We had to change at Carmarthen and as we stood on the
platform, there was a wonderful sunset – the most vivid red
sky I have ever seen. The stationmaster came up to us, and
your uncle remarked to him on the blood-red colour of the sky.
"Yes," he said, "it's caused by the blood of the poor fellows
who have just fallen in the battle of Sedan."

'Then, as we went on to Tenby, your uncle told me that he also had a battle on his hands. He had decided to set up a new tin-plate works near Pontardawe and fight the rival Gilbertson Works – "We'll be rich beyond the dreams of avarice", he told me, Wynford, and I thought it was the most wonderful wedding present anyone could have, for your uncle David was a marvellous talker.'

Rich Aunty Bess certainly became. Mother used to tell us how she would return to visit the family in Pontardulais in her smart carriage driven by her servant, her golden tresses piled into an elaborate coiffure. Then mother's voice would drop in admiration, 'Ah, she was a beautiful woman, and the first person to wear a bustle in Pontardawe.' There came the fatal day, however, when all the glory suddenly departed. The Gilbertsons discovered a flaw in the lease of the land over which Uncle David's short railway connection ran to the main line. With the ruthless determination of Victorian industrial barons, they throttled their rival. Uncle David could no longer move his tinplates the hundred yards that meant profitability – he had perforce to hand the lot over to his competitors. There was only one thing to do – go off to America and start again.

Uncle David sailed first and naturally went out west to seek his new fortune. Montana was being opened up. There were stories of rich gold strikes, of silver mines that paid enormous dividends, of 'Big Jim' Hill getting ready to drive the Great Northern Railway through the Last American Wilderness. This was clearly the place for a man of enterprise. A year later came the anxiously awaited telegram, 'Great prospects. Join me at Great Falls as soon as possible.'

No one in Pontardulais could find Great Falls on the atlas, but undaunted my aunt set off and landed at New York in the spring of 1876. She went, on her own, towards a west that turned out to be far wilder than she ever expected. All her American stories began with a magic formula, like the 'once upon a time' of the fairy tales. My aunt's formula ran, 'In those days, Wynford, the railway had gone no further west than Fort Benton.' Where Fort Benton was I had not the remotest idea, but for us boys it became the enchanted springboard for an Aunty Bess adventure.

'We joined a party going west and our wagons were four days out when a scout came from General Crook's force to warn us that there was trouble ahead. We were to form a corral and wait for further orders. No one had told me – or if they did I hadn't understood – that we were going through Indian territory near the Big Horn River and that the Sioux were in rebellion.'

The Sioux, as pronounced by Aunty Bess, were a sinister war whoop in themselves, and their allies, the Nez-Percés, sounded even more sinister. Sitting Bull and Chief Rain-in-the-Face were obviously on the warpath and while the main body were scuppering General Custer, Sitting Bull had detached a small flying column to mop up any odd wagons that might be wandering around, including the one containing my Aunty Bess, the bold adventurer from Pontardulais. Soon the Indians appeared, as in my aunt's stories they always did.

'They were very, very dirty, Wynford, and their ponies were smelly as well. But they were shouting and shooting arrows and some of them had guns. I was frightened, I can tell you. They'd never told me anything about this in Wales, and I was even more frightened when our guide said to me, "Can you shoot?"

' "No, I don't know how."

' "Well, now is the time to learn, lady, if you want to keep that lovely golden hair you've got." He gave me a gun, and I shut my eyes and pulled the trigger.'

'Did you kill an Indian, Aunty?'

'To tell you the truth, I'm not certain what happened except that there was a loud bang and I got a bad bruise on my shoulder.'

'What happened to the Indians?'

'They went off shouting, and we didn't see them again, but that evening another scout came in from General Crook to say that General Custer's force had been wiped out, but that they were driving the Sioux north. We were safe to go on, and in two days time I was in the arms of your Uncle David.'

'And did you then become rich again, Aunty?'

'I should have, and indeed your uncle did brilliantly.'

Then followed the final part of the adventure, when uncle

made a fortune by catering for the building of the Great Northern Railroad and put his money into silver mines in the Rocky Mountains which turned out to be as rocky as the mountains themselves. My aunt still retained trunkfuls of share certificates which depicted vividly-coloured Indian chiefs, clad in full eagle-feathered head-dresses handing glittering nuggets of precious ore to bearded, red-shirted miners and entitling uncle to a thousand shares in such cast-iron certainties as the Silver Eagle El Dorado, the New Alder Gulch and the Montana Happy Surprise Mine. Unfortunately, just as uncle was going to coin the cash, the United States began to change its monetary policy and proposed making gold the only legal backing for the dollar. The silver dollar was threatened with extinction.

'Ah, but the miners and the farmers had a great champion, who had a silver tongue and defied those big money men of the East – The Rockefellers and the Morgans and the rest of them. Never forget his name, Wynford – William Jennings Bryan.'

I haven't. I can still hear my aunt's voice as she gave Bryan the highest praise in her power. 'He was the greatest Talker I ever heard.' Talk is a wonderful thing. Nothing can be done without it and he was magnificent. And the greatest thing he ever said was, 'You cannot crucify mankind on a cross of gold.' Unluckily my Uncle David believed him. He hung on to his mining shares, the US abandoned silver and away went another of Aunty Bess's numerous dreams of fortune. Uncle David decided on a last throw. He joined the Yukon gold rush. Like Charlie Chaplin he found himself out of his depth in the icy north. He lost most of his goods climbing the Chilcoot Pass, caught pneumonia, came home to Great Falls and quietly handed in his last share.

Aunty Bess's adventures in the Wild West had one more chapter before they closed.

'After he died, Wynford, I discovered that he'd handed the deeds of the house and business to some Jewish moneylenders from Helena in order to raise cash for the Yukon trip. I was penniless. But I had my friends. The mayor of Great Falls and the mining surveyor and Mr Pritchard the big rancher and Big Jim Hill's secretary – they invited those moneylenders to meet

them with the documents, and when these wicked men
arrived, Uncle David's friends simply drew their guns and
made them hand over the documents and sign everything back
to me. That was real western justice.'

Montana was the first foreign land I travelled in without
ever setting foot in it. For years I knew it better than I knew
that even more mysterious, far-off, dangerous, unsettled country – England. There was, however, another land far closer
than England in which I could actually travel – a country of
bright rocks and clean golden sand, where it was always
summer and the air was humming with the sound of honey-
laden bees and there were no trams or schools or wet streets
full of hurrying people with umbrellas; my land of heart's
desire and my annual trip to paradise.

The Gower Peninsula lies on the very doorstep of Swansea
and is a surprising piece of unspoilt country to find tucked
away in the heavily industrialized coalfield of South Wales. It
was a secret we hugged to ourselves. Even today, when the
suburbs of Swansea have crept out to the west and caravan
parks have clustered around Port Eynon and Llangennith,
much of the Gower of my childhood remains, rescued by the
devoted defence of the Gower Society. These delectable sixteen miles of moorland, commons and limestone-girt bays
were also saved by the trick of geography. The peninsula has
the sea on the south, and on the north are the wide flats of the
Burry Estuary, where the oystercatchers run piping along the
edge of the sandbanks and – when I was young – the women of
Penclawdd used to follow the falling tide, driving their pannier-
laden donkeys before them like a Bedouin tribe on the march,
to rake up the cockles we bought in Swansea market. Gower
has happily remained out of the spotlight of history since the
day, back in the twelfth century, when it was conquered by
those medieval Bedouins, the Normans, who flung out the
Welsh and imported settlers from Devon and Somerset. Like
Southern Pembrokeshire, Gower, too, became a Little England beyond Wales.

Into this magic country we journeyed on our summer holidays towards that coastline of shining cliffs which ended at
Worm's Head. The old Vikings knew what they were doing

when they christened it the Worm. It really does wriggle out to
sea like a strange serpent rearing up its limestone head before it
takes its final plunge under the waves. There was no railway.
We travelled in creaking buses, grandiosely christened the
Vanguard and the Pioneer, which threw up clouds of white
dust in the endless sunshine beating down on the traffic-free
roads. As we grew older we were allowed to sit on the roof of
the Pioneer, packed in among the parcels. We trembled with
excitement as the driver took the bus with infinite care
around the sharp bend of the Devil's Elbow, for once a Vanguard bus had actually toppled over on this terrifying guardian
entrance gate to the Gower paradise. Ponies went racing away
with tossing manes across windy Fairwood Common. In
triumph we arrived at the School House, among the thatched
cottages of Port Eynon, where for a blissful month we lived, it
seemed to me, on another planet.

We ran down every morning to plunge into clear waves
creaming in over golden sands. We conducted daring expeditions out onto the rock pools at low tide, lifting up tangled
seaweeds with our nets to find them full of leaping snapping
prawns; and once a week, Mr Grove harnessed his pony in the
'gambo' (Gower's special variety of trap) and we trotted away
through the lanes overhung with brambles loaded with black-
berries to picnic on Worm's Head, or we went on to Llangennith, the Ultima Thule of the peninsula, where the downs
looked out over Carmarthen Bay and beyond which no boys
we knew had ever penetrated.

There, in the stillness of the evening, broken only by the
distant crying of the gulls on the rocks of Burry Holmes, the
clear tenor voice of Phil Tanner would soar into the warm air –
Phil, the Gower Nightingale, a nobly-bearded patriarch with a
wicked twinkle in his eye, a fund of songs and stories, and a
friendly sheepdog that thrust a cold trusting nose into our hot
hands. Phil always sat on his bench outside the King's Head,
tactfully supplied with ale by his admirers and ready to bring
us all the flavour of that unspoilt Gower of the last days of
Queen Victoria. He came from a famous family of weavers,
and all the time I knew him, I never saw him wear any other
suit than his pepper and salt coat and trousers of Gower tweed.

Rumour had it that when he retired at night to his little cottage on the slope of Stormy Down he put it to stand up in a corner like a suit of armour. Yet Phil was never a real, dyed-in-the-wool weaver. He tried his hand at every country craft, including a short spell at innkeeping; but his real love was singing. He became Gower's best-loved folk singer, and in a way, our Gower Aunty Bess.

We boys listened wide-eyed as he told us about the Gower bidding weddings. Phil was the 'bidder', the man who walked around the parish carrying a staff decorated with red, white and blue ribbons and 'bid' everyone to come to the wedding bringing cash, which would be repaid when the guests, in their time, had a wedding in their own family. Phil had his patter by heart and I can remember it myself, for I heard it again and again from his lips:

I'm a messenger to you and the whole house in general
To invite you to the wedding of Morgan Eynon and Nancy
        Hopkin.
The wedding will be next Monday fortnight
The wedding house will be the Ship Inn at Portynon
Where the bride will take breakfast on plenty of good beer,
        butter and cheese.

And on would go Phil, detailing all the delights awaiting the guests at the Ship Inn, including 'fiddlers, fifers and drummers and the devil knows what besides', until he reached the final inducement:

And if you come to the wedding
I'll do all that lies in my power that evening if required
To get you a sweetheart if I don't get drunk,
But the bride is wishful you should come or send.

If no fiddlers arrived Phil would supply mouth music, and set feet tapping with its infectious lilt; but his songs were his real glory. He picked them up from all sorts of sources, music halls, travelling tinkers, song handed down from the distant past. He would clear his throat, call, 'Order order, gentlemen, singing is a serious matter,' and ring out the first verse, while the dog would whimper in protest.

I must go down to some lonesome valley,
Where no man on earth there may me find,
Where the pretty little songbirds sit tuning their voices,
And always blows there a most healing wind.

('Down bitch. Drat her, what's the matter with her? She was musical enough, boy, as a puppy!')

Stand back, young man, and don't be so deceitful
For 'tis you're the cause of all my pain,
'Tis you have made my poor heart to wander
And for to cure it now, 'tis all in vain.

There was an Irish one in which we all joined in the chorus. It had a splendid swinging tune.

It was back in Tipperary I was born when I was young
That's the reason that I've got the Blarney on my tongue.
I was the image of my daddy, even the doctor did allow
And the girls all came to kiss me – Oh, I *wish* they'd do it now!

Chorus. How I wish they'd do it now! How I wish they'd do it now
They would tickle me down all over – Oh, I *wish* they'd do it now!

Then there were what Phil called the 'naughty ones'. Looking back on them how innocent they all were, those 'naughty ones' of Phil's. Our permissive society wouldn't turn a hair, as Phil, glancing around hurriedly to make sure no ladies were present, gave us the Gower Toast:

Here's to the maiden bright with honour,
Many's the time I've lain upon her,
I've done it standing. I've done it lying.
And if I'd wings (*whistle*), I'd have done it flying!

At which point mother usually appeared and said firmly, 'Time we started back.' Into the gambo we crowded, and the old horse clip-clopped his way through the gathering dusk, with our voices still singing with gusto, 'How I wish they'd do it now'.

So I came to the day which I felt was the day when I first started to grow up – the Day of the Lobster.

Beyond the safe sands of Port Eynon beach lay a mysterious, even dangerous land which we were forbidden to explore. In his rich Gower dialect – a musical compound of Devonian and Somerset, sprinkled with some strangely metamorphosed Welsh words and spoken with a Celtic lilt – Mr Grove called it 'the huvvers and scarras', which made it more mysterious and attractive still. At low tide a wide rock shelf is exposed at the foot of the high Gower cliffs. It is pitted with deep, clear pools fringed with waving seaweed. Here, we knew, lived monsters – giant crabs that could eat small boys who disobeyed their parents' orders to keep to the small pools on the edge of the sands. There were even stories of lobsters with claws as big as a man. It would take heroism of the highest order to venture out on the edge of the falling tide and tackle these strange danger-ous dragons in their lair. When Mr Grove offered to take me, I felt as honoured as if Captain Scott had invited me to join his expedition to the South Pole. There was a family conference. Yes, I could go, provided I implicity obeyed every word from Mr Grove. Mother added (knowing me only too well), 'No daydreaming.'

First, I had to be properly equipped with my own crabbing hook, and for this we went up the hill to the smithy, where the great horses that helped to drag the lifeboat into the water when they were not ploughing, stood patiently to be shod. With a series of ringing blows and showers of sparks, the smith fashioned an iron bar into a hook, known as a penny bender for the ideal curve for a Gower crabbing hook should go around the circumference of a penny. 'With my crabbing hook on shoulder, faith, no one could be bolder,' as I proudly followed Mr Grove out over the rocks, beyond the lichen-covered hump of Skysea, where the gulls were crying among the white breakers thundering on the edge of the 'huvvers'.

Now crabbing in Gower is at once an art and a sport. The countryside cherished the memory of great performers as zeal-ously as cricket fans remember Jack Hobbs or Sir Don Brad-man. They saluted Kitty 'Crabs', of Oxwich, who was one of the few women champions, and Billy Hopkins of Porteynon, who won fame as the only man who went crabbing by moon-light. Mr Grove didn't bother to look under every ledge. He knew exactly where the big holes lay in which the best crabs and lobsters retired to hide as the tide went down. We came to a deep pool just uncovered by the tide. He warned me, 'No good ever came of meddling here.' And he told me of the terrible experience of John Taylor who was working this hole long ago, convinced that he'd got a giant lobster. He spent a long time getting it out but to his horror it was no lobster that floated out but the body of a sailor, one of the lads drowned in the wreck of the *Agnes Jack* in 1883. I turned slightly pale at the story and stood, in some trepidation at the next big pool, which Mr Grove declared perfect for the job. He stood up to his waist in the salt water and felt carefully under the swaying seaweed with his hook. 'Aye, he's here.' I had a momentary fear that 'he' might be another sailor from the *Agnes Jack* but Mr Grove's smile reassured me. 'Now, boy,' he said, 'never shuv or thrash 'un about. Just you give 'un a hint with the hook, boy, an' out he'll come.'

Gently Mr Grove probed into the depth of the pool with an artist's touch; no crude pulling that could break off a claw or a limb. And then, suddenly, an astonishing sight – as amazing as if a pterodactyl had appeared at the National Eisteddfod! Out into the clear water of the pool floated that strangest of prehis-toric survivals, a lobster. My first shock was to find that he wasn't red like all the lobsters I had previously seen, already boiled for my gastronomic pleasure. There he was, antennae waving, claws open and coloured a lovely, suffused dark blue, with touches of white and red, one of the most beautiful sights I know on the seashore. 'Now, boy,' said Mr Grove, 'he's yours. Put your hand on the back of his neck, and he can't touch you!' I lifted him up, and no one catching his first salmon could have felt a greater thrill. I dropped him into the sack at last, after placing him on the seaweed and looking at him as if he had come from Conan Doyle's *Lost World*.

Ruskin, in an eloquent passage in *Modern Painters*, describes the moment of revelation that came to him as a boy when he first saw the Alps. In his organ-voluntary prose he describes how his parents were taking him, in the pre-railway days, to Italy in their specially hired personal coach. They had reached Basle in the afternoon and then gone for a stroll on the hill behind the town. They looked southwards and saw what they took to be banks of white cloud. They looked closer and to their astonishment the clouds changed into solid peaks buried in snow, and into glittering glaciers starting to turn rose-coloured in the evening sun. Could these ethereal mountains, floating clear of the mundane earth, actually be those Alps, which says Ruskin 'none of us thought could be attained without profane exertion' – by which I presume he meant rock climbing. 'The seen walls of lost Eden were not so glorious as these,' he declared, and from then on the sheer physical beauty of the surface of the earth 'haunted him like passion'. Wordsworth had the same revelation as he skated when a boy along a frozen stretch of Windermere. Thereafter, the physical world, the astonishing, mysteriously beautiful and ever-surprising world that surrounds the logical, practical world created by the mind of man, became the real world to Wordsworth and Ruskin. In a modest way I got my own moment of revelation on the Day of the Lobster.

Dates become confused, tangled with each other, as you try to think back into your own early years. I now realize with a slight shudder, as I check on the period we holidayed at Port Eynon, that my Day of the Lobster must have occurred in the summer of 1917. Far away from my tranquil Gower, Europe was tearing itself to pieces on the barbed wire and in the blood-stained shell holes of France and Belgium. 1917 was the year of Passchendaele. But the world crisis – the horror of the collapse of our western civilized order – went over my head. I was simply occupied in the exciting business of growing up.

Sometimes as I talk today about the 1939–45 war, my war, I detect a slight look of bewilderment coming into the eyes of anybody under thirty-five when I mention names like Anzio, Dieppe and El Alamein or talk of the Blitz or D-day. What were these 'old unhappy far-off things'? What have they to do with the world of the young? I start to grow indignant. Surely the young ought to know, must appreciate, should be made to understand that 'we stood alone' in 1940. They should cheer their fathers in their 'Finest Hour', and not suggest that the

1 The author's father, Dr David
Vaughan-Thomas

2 The author's mother, Morfydd
Vaughan-Thomas, 1902

3 Aunty Bess in the centre of the family group, 1919. The boys, from left to
right, Spencer, Wynford and Vaughan

4 The top form at Terrace Road School (W. V.-T. at the right end of the middle row)

whole business was somehow due to the bungling of my generation. No, no a hundred times no. We were surely saving Europe by our example. We were heroes! We were . . . and there I stop in full flood of indignation, for I try to remember what I did in my father's war.

I was six when it broke out and ten when it ended. I can't remember anyone telling me that Britain had come to the rescue of Gallant Little Belgium and that the Lights of Europe were going out one by one. Suddenly the War was there. A map appeared on the wall of father's study depicting the mysterious land called the Front, which we marked with small flags to show the progress of the Russian Steamroller. New figures, half menacing, half comic, entitled Kaiser Bill and Little Willie entered our imagination, for we lived in fear that one day they might march down Walter Road, Swansea at the head of legions of spiked-helmeted, goose-stepping, sausage-eating Germans, who would confiscate all our potatoes and ban liquorice all-sorts from the school shop. In the school yard we sang songs which seemed to us the height of brilliant wit.

> Oh, have you heard of Charlie Chaplin,
> Whose boots are cracking
> For the want of blacking,
> And his old baggy trousers wanting mending
> For they're going to send him
> To the Dardanelles.

There came a strange Easter holiday when we were on Swansea sands with Aunty Bess, and I wandered off to buy ice cream in the warm sun. I passed a portly gentleman asleep in his deck chair, his face covered with his newspaper. I had just started to read easily and stopped to exercise my skill by picking out the headlines as they gently rose and fell in time to his snores. 'Rebels occupy the centre of Dublin,' I read and, ice cream in hand, walked back to Aunty Bess. 'Who are the Rebels?' I asked.

'Well,' said Aunty Bess, 'they used to come from the southern states of America when I was a girl, but this must be a new lot.' And that was all I knew of the Easter Rising and the birth pangs of the Republic of Ireland.

The war became more serious when my Cousin Artie came

to call on us in 1916 before he went to France with the first
wave of the New Army. We were already singing at school:

> I'm going to 'list. I'm going to 'list
> I'm going to 'list in Kitchener's army,
> Ten bob a week and bully beef to eat.
> Hob-nailed boots and blisters on your feet.

And here was Cousin Artie actually one of Kitchener's gallant
men. He drew a shining sword from its scabbard. This was
apparently considered essential equipment for a young
lieutenant engaged in modern warfare in the trenches. I pictured him waving it as he led his brave lads over the top, but
poor Artie was severely wounded on the Somme without ever
wearing it in action. Like Bruce Bairnsfather's officer, all he
used it for was to make toast over a brazier when his unit came
out of the line.

I had often been taken by mother, on our way to the market,
past the Mond Buildings and seen the women with their children waiting in an anxious crowd on the pavement while their
husbands were inside going through their medical after con-
scription. I had heard the crying of the mothers as they clung
desperately to the men who had been passed fit, and the
wailing of the children clustered around. I saw myself already
crying in the street. The scene had a dramatic attraction, but it
never took place. Father was rejected as unfit and returned to
do voluntary war work, while mother practised bandaging
and we entertained wounded soldiers to tea.

There were thrills when a ship was torpedoed in the Bristol
Channel and when the first American troops landed in the
docks and paraded through the cheering crowds, while the
bands played, 'Over there, over there, the Yanks are coming
over there,' and we threw cigarettes at the marching ranks.
Then suddenly, on a damp November morning, the sirens
started to wail and every ship in the harbour sounded its
hooter, and our neighbour ran in shouting, 'It's over. It's over.
Thank God, it's over.' We seized our flags – we seemed to have
flags galore in those days ready for every occasion – and
walked through a town gone mad, with everyone out in the
streets, people in tears, sounds of singing coming from every

pub, impromptu processions formed to march nowhere in particular and, in the air, the sense of a great cloud lifted. 'It' was definitely over, and my world narrowed into one overriding consideration, far more important than any World War to me. Would I get a 'schol' to Swansea Grammar School?

For, I have to remind myself, through all these eventful years I was being educated; or as the Mayor of Swansea used to remind us on every speech day, 'being trained for the Great School of Life'. My first training session took place in a private school in Walter Road, kept by a lady picturesquely named Miss Bonnet. My elder brother and I were taken there every morning but our maid, Hannah – an exciting walk under the avenue of tall trees that then lined Walter Road. The trams came clanging down beneath the overhanging boughs, and we could wave at our doctor's car, one of the first cars in Swansea. It was driven by electric batteries and went by with a sedate, well-bred purr of lucrative satisfaction. There were strange signs painted on the gable ends of some of the houses. For years I puzzled over the meaning of the inscription on the grocer's, 'Phillip's Fine Teas. They stand the second water'. At Miss Bonnet's we were given slates with pencils that made a penetrating scratching sound that set your nerves on edge, and with which we laboriously formed the letters of the alphabet. In accordance with some advanced educational principle of the period, we were encouraged to use our hands to express our supposed eager desire for concrete knowledge of the Big World Outside. Thus our geography lesson always started with a large bowl of damp sand being produced, and a rather formidably bosomed lady – could it have been Miss Bonnet herself – dumping a lump on each slate with a brisk command, 'Now, everybody, make a peninsula'. I had no idea what a peninsula was, but I can still remember the pleasant cool feel of the damp sand and voices coming from the next room singing to the tinkling piano the touching ditty of 'Barbara Allen'.

At five I left my damp sand and entered the wide world of Terrace Road School. This was a formidable stone fortress constructed by the local authority in the 1890s on a sort of shelf carved out of the hillside and surrounded by a palisade of tall, spiked railings through which small boys regularly stuck their heads and had to be released, amid pleasurable excitement, by the local fire brigade. We had to climb up a succession of extraordinary steep streets to reach it, for our house lay on the level land at the foot of Town Hill, which was itself over four hundred feet high. No school transport or midday meals were supplied in those days, so we had to climb up three hundred feet every morning, down again for lunch, up again for afternoon school, then a glorious run home at 4.30 for tea. Occasionally a hard frost would prevent the big horsedrawn coal carts from bringing in supplies for the boilers over the semi-perpendicular glacis that defended our education Bastille, and we had days of unexpected freedom which we employed on expeditions to Swansea sands, walking behind the carts that went out in any weather to collect the fish trapped in the nets that made Paul Klee-like patterns across the bay at low tide.

We seemed to imbibe all our learning in the lower forms at Terrace Road through a sort of mesmerizing chant. The rows of little boys swayed like dervishes in a hypnotic trance as they memorized the twice-times table. I can still make the roll call of the Rivers of Britain, ending triumphantly with the musical

Terrace Road School.

finale of, 'the Witham, the Welland, the Nene and – (glorious sound for a Fenland river and always pronounced *double forte*) – the Great Ouse!' Dictation was another matter. I was always bottom of the class when it came to spelling and have remained so throughout my life. I cannot find any clue to the vagaries of English orthography. When it comes to long, complicated words I simply dive in, splash about among the consonants and hope for the best. I even find myself in shameful hesitation before such commonplace traps as 'committee' and 'diarrhoea' (I admit I have just carefully looked them up in the dictionary before writing them down!).

I floated happily upwards through the school to arrive eventually at the scholarship class; but then, I had a hidden advantage denied to so many of the boys who floated up with me. I could always go and curl up in a chair after raiding father's library. All sorts of strange volumes swam into my astonished view, from Darwin's *Origin of Species* (naturally not understood at all) to Cary's translation of Dante (with the horrific pictures of Gustave Doré, only too well understood). I read indiscriminately as I grew up. My mind, at the time, must have been a wonderful hodgepodge, with the tales from the *Mabinogion*, the great Welsh medieval treasure house of romantic stories, all tangled up with *Pickwick Papers* and *Lays of Ancient Rome*, and the whole mixture peppered with surreptitious lacings of the adventures of Harry Wharton, Bob Cherry and other Frank Richards heroes. Perhaps it has remained a bit of a hodgepodge ever since!

Modern children will measure the rate at which they grew up by the changes in the jingles they heard on commercial TV. I evoke my past by remembering the adverts I laboriously deciphered as a small boy in the newspapers or on walls. I remember that magic formula, promising the reform of the world:

> They come as a boon and a blessing to men
> The Pickwick, the Owl and the Waverley pen.

Then there was Tiz for Tired Feet, with a picture attached showing an exhausted commercial traveller, bowler hat on a nearby chair, sitting with his pinstripe trousers rolled up and his feet in a bowl of hot water, into which his wife had emptied a packet of 'Tiz'. The commercial traveller's face was suffused with a blissful smile of relief. A wife and a packet also featured in the Turvey Treatment for Alcoholics, but in this case the lady poured the packet into the gentleman's tea – without his knowledge. Why an alcoholic was so keen on tea drinking was never explained!

Are they still around, these mystic rubrics from my long lost youth? Where have all the Zambuks gone? Where are the Yardils of Yesteryear? Never mind Rupert Brooke's anxious enquiry whether there is honey still for tea at Grantchester. I want to know if Scott's Emulsion still carries a label depicting a sturdy Newfoundland fisherman clad in heavy oilskins and humping the Biggest Cod in the World on his back. Mother had a touching faith in this glutinous, fishy-smelling compound, the apotheosis of cod liver oil. It built up resistance against all the ills that lay in wait for small boys in damp winters, but mother also believed that it developed brainpower. This was important, since she was determined that we three boys should go to Oxford and that meant, in the state of father's finances, that we had to win scholarships to do so. My early life became a sort of scholarship steeplechase. Mother sent us off to examinations in the spirit of a Spartan mother: 'Come back with your shield or on it.' To make absolutely sure of success on the day of my first test, she gave me a double dose of Scott's Emulsion. It did the trick. I passed, first to the Municipal Secondary School, known to everyone naturally as the Mun. Sec., and was later transferred to the Swansea Grammar School.

CHAPTER TWO

Growing Up in Swansea

When I entered it in the early twenties, Swansea Grammar School was the complete and glorious antithesis of all the educational establishments admired today. The comprehensive concept, coeducation and the rest of the progressive stock-in-trade of the modern educationalist would have seemed like the ritual exercises of some strange African tribe to the governors, the masters and the pupils who sauntered through its pseudo-Gothic portals. In essence, their idea of the true end of education remained that of Bishop Gore, the kindly, Restoration-type prelate of the Irish Establishment, who had founded the school in 1687 and proclaimed its motto as: 'Virtue and Good Literature'. I am not sure about the results on the side of virtue, but it certainly did its bit for literature – it produced Dylan Thomas. Looking back on it, Swansea Grammar School was the only school that could have produced him.

The buildings were a sort of 1850-ish mid-Victorian dream of what a school would have looked like in the later Middle Ages. As this was Swansea, it was naturally built on the side of the steepest hill available, but the hill rejoiced in the poetic name of Mount Pleasant. You entered through a doorway that looked like a leftover from some hurriedly dissolved minor monastery. Over it rose a castellated tower, designed for defence against all attacking educational theorists. Here the governors could defy every education act passed since 1687. Immediately beyond the doorway was a large, stone-flagged entrance hall which echoed continually to the footsteps of boys changing classes and from which you could catch a glimpse of the headmaster's study and even of the headmaster himself, Dr Trevor Owen, sitting at his massive mahogany desk. No trendy, open-necked, jean-clad, still-with-it-at-fifty-lefty he, but an impressive, statuesque figure, perpetually clad in MA (Cantab.) gown and mortarboard, as all headmasters should be. On the right was the assembly hall, oak-beamed and gothic-windowed, where we gathered for morning prayers, when the lessons were read by the prefects in turn, standing at a lectern supported by a bronze eagle. On the slightly raised platform behind it, the headmaster sat at a finely polished table. The effect of scholastic dignity was slightly damaged when you noticed two large lines scored on the polished surface. These had been made by certain young gentlemen who sneaked into the hall during unauthorized hours to use the table as a shove-halfpenny board. As for the rest of the buildings – classrooms, labs, gym, etcetera – they had been added to the original school in a series of afterthoughts. The whole place was a wonderful piece of architectural knitting.

The masters fitted perfectly into the architecture. To the eye of youth they had a slightly Gothic look about them. They were characters who had all found attractive niches in this unusual educational hide-out. Many were men of intellectual distinction who could have sought a university career, but who preferred to stay in a town that had the Gower paradise on its doorstep and rejoiced in a school conducted on highly civilized lines. Boys being boys, we had no appreciaton of our mentors' attainments. Masters are fair game in the perpetual battle between the educator and the educatee.

Our classics master was an outstanding scholar who had made valued contributions to the *Classical Review* but who was a nonstarter when it came to discipline. He would sit at his desk pondering over such deliciously obscure and fascinating problems as the interpretation offered by the great Willimoitz-Mollendorf of the use of 'quoque' in the 2nd Satire of Juvenal, or the validity of Lachmann's emendation of line 462 in the second book of Lucretius from 'videmus Sensibus Sedatum' to the controversial 'venenums Sensibu sed rarum'. Meanwhile pupils were pondering an equally difficult problem

– how to attach strings, without being noticed, to all the lamps in the schoolroom and how to pull those strings so that the lamps would sway alarmingly at a given signal. The strings were successfully tied and suddenly the whole class leapt up shouting, 'Earthquake, sir, earthquake'. The startled master looked up and felt the world collapsing around him. He resolved to calm the panic in the most effective way possible. 'Don't panic, boys. Don't panic. It's quite natural. Remember the words of Seneca the Younger, "Hic aliquo mundus tempore nullus erit". Translate, Jenkins.' For once, the master had won!

Every lunch time he walked up the hill to the nearest local to enjoy an innocent pint with the English master, D. J. Thomas, who also happened to be Dylan's father. This was enough for the whole class to sing a greeting to him on his return for the afternoon session, to a well-known Welsh hymn tune. 'Where does Soapy get beer from?' they chanted, 'Where does Soapy get beer from?' ending with the answer, shouted *double forte*, 'From the Mountain Dew'. For the first quarter-of-an-hour, poor 'Soapy' struggled manfully to get the class under control. 'To work, to work!' he would plead. 'Where there's a will, there's a way.'

'Ah, yes,' replied the class. 'And where there's a swill, there's a sway!' The afternoon ritual duly completed, work actually began in the Classical sixth from.

D. J. Thomas's English class was a different affair altogether. He was a disciplinarian with the disconcerting habit of rapping you over the knuckles with his pencil if you misplaced a quotation. The English language and its correct usage was a passion, and he was outraged at the mangling it underwent at the hands of boys, many of whom came from a mixed Anglo-Welsh background. He had a gift of irony which could hurt. In moments of exasperation with his class he would look over his glasses and misquote with a certain contemptuous relish as the quiet noise made by the boys reached the Olympian heights of his desk: 'Ah, the murmur of innumerable B-F's.'

I think that, at this time, he must have been a disappointed man, who had hoped for better academic things than drilling

Chaucer into what he called 'the thick Neanderthal skulls of ignorant adolescents'. He certainly drilled Chaucer into me, savouring on his tongue all the more anti-clerical asides of the poet as if they were glasses of thirty-year-old vintage port. I can still see him, wrapping his gown around him and quoting with gusto the portrait of that worldly fellow, the Monk:

> His head was balled, that shoon as any glas,
> And eke his face, as he had been enoynt,
> He was a lord full fat and in good point.

'As indeed,' D. J. would add, 'is a certain Welsh bishop I could name today.' But when he came to deal with the young squire, his whole voice seemed to lose its usual hint of acid and become soft and tender. A rare smile played around his lips as he recited:

> Synginge he was, or floytynge all the day;
> He was as fresh as is the month of May . . .
> He koude songes make and wel endite.
> Juste and eke dance, and well purtraye and write.

And so to the charming end of Chaucer's portrait of the perfect son:

> Curteis he was, lowly and servysable,
> And cerf biforn his father at the table.

Could we doubt for a moment that this particular father had his own son in mind – young Dylan, who had now entered the school and, even at the tender age of twelve, showed evidence of his precocious poetic gifts. D. J. saw all his own ambitions as a young man being fulfilled in Dylan. I was considerably older than Dylan, and had attained the power of a prefect while he was still in the lower forms. It was some years later that I got to know him properly, but he was naturally pointed out to us all as 'D.J.'s boy', and we were careful how we applied discipline to him. At this period he looked like a mischievous Botticelli angel, and I am pretty certain his father's influence was exerted to spare him too many of the boring periods of school life. What was the point of instilling French and maths into the mind of someone who was growing up to be a Great Poet?

Dylan felt this strongly as he and his classmate Dan (who

later became the distinguished Welsh musician, Dr Daniel Jones), sneaked out of school to dodge the French class. The headmaster happened to look out from his study. 'What's this, boy? Where are you going?'

'Down town to play billiards,' said Dylan, putting a bold face on it. 'Any objection?'

The headmaster looked at him doubtfully. 'Oh, you wicked boys. I hope you get caught.'

Ah, but Swansea Grammar School, in my day, was the one establishment where a genius need never be caught in the toils of needless discipline. The headmaster reassured my father when I became a pupil, 'Dr Thomas, if your boy has anything in him, we'll make certain he'll get a scholarship to Oxford – even to Cambridge; and if he's got nothing in him but is just a nice fellow, we'll make his passage through school as pleasant as possible.' Of course, the school was no educational Abbey of Theleme with the motto *Fais ce que Voudras* – Do what thou wilt – inscribed over the Gothic doorway. It simply took the civilized view that teaching was impossible unless the boys were willing to be taught, and in those far-off days, before society dragged everyone, willing or unwilling, through the educational machine, most of the boys with me were willing to be taught, or at least put up a pleasant show of being willing to please the masters. As a result, the school had a fine record of winning scholarships to the senior universities. When my moment came, I too was successfully propelled into Oxford as an Exhibitioner at my father's old college, Exeter.

In the meantime, as at my first school, again I simply floated happily through the long business of education – all the more happily because the school had no compulsory games. I am not even certain that it had proper playing fields. There were two bare earth patches known as the 'upper' and the 'lower', on which we disported ourselves during the morning break, and some fives courts tucked in near the break-neck flight of steps that conducted you to the main buildings, if you had enough stamina to climb them. I deduced that there must have been rugby and cricket teams because their somewhat chequered records were chronicled in the school magazine; but no one ever suggested to me that I ought to 'turn out at nets' or attend a training session in rugby tactics. Instead I went off for long bicycle rides on those still traffic-free roads of the early twenties, or puffed down to the sands of the nearest Gower bays, riding on the glorious Mumbles train. This strange and magical railway was Swansea's pride, for it was the oldest continuously working railway in the world. The line curved on the edge of the tide around Swansea Bay – once described by Walter Savage Landor as more beautiful than the Bay of Naples. Now it has gone, and I hear only the ghostly sound of its clanging tank engine and see, through the mists of time, the holiday crowds clinging to the long string of 'toast-rack' open carriages, like the passengers on the Calcutta trams.

The Mumbles train deposited us first at the village of Oystermouth tucked under the steep limestone crags left by quarrying operations in the early nineteenth century. Oysters were still sold here in the early 1920s, although the great days of the Oystermouth 'natives' were over. The Romans had first given the seal of approval to what my uncle Arthur insisted on calling 'this delectable bivalve', and in the 1880s, over two hundred ketches operated out of the village, dredging up the oysters from beds down-channel from Mumbles Head. But the beds were overfished and by the time we came to patronize the oyster bars, the oyster fleet had dwindled to a few boats, and maybe the oysters themselves did not all originate in the Bristol Channel. No matter. We delighted in standing beside the trestle table outside the oyster bar and watching the proprietor opening the shells with a deft twist of the knife, while the salt tang from the shells in their wooden buckets pervaded the whole promenade.

It is curious how a perfume, a smell remembered, has a persistent power to carry you back into the past. I still cannot swallow an oyster without hearing Uncle Arthur's voice declaiming 'delectable bivalve', and seeing us gathered around him at the Gladstone Oyster Bar as he instructed us in the correct way of swallowing an Oystermouth native, and impressed on us that if we swallowed oysters regularly we would never suffer from rheumatism for the whole of our lives. The enlarged photograph of the great Liberal leader looked down on us approvingly as we swallowed the oysters as eagerly as

uncle had swallowed his speeches. The very act of letting the
shellfish slide down our throats was, in a small way, an act of
defiance against the Great Liberal Bore. No one could remind
us when it came to oysters that we should not bolt our food
because Gladstone always masticated each bit ten – or was it
fifteen or twenty – times before he swallowed it.

Uncle Arthur however, had the Victorian's reverence for
Great Men, no matter how they had become great. Thus he
drew our attention, with almost the same tone of respect he
had bestowed on Gladstone, to another place of pious pilgrimage in Oystermouth. In the churchyard lay the solidly
ornate grave of the Reverend Thomas Bowdler, the early
nineteenth-century cleric who published expurgated editions
of Shakespeare and other classics, from which he carefully
removed 'all passages which might bring a blush to the innocent cheek of youth', and in the process added the new word,
to bowdlerize, to the English language. The naive performance brought sardonic comments on many occasions from
Dylan's father to his sixth form, and later on, the rector
refused permission – perhaps wisely – for an elaborate ceremony of homage to Bowdler to be held in the churchyard. It
was to have been organized by Kingsley Amis in his *Lucky Jim*
days as a lecturer in Swansea University. The climax would
have been the laying on Bowdler's grave of an enormous
wreath – of fig leaves!

At the age of twelve, however, I confess I was not interested
in the status of poor Bowdler amongst modern intellectuals. I
never went into the churchyard of Oystermouth Church, but
marched resolutely onwards, through the Cutting, to the
delights that awaited us on Mumbles Pier. This splendid
flowering of late Victorian pier-culture was built in 1898. The
railway directors felt that no self-respecting holiday line could
be complete without a pier, so they built a glorious one,
covered with curly cast-iron decorations, clanking wooden
planks, and little kiosks at regular intervals, in which you
could crank up ancient photo machines for a penny and enjoy
the forbidden delights of 'What the Butler Saw' – not very
much, I remember, in those non-permissive days!

There was another temptation on the pier which inevitably

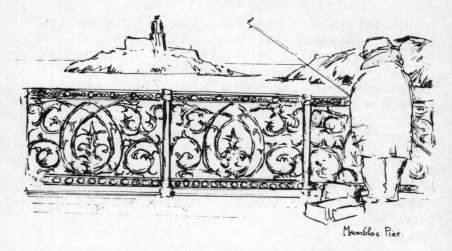

Mumbles Pier.

lured us off the straight and narrow path of middle class rectitude in which we were brought up. In front of one of the kiosks was a rack containing a choice selection of those fruity seaside postcards which are a traditional joy of all British piers and promenades. Here was a strange mad world that I had no idea existed, a dream country inhabited by red-nosed gentlemen pinching barmaids' bottoms; landladies with breasts like vegetable marrows waiting up with frying pans to deal with lodgers smashed out of their minds; drunken husbands falling into horse troughs; Bertie Woosterish figures, on piers that led out over seas of permanent Reckitt's Blue, lifting their straw boaters to young flappers who seemed built for winning the hundred yards Olympics below the waist and for instant motherhood above it. Or a pert schoolteacher, bulging in all the places never mentioned in education authorities forms, standing in front of her class as a pupil raised his hand, 'Please, miss, can I have a rubber?'

'No, use the little boy's behind.'

At the pier's end, rows of rather depressed-looking fishermen waited patiently for the bells to ring at the ends of their rods. Then they hurriedly reeled in their lines to find large, uneatable green crabs clinging to the lugworm bait. Back went the lines, with a splendid swing, far out from the iron pillars of the pier, buoyed up with the knowledge that once, in the early

years of the pier's existence, a fisherman had actually caught a
noble salmon bass on this very spot. The lines got tangled and
were rushed out of the way as the hooters announced the
stately approach of the cross-channel paddle steamer of Messrs
Campbell's White Funnel Fleet.

Once a year we boarded the *Lady Moira* or the *Glengower*
for our annual trip to 'Combe. On clear days across the
twenty-five-mile-wide Bristol Channel, we could see the long
line of the hills of Exmoor ending in the graceful tors high
above Ilfracombe. 'Rain tomorrow,' prophesied the know-
ledgeable Swansea residents, but somehow I always seem to
remember calm seas for our voyages. How else could we have
encountered the strange figure of 'Cyclino', billed as Swansea's
own star of variety, pedalling his bicycle fitted with floats on
his annual bank holiday trip across the Channel? 'Cyclino'
received his salute of cheers and a fanfare on the steamer's
hooter, and as he dropped astern, still madly pedalling, we
went down below to see the great engines, with their glistening
brass rods and hissing steam connection driving the vast
paddles dripping and clanking inside their wooden cage. Our
trips always took place on a Saturday, for the Sunday trips
were crowded with escapes from the Welsh licensing laws.

Our returns from Ilfracombe were more sedate. Crammed
with Devonshire cream, we were met by Aunty Bess with
tickets for the evening concert in the Winter Gardens. These
curious cultural get-togethers were probably on their last legs
in the years immediately after the First World War, the fag-end
of the great tradition of palm court entertainment at the seaside. There was always a choir, singing an arrangement of 'All
Through the Night', a tenor who competed with the seagulls
and the waves slapping against the pillars of the pier with a
version of 'Largo al Factotum' and a big-bosomed lady carrying all before her as she took us back to old Kashmir or
brought the house down with, 'There's a long, long trail
a-winding, into the land of my dreams'.

It was at a pier concert that I last heard a recitation, to
public applause and not laughter, of Swansea's own special
tear-jerker, 'The Women of Mumbles Head'. In January,
1883, the barque *Prinz Adelbert* of Danzig went ashore on the

outlying rocks of Mumbles Head, and the lifeboat was launched in a desperate attempt to save the crew. The lifeboat itself was flung against the wreck, and coxswain Jenkins and two of his sons were drowned. But two men were saved by the courage of the lighthouse keeper's daughters, the sisters Ace, who went down into the swirling surf, threw their shawls to the drowning men and dragged them to safety. At last, Wales had its own Grace Darlings.

Clement Scott, the Victorian critic and ballad writer, was quickly on the scene with a splendid piece of rhymed rhetoric that made the round of the music halls and is remembered by the old folk in Swansea to this day. The climax gave the elocutionist every chance to pull out all the stops in his art:

Wait for the next wave, darling, only a minute more
And I'll have him safe in my arms, dear, and we'll drag him safe to
the shore
Up to their arms in water, fighting it breast to breast,
They caught and saved a brother alive! God Bless us, we know the
rest —
Well, many a heart beat stronger, and many a tear was shed,
And many a glass was tossed right off to the Women of Mumbles
Head.

Stirring stuff! But perhaps it represented a slight drop in standards from the pre-First World War concerts when Sims Reeves and John McCormack and the great Adelina Patti herself had graced the pier with their presence.

Patti — Madam Patti, to everyone in Swansea — was a strange, exotic bird to find nesting, at the close of her career, in the Celtic wilds of the South Wales hills. My Uncle Arthur with his love of the ripe, rotund word, always referred to her as 'the diva of Craig-y-Nos'. It was an odd quirk of fate that sent the most glamorous operatic star of the nineteenth century to settle by the Crag of Night (Craig-y-Nos) at the lonely top end of the Swansea Valley. Patti was born in Madrid but was brought up in New York. She dazzled Europe with her singing, her beauty and her love affairs. Her voice was a melting soprano and earned her fabulous wealth. For a single performance in New York she received £1,000, then the biggest fee ever paid to an opera singer. But her spectacular success only led to unhappiness in her love life. She had been married to the Marquis de Caux, Equerry to Napoleon III, but the marriage was a failure and she had turned for consolation to her leading tenor, Ernest Nicolini, a Frenchman by birth, who had sung Romeo to her Juliet in Gounod's opera and Radames to her Aida. She needed a romantic hide-out, where she could retire from the world in between operatic tours.

An old admirer, Sir Hussey Vivian, later Lord Swansea, suggested the lonely country at the top of the Tawe valley, where there was a big house for sale at Craig-y-Nos. Patti took his advice in 1878 and Craig-y-Nos became her home for over forty happy years. What newspaperman would think of hunting her down at the end of a Welsh mining valley?

The secret lay, of course, in the little-known fact that the River Tawe in its upper reaches passes out of the coalfield into wild, lonely country which even today is comparatively unfrequented. Here are glittering limestone crags and great hills which rise over 2,600 feet and hide lonely lakes under layered cliffs of Old Red Sandstone. I have a deep affection for the 'Patti Country' for it was the first bit of wild landscape I discovered, as it were, for myself. Gower, my first love, had been given to me by my parents, and Ilfracombe by Aunty Bess, but the secret land above Abercrave, in the upper Swansea valley, was a personal find. I knew about it, of course, for father had written a vivid dramatic cantata around the legend of Llyn y Van Fach, the lost lake cradled under the most savage of the Old Red Sandstone cliffs. I suppose that every child in South Wales in my day knew the story of the farmer's son who married the fairy maiden who rose out of the lake, and how he prospered until he forgot her one stipulation – that he must never strike her without cause. Thoughtlessly he did so, and after the third time, the lady of the lake returned to the still waters taking all the cattle and the farmer's wealth with her. Of course, he died of a broken heart, but the mother reappeared and instructed her sons in the mysteries of fairy medicine. So began the famous line of the Physicians of Myddfai, renowned from the Middle Ages almost down to our own day. The last of the line, Dr John Williams, became the personal physician to Queen Victoria and did not die until 1920.

My brothers and I set off one memorable Easter holiday, loaded with rucksacks full of lunch and with much careful paternal advice, to climb the 2,600-foot peak of the Carmarthen Van, and to walk along the high escarpment to where the dark cliffs encircle the lake of the legend, the lonely pool of Llyn-y-Van. I remember all the incidents of that day, as I remember the Day of the Lobster in my childhood. I was many years older, but once again I felt a new revelation of the beauty and excitement of the physical world. This time, I was to be given the freedom of the high hills. It has been with me ever since, one of the basic forces that sustains me through life. I was thirteen at the time and not given to biblical quotation, but later on I read the psalmist's exhortation, 'I will lift up

mine eyes to the hills, from whence cometh my help'. I have never felt any need to read further.

The approach to paradise was prosaic enough. The bus took us through the long line of straggling townships – Clydach, Pontardawe, Ystalyfera, Ystradgunlais, with names that baffle the English in print, but are music to the ears of Welshmen. Maybe this was the only delightful thing about them, for in those days chemical works, steel works, tin-plate works and colliers were still busy in the Tawe Valley. They are all gone now, and the hills ahead are always visible in the clear air. Then we caught only fitful glimpses of them through industrial smog. We cheered ourselves up by playing the celebrated game

Rhyd g peisant. chapel.

classic symplearly. while washed
sketch r w pine gard.

of oratorios. At Easter, every one of the chapels we passed staged a special musical dramatic production with its children's choir. You tossed for sides, and right played left. As the bus lumbered through the twenty miles of strung-out Bethels, Bethesdas, Carmels, Bethanias and Caesareas you tried to collect the greatest number, on your side, of the same Easter musical offering. I scooped the kitty with twelve performances of 'Esther, the Beautiful Queen', between Pontardawe and Ystradgunlais.

The bus passed the last colliery at Abercrave and the revelation began. The whole valley made a sharp turn and dramatically changed character. The clean, white limestone crags tumbled down to meet us and the Tawe ran clear of coal dust through the woods. Trout leaped in the deep pools. In the shadow of the crags rose a castellated construction, all spiky turrets and high dormer windows, a miniature Welsh version of Scott's Abbotsford. This was Patti's hide-out. In the new crystal-clear river, her fishing-mad consort, Signor Nicolini. angled for trout between arias. Beyond rose the high peak of Van Gihirech. A perfect place to retire from the world. I was carried away by it as passionately as the diva had been.

We began our climb at Patti's door – up through the high farms where the limestone changed to Old Red Sandstone under our feet, then out onto the bare mountain side, following the moraine left by the glacier that once lay under the cliffs of Van Hir. From the dark Van Pool, we climbed up the steep sheep track for the last six hundred feet to my first real mountain summit. It was a clear day, with a sky of eggshell blue and a few cloud wisps drifting slowly across it in a light wind. All Wales seemed to lie below us. The long, breaking wave of high summits that marked the Brecon Beacons was still speckled with snow. Away to the north stretched the mysterious untrodden wilderness of Central Wales. To the south, beyond the smokes of the valleys, glittered the Bristol Channel, widening out to the great, open sea. There was a lark singing above me.

I have climbed many mountains since – wilder, ice-covered, higher and more savage and infinitely more dangerous; but the Carmarthenshire Van, like first love, was the mountain that taught me what it was all about. I have never since that day been able to give any rational explanation of why I climb mountains. All I can say is – I don't think about it. I feel it. And I first felt it on that Easter Day on the high summit above the dark lake of Llyn-y-Van.

You cannot stay on Exultation Summit forever. We walked back following the river down to the valley and came to the Gwyn Arms, which was then kept by Mr and Mrs Price. It was everything an old-style Welsh inn should be. George Borrow might be approaching it at any moment to demand *curw da* (good ale) and astonish the locals with the Welsh he had acquired on the Norfolk Broads. There were open fires in the bar and a kitchen behind, with hams hanging from hooks in the roof like gastronomic stalactites. Mrs Price had been in service at Craig-y-Nos in Patti's day, and kept a photograph of the diva on her wall. She told us of the great days at the castle. 'Madam', as she always called Patti, kept almost royal state. Not for nothing was she called the queen of song. Mrs Price remembered how she entertained her visitors in her private theatre which held 150 special guests. It is still there, complete with the curtain depicting Patti riding in a chariot drawn by two spirited horses, and enacting her favourite role of Semiramide in Rossini's opera of the same name.

Patti used to travel down to Swansea in her special train. Her private station and waiting room remain high up on the mountainside. It was last used for the film of *Young Winston*, when actors dressed as Boers and British soldiers scrambled around Penwyllt station to re-enact Churchill's capture in an armoured train during the South African War. I do not think Patti would be amused. She travelled in more dignified style, and was always met at Swansea Station by the mayor. Then she was driven through cheering crowds in an open carriage, with an escort of yeomen cavalry, to preside over charity concerts. I have a vague memory of being taken as a little boy to see her pass. Every concert ended with Patti being persuaded to come onto the platform to sing 'Home, Sweet

Home': 'Be it ever so humble, There's no place like ...
Craig-y-Nos Castle!' They knew how to treat a great artist in
those days. They gave her the public homage that we now
reserve for pop stars.

There is one strange relic of Patti's long love affair with
Swansea. Her ghost still haunts the Grand Theatre – well, at
least, I have the evidence of a distinguished Thames Television
producer to prove it. The producer was rehearsing one morning on an empty stage when she looked up at one of the boxes.
She saw a beautiful lady in rich Edwardian costume lean
forward and give polite applause to the act. She turned to a
stagehand to ask who was in the box but when she looked up
again the lady had vanished. Said the stagehand, 'We all know
her – it's Madame Patti.'

With father earning his living by music, our house was
naturally filled with sound, but it was strictly classical sound.
Outside in another world, jazz was starting to creep across the
Atlantic to subvert the old settled routine of English light
music. We picked up plenty of its early frolics at school, but we
never brought jazz home. I would have felt it sacrilege to try
and play 'Yes, we have no bananas' on father's Broadwood. At
home we tackled, or hacked our way through, Brahms and
Mozart and Bach's '48'; in fact, everyone up to Debussy and
Ravel was fair game. The curtain only came down on Verdi, or
Donizetti or Puccini. Father, I think, secretly felt that they
were vulgar, the musical equivalent of the cinema and
Hollywood. He made one exception, and that, curiously
enough, was in favour of Wagner. Wagner, after all, still held
the field as the man who had remoulded music into a new
exciting image when father went up to Oxford in 1891. Had
not Bernard Shaw set the seal of British approval on him in *The
Perfect Wagnerite*, published in 1898. True, Wagner had been
dead for fifteen years, but Britain had finally caught up. To
father, Wagner was Opera.

Not to me. Father did his best to make me enchanted with
the vast musical labyrinth of *The Ring*. He played me chunks
of *Siegfried*, but I recoiled from the goings-on of that foretaste
of the ideal Nazi thug. It is all irrational, unfair, even uneduc-
ated, but my anti-Wagnerian prejudice remains with me to this

day. One half of me admits that here is one of the giants of music, a daring innovator, a very great composer indeed. The other half remembers Hermione Gingold, dressed as Brunhilde 'with storm troopers down in my basement' singing

> Oh, the brass, Oh, the wind
> And oh, the relief when they got me unpinned.

I have to leave it at that, and turn to composers more suited to my rather light-hearted taste. To Wagner, I felt bound to give a Wotan's Farewell.

Still, the urge – the temptation – to find out the Truth about Opera nagged away at the back of my mind. After all, this was the magic world of the diva of Craig-y-Nos. This was the area in which Patti, Swansea's pride, had scored her triumphs, in which her voice had soared to glory and an enormous fortune. The voice was the key to it, and at this moment of growing up I had acquired a rather morbid interest in one voice – my own.

When I was small I had a pleasant, boyish alto and could warble 'Orpheus with his Lute' by Sullivan, and Arne's 'Water Parted' to please visiting elderly relatives at tea time. I was no Master Ernest Lough, whose record of 'Oh for the Wings of a Dove' was hovering in the wings ready to wow the sentimental heart of the nation a few years further on. I had just reached the stage of suitable Schubert when my voice broke. I wasn't supposed to use it or strain it for the next year or so – and then, who knows – I might develop a glorious tenor. Everyone assumes that Welshmen all have tenor voices that propel them immediately into the nearest choir. Alas, no ravishing tenor voice appeared after my vocal closed season and today I still croak my disappointment. I envy the men and women who have glorious voices.

Then, in 1924, the 'Grand' announced a special and important Sunday concert. Madame Tetrazzini would appear at Swansea on her final world tour before retirement – Louisa Tetrazzini, who had been acclaimed as the nearest approach to Adelina Patti, the toast of opera goers throughout the heady days of Edwardian opulence. There was no objection to me attending a concert. I would thus hear the acknowledged great operatic arias free from the gaudy scenery, lurid plots and grimacing, overacting singers. I sat eagerly in the grand circle waiting for the entry of the diva. To my astonishment, there suddenly popped out, almost from inside the grand piano, not the reincarnation of the 'Diva of Craig-y-Nos' but a portly smiling little tub of a woman, in a black dress covered in more sequins than ever graced the costumes in 'Come Dancing', and which fell as straight as a plumb-line from her ample bosom to the floor. When she moved she looked like a Dalek chasing Dr Who. She acted as a prima donna, it is true – kisses to the audience, cascades of notes in long-forgotten arias from Cherubini and Donizetti, vast bouquets of flowers presented in tribute at the end; but that squat almost dwarf-like figure was a killer. She had killed, with one expensive warble, my picture of the delights of opera going.

I did make one more attempt, a few years later, to recapture the dream that had started with the romance I had with the memory of Madam Patti. The Carl Rosa arrived for their annual visit and I was now old enough to go if I pleased. I felt, however, in deference to father's views, I ought to select the most worthwhile of the offerings that week at the Grand – not sugary Puccini but mature Verdi. I went to hear *Otello*! The plot, it is true, seemed puzzlingly different from Shakespeare's play, but the music was thrilling. This, I felt, was more like it – and then, once again, came the disaster that dogged all my first footsteps in opera. Otello was sung by the genial Frank Titterton. In the handkerchief scene, Otello faints and falls, with a *double forte* crash, to the ground. Iago then places his foot on him and sings an aria of contemptuous triumph. Frank Titterton duly fell, raising a slight cloud of dust from the boards. Iago stepped forward and lifted his foot – but, horror, poor Titterton had put on weight and would perhaps have filled the role of Falstaff better than that of Otello. Iago tried again, singing gamely, and failed. A last supreme effort – and his tights split! My temporary flirtation with opera was over.

Years later, after I had heard *Don Giovanni* and the Mozart masterpieces, when tenors and sopranos had become slim and handsome and designers splendidly ingenious and lavish, I returned to the opera house and was ravished by what I saw and heard. I have become an opera fanatic in my old age.

Could I even be ready to go to *Götterdämmerung* at last? Fifty-odd years or so ago, however, I had put opera firmly on one side, and when in search of sensation turned to the cinema instead.

When I was growing up, the cinema was growing up too. It had long passed out of its nickelodeon phase. The Carlton, Swansea's leading picture house, had a marble front on to Oxford Street and you were shown to your place in plush seats by usherettes, flashing torches. The music was still supplied by the pianist in the pit, who had an appropriate tune for every change of scene. The cowboys and Indians still went charging over the screen to the rhythm of Suppé's *Light Cavalry* overture.

In the Carlton they always gave you full value for money; two features, a serial and a comedy short. It was the serial and the comedy shorts that remain with me. We were allowed to go when mother was satisfied that the features were 'healthy for us', as she put it, in other words, adventure or cowboys and Indians. The Indians in those days were Aunty-Bess-type red men – mean, dirty and dangerous – not noble savages, to whom American film makers now conduct an endless apology for the harsh way the west was won. The cowboys were our heroes, and we cheered when each Indian bit the dust. The serial always seemed to be Pearl White in *The Exploits of Elaine*. She really was left tied to a railway track, or strapped on a belt carrying her towards a circular saw, at the end of each episode. The audience was as unsophisticated as I was, for the intelligentsia still despised the cinema in those immediate postwar years. As the villain's hands closed around the neck of the unsuspecting heroine, the elderly ladies in the six-pennies gasped in chorus, 'Look out, Pearl, he's gotcher!' But it was comedy that we longed for, and I used to tremble with excitement as the screen announced, 'Clyde Cook in *The Guide*'. They didn't waste hours giving credits in those days. Up came the subtitles, 'The Guide, who has known the Alps since they were little knobs'. And I would roll in the aisles with laughter. Or Charlie Chaplin would appear, bowler-hatted and cane in hand, in the middle of a high society ball; subtitle 'Dresses by Omar the Tentmaker'.

Unknowingly, I was living through the early days of the communications revolution. After the cinema would come radio and after radio, TV, and the world in which I was brought up would never be the same again. The symbol of the change was the transformation of the Albert Hall. This was Swansea's assembly hall, a solidly built Victorian structure, with a wide balcony and an organ, where father had produced Elgar's *Apostles* and where I had attended Miss Langdon's dancing classes at the age of eight, with two dozen small boys and girls of the same age. The elder Miss Langdon played the piano, while the younger one marshalled us into line and we learnt the waltz, the schottische and other evolutions that seemed to have come straight from some Dickensian dancing academy. Across the Atlantic a dancing revolution was accompanying the advent of jazz but no anticipatory rumbles reached the ears of the Misses Langdon. They were busy banning such war horrors as the bunny hug and the turkey trot. The older girls were taught a sedate tango. At the annual ball, the parents sat proudly around the walls, as my brothers and I performed a stately giration dressed as Pierrots with three little solemn-faced girls dressed as Columbines, and then made low bows to them – 'as little gentlemen should'.

All this was designed to make us well-behaved at the parties to which we always seemed to be invited around Christmas – parties full of jellies, crackers, and games organized by jolly uncles. I was also to teach us the now lost art of deportment and the rituals expected of boys growing up in polite society. In 1920–1, the demolishers moved in. Down came the pitch pine gallery and the organ. In went the screen and the Wurlitzer. Out went any pretensions to polite society.

The metamorphosis of the Albert Hall also marked a change in the whole political climate of Swansea, for it began the decline of the great mass meeting. The cinema supplied more excitement than any political orator could muster and soon radio would make it easier for an audience to stay at home, crouched over their crystal sets, than to struggle out to the Albert Hall on a wet night. Not that I knew much about politics, I was unaware of any of the issues involved until I was about fourteen; but in the days immediately after the First

World War, elections seemed to arrive at regular intervals, bringing glorious holidays, processions around the town, people wearing gigantic rosettes and the inevitable final rally at the Albert Hall. I remember being taken to one by Aunty Bess, who could never resist a good speech and this one was to be delivered by the greatest performer of them all, Lloyd George himself. He was at the peak of his power as an orator. He may have ceased being prime minister but he was a youthful sixty and could sway any audience, above all a Welsh audience, by a mere wave of his gold-rimmed spectacles. He made great play with them, and I was mesmerized by the way he pointed them at his audience, stabbing them in the air with gusto as he tore apart a supine figure called Mr Baldwin. His voice carried with flute-like clarity, without any microphone's aid, to the back of the crowded hall. The laughter, the cheering were his to conjure up at will.

'What is he saying, Aunty?' I asked.

'Never mind what he's saying, Wynford, but what a wonderful way to say it,' Aunty Bess replied, giving me my first insight into the art of politics.

Swansea was traditionally a Liberal stronghold but the local standard-bearer was hardly a figure to set a young boy's imagination on fire.

I suppose that Sir Alfred Mond had stood for the seat of Swansea West because of the important industrial interest he had in the big Mond Nickel Works at nearby Clydach. His father, the brilliant German industrial chemist Ludwig Mond had set up the process on the outskirts of Swansea, and his statue – in bronze and not nickel-plated – still stands outside the plant. With his wide-brimmed hat, walking stick and great square beard he looks like one of the more elderly generals in the Boer War. Sir Alfred did not exactly improve on his father when it came to looks. He appeared to have modelled himself on a *Communist Review* cartoon of the typical portly and wicked capitalist, pinstripe trousers, cut-away morning coat, silk hat and all. Added to which, he looked extremely Jewish and spoke with a guttural German accent. Poor Sir Alfred! He would not have much chance of being adopted as a candidate today, but he was first elected for Swansea when it was a solid

and safe Liberal seat, and a word from Lloyd George guaranteed acceptance. Behind that somewhat unprepossessing
exterior lay a brilliant industrial organizing power – he created
I C I – and a shrewd political brain; but his safe seat at
Swansea was now being rocked by a whole series of unexpected storms. The Liberal Party was torn into two by the old
feuds between Asquith and Lloyd George. The new Labour
Party zealots were advancing upon him with menacing strides.
He longed for a more dignified political asylum, but he had to
fight tied to his stake at Swansea West. The battle supplied
cruel and endless entertainment to us as growing boys.

I see Sir Alfred walking with his committee to a rally of his
supporters followed by a mob of ragged urchins in the Labour
colours, shouting – in response to some action of his as Minister of Health – 'Who stole the baby's milk? Who stole the
baby's milk? Alfie Mond! Alfie Mond!' Or pursued by derisive
cries of 'Votes for the Welsh', a slogan from the days of his
early advocation of Welsh home rule which had earned him a
savage mauling from Lord Birkenhead, who described him as
'a fiery crusader . . . crying out in the wild accents of his native
Wales'. As he ended his speech at his meetings, he had to put
up with the inevitable scabrous enquiries from the back of the
hall, 'Have you finished, Sir Alfred?' To his polite reply, 'Yes',
came a thunderous, ribald shout of, 'Pull the chain!' No wonder he eventually gave up Swansea West and the Liberals as
well. He joined the Conservatives while Lloyd George taunted,
'Many a man has crossed the floor of the House before him,
but none has left such a slimy trail of hypocrisy behind him'.
Sir Alfred soon sought happy and safe seclusion in the Lords.
He was the first politician I had seen in action at close quarters,
and he left me deeply puzzled – as I have been about politicians
ever since. Indeed, I was bewildered by politics altogether.
Which was the right side to support? My family was neatly
divided.

Mother's side, I felt, leaned towards the old-style Liberal –
even Conservative – outlook, and in my youthful eyes the
figure of my Uncle Arthur seemed to symbolize wealth, position, power. He was mother's elder brother, and by his
own ability had become the managing director and a large

shareholder in the Ashburnham Tin Plate works in the little town of Burry Port on the north shore of the Lougher estuary. The tin-plate world was booming when Uncle Arthur entered it and he was obviously a far shrewder businessman than Aunty Bess's over-optimistic husband Uncle David. He had his car, a large house with extensive gardens and membership of every important industrial committee in addition to being chairman of the Bench at Carmarthen. I looked on him with a certain amount of awe, almost as a being from another world. We used to go every year to spend Christmas Day with him and his family, riding down in his chauffeur-driven car, in which I secretly hoped some of the boys in my class would see me. The house contained two delights which seemed to me when very young to be the epitome of the power of wealth. There was a parrot who spoke such witty phrases as 'pretty Polly', and 'I don't like Lloyd George', and there was a billiard room in which we were allowed to play in the afternoon, after the gigantic Christmas dinner, carefully supervised by my cousins.

Above the fireplace of the billiard room was a vast dark painting of Loch Lomond by W.B. Leader, R A. 'They tell me it is excellent value for the money,' Uncle Arthur assured father, and I kept glancing up at it in admiration as I played, to the consternation of Cousin Artie. Even at the age of eleven or so, our characters in later life must already have been clearly prefigured. My elder brother, Spencer, played carefully and correctly. He became a schoolmaster and had a successful international career in educational administration. My younger brother, Vaughan, was a brilliant games player, who eventually performed the curious feat for a Welshman of becoming a hockey international for Scotland. He served with distinction on Mountbatten's staff at Combined Operations and rose to the rank of Brigadier – good going for an amateur soldier. He went on to become a successful businessman and lives happily in Sussex in the shadow of the South Downs. He potted everything with unerring aim, even from the far end of the table. As for me, I was brilliant at cutting in delicately poised reds over pockets but equally brilliant at almost ripping the cloth with a careless attempt to get at an impossible black. Luckily our assaults on the billiard table were always interrupted by the maid announcing, 'It's time for Thora, they are all waiting in the hall'.

We would gather near the door in the hall, uncle with his glass of port and cigar in hand. Outside the cold, rainy winter's evening brought a slightly melancholy darkness and we could see the shadowy figure of the singer through the glass of the door. Then his untrained but sweet tenor voice rose in the quiet of the evening, 'Thora, Thora, speak to me Thora'. The old sentimental Victorian ballad of the vision of a lost wife warbled away outside, as it did every Christmas. The ritual never varied, and as the last notes faded, Mr Rees, who was a 'doubler' at the Ashburnham Works, was invited inside for a glass of whisky and a one-pound note. Uncle's eyes were always filled with tears as he presented the note. Then I remembered, of course, his wife – Aunt Bella, whom I never knew – had died long ago. Yes, I thought with the sententiousness of eleven, the rich too have their sorrows and our own little family group, although we had no parrot or car or billiard table, suddenly seemed snug, safe and desirable.

Especially when Uncle Arthur started to tell us (rather guardedly in front of the children) about the problem that had arisen with his neighbour and indeed his solicitor, Mr Harold Greenwood. 'They've arrested him. They say he's poisoned his wife. I can't believe it. I knew them both. It's not possible. After all he was a solicitor. Solicitors may embezzle funds but they never poison people.'

It is strange how certain events, right outside the narrow circle of your own experience, affect you powerfully when you are halfway through the process of growing up. Suddenly a danger you never knew existed impinges on your secure little world. A man could poison his wife! I took a macabre interest in the affair, as indeed did the whole of South Wales. Greenwood was a highly respected resident of the little town of Kidwelly, whose wife had suddenly died after drinking from a bottle of port wine. When Greenwood married a young and pretty girl three months after his wife's death, local tongues began to wag. Eventually poor Mrs Greenwood's body was exhumed and traces of arsenic were found in it. Greenwood went on trial and the great Sir Edward Marshall Hall was engaged to defend him. Those were the days when court advocacy was gloriously florid, a quality deeply appreciated in Wales. Crowds lined the streets to gaze on Sir Edward and gave him a hero's ovation as he walked to the regency courthouse from the Ivy Bush Hotel. Uncle Arthur stationed me where I, too, could almost touch the great man as he entered the court. He looked like Sir Henry Irving in the role of the Silver King, superbly handsome in a Roman way, white-haired and commanding. He had something clutched in his hand which Uncle Arthur – rightly or wrongly – told me was an expensive jewel. So Cicero must have passed through the forum on his way to denounce Cataline.

As I recollect, the whole case turned on who had also drunk a glass of wine at the lunch which had taken place outside, on the lawn, on that fatal day. Marshall Hall produced Greenwood's daughter at the critical moment in the trial. She gave evidence that she too had sipped the wine from that dangerous bottle. This may have been the turning point when it came to the law, but what the Welsh public really wanted to hear was Marshall Hall's final address to the jury. This was the performance for which the Great Advocate (always pointed in capitals by the local newspaper) was famous. He did not disappoint us. I have looked up the report of the speech in the back numbers of the *Carmarthen Journal* and it is stirring stuff, a sort of legal symphony of the nineteenth-century romantic school, ending, first with a long passage for muted strings:

'Your verdict is final. Science can do a great deal. These men, with their mirrors, multipliers and milligrams, can tell you to the thousandth or millionth part of a grain, the constituents of the human body. But science cannot do one thing – that is, to find the final spark which converts insensate clay into a human being.'

Then, *piano* – almost a whispered note on the cellos – as he quoted *Othello*:

Put out the light and then put out the light . . .

on to the close of Othello's words over the sleeping Desdemona:

But once put out thy light
Thou cunning'st pattern of excelling nature,
I know not where is that Promethean heat,
That can thy light relume.

He turned to the jury and slowly pointed his hand at them, 'Are you going, by your verdict, to put out that light?' The ringing voice, *double forte* now, playing on every chord backed by the whole orchestra, 'Gentlemen of the jury, I demand at your hands the life and liberty of Harold Greenwood'.

Of course, Marshall Hall got them, for this was a Carmarthen jury and Carmarthen juries are famous for their tender hearts. Unkind people from the rest of Wales say that they always have a fellow feeling for the accused, 'Better let him off. Could be one of us!' In the Welsh Bar mess, they tell the story of the distinguished Q C, who was watching the last stage of the successful run by the Dynefor Hunt, when the hounds were almost right up with the fox. 'They've got him. They've got him,' he shouted excitedly. 'Only a Carmarthen jury could save him now!'

The Greenwood case gave me a shuddering fascination for sensational crime which I have never been able to eradicate. I suspect most people will admit to this, for how else do you account for the circulation of the *News of the World*. The shudder section of my fascination with crime, however, received a sobering reinforcement a few years later with a strange incident during – of all things – a school excursion conducted by our history master. In a sort of converted lorry, fitted with wooden benches, which was the cheapest form of transport available in those days, we set off to inspect a series of castles on the way to St David's Cathedral. Our first stop was Kidwelly, and while the serious boys were making a last survey of this splendid concentric castle, I couldn't resist the thrill of suggesting to certain backsliders that I could show them the exact spot where Mrs Greenwood drank her port. We sneaked away and went down to peep through the gates of the House. I showed them the great tree under which Mrs Greenwood had sat when Hannah Williams, the maid, poured out that sinister glass of port (the tree is still there, so is 'The

5 *Top*: A group of fellow students at Exeter College, 1927 (W. V.-T. second from the left in the middle row)

6 *Above*: As forward in the Exeter College hockey XI, 1929

7 *Right*: Climbing on Glyder Fach, North Wales, 1930

8 The start of a commentator's career with the old style lip-mike

House', but it now used as a Sunday school). My comrades felt that I was in close contact with the men of inside knowledge and power and I glowed with pride and self-satisfaction – until we came to Carmarthen.

Our master, I suspect, wanted to retire for a brief spell to the Ivy Bush Hotel for a powerful whisky and soda. I don't blame him, for he had a long afternoon and evening ahead, coping with fifteen unruly youngsters. He instructed us to look at the scanty remains of the castle and return to the lorry by two o'clock. We found the castle all right, but within the circuit lay the old jail scheduled to be demolished. At the gateway we were met by the temporary watchman, who sized up a collection of innocent suckers if ever there was one. 'Looking at the castle?' he enquired. 'Well, I can show you something far more interesting – something you will never forget. It's highly educational, too. How much money have you got?'

'Well, we've got two shillings left after lunch.'

'That's exactly the entrance fee.' He collected all the money we had and led us across the bleak, echoing deserted jailyard to a small red brick, slate-roofed shed built against the high wall. Inside, all that we saw was a lever like those in a signal box, placed under a thick beam. Our guide invited me to pull it. I tugged and two flaps suddenly fell open revealing a deep pit at my feet. 'Now, my boy, you've done something few people have ever done. You've worked the Drop.' A horrible realization came over us. We were in the execution shed! Here poor Greenwood might have come if the jury had found him guilty. I gasped and led the rush out from that hateful little room into the clear air outside. No one else wanted to try and we fled across the prison yard. As we assembled outside the castle, we all agreed 'Don't tell a soul. Don't tell anyone at school.' I never did, but there have been moments ever since when that nasty little memory comes uninvited back to me. I didn't dream then that I would one day find myself in Belsen. Carmarthen gave me a strange anticipation, twenty-five years before, of the dismal horror of the concentration camps. Never ask me to support capital punishment.

All of which has taken me very far from Christmas and the kindly, considerate figure of my Uncle Arthur. His Ashburnham

Tin Plate Works were placed in a vast, dark, echoing cavern of a shed. A giant flywheel turned in the centre and drove the banks of mills where the tinplates were rolled after they were drawn red-hot from the furnaces. Rolling was a spectacular affair. I watched with awe as the doubler – Mr Rees who had sung 'Thora' at Christmas – seized a hot plate with huge iron tongs and flipped it through the mill. On the other side, his behinder turned it over and passed it back through the mill. Then Mr Rees doubled it with his foot protected by layers of leather and steel – and back it went again through the rollers until it was rolled to the required thickness. Mr Rees and his behinder paused and refreshed themselves with cans of beer.

There were other marvels to be seen in that clanging, hot shed – the Melingriffith Pot where the plates were dropped into a hot bath of shining tin, and the benches where rows of husky girls split the glittering packs apart with the noise of ripping silk and traded fruity dialogue with all the young workers who came near them. It seemed the epitome of industrial power to me; I did not know that new techniques were already being developed that would put all the individual tin-plate works out of business. Giant strip mills were being set up in the United States which would do, in an hour, in one continuous process, all that Mr Rees and his behinder, the Melingriffith Pot, and the rows of girls on the benches could do in a day. It took the two world wars to do it, but the old tin-plate world was bound to disappear in the end. Today, the Ashburnham Works are deserted. The old machinery has rusted, some of it sold for scrap. There is even talk of restoring Ashburnham as a piece of industrial archaeology – a tourist attraction and a museum where modern schoolchildren can learn about their past. I shudder at the thought. My Uncle Arthur and his world a chunk of industrial archaeology, a Welsh byegone, a peepshow for the curious! Never. Let it all fade with dignity into the shades.

As I look back, I tend to think of my father's relatives as the left wing of the family. An illusion, of course, for my uncles and cousins were solid citizens with the best of them, supporters of the chapel and lovers of choral music as all good

Welshmen should be. But as many of them lived in industrial villages like Pontardulais or in mining valleys like Cwmavon, I felt I was venturing into another world when we went to visit them. The train puffed and twisted up the narrow slits in the earth's surface, crowded with long terraces out of which sprouted chapels and welfare halls, like brick icebergs floating on a dark sea of houses. The wheels of the colliery winding gear spun high up in their cobweb of girders to drop men 2,000 feet down into the darkness of the coal seams, and to pull up the waste rock that was carried by aerial ropeways to build sinister pyramids high on the mountain sides. Through the streets the miners walked home with blackened faces, for the pithead baths had not yet been installed, and in a thousand two-storeyed 'Cartref's' the wives waited with hot water in big tin baths, ready to scrub their husbands' backs in front of the kitchen fire. All this was different – even frighteningly different – from the everyday routine of my life in Swansea.

Swansea, it is true, was a heavily industrialized town, but it was possible to live there, as I did as a small boy, without coming into daily contact with industry at all. Dylan Thomas summed it up to me one evening in our sardonic twenties, when we were panting on our way up the steep hill to his house in Cwmdonkin Drive, 'You've got to be a Welsh Sherpa to live in a place like this'. Then he looked out over the streets of Swansea tumbled carelessly at our feet around the long curve of the bay, 'This town,' he said, 'has more layers than an onion, and every one can reduce you to tears.'

The section of the town which held our house in Walter Road faced the sea. The roads climbed to the uplands and the edge of the Gower commons, or curved around the bay to West Cross and Oystermouth. This was the expanding area of desirable villas, of the old mansions of the nineteenth-century copper kings where the tramlines ended and the houses began of the people who had the first motor cars in Swansea. Beyond lay all the unspoilt glories of Gower. True you could also see the long piers of the harbour from our bedroom windows and hear, on still summer nights, the far-off rumble of the coal elevators in the docks pouring down anthracite into the eager holds of tramp steamers and colliers from the far corners of the world. Those coal tips are silent now, and the long line of vessels anchored off Mumbles Head awaiting their turn to enter the docks has long since disappeared. When I was a boy the port was a thrilling adventure, a place where men sailed to the exciting outside world, far more stirring than any airport. We explored it on Saturday afternoons, and looked with awe and fascination at the tracery of cordage and yards on the masts of the great sailing ships that still tied up at Weaver's Wharf with grain from Australia.

How lucky we were in Swansea to see a little of the last days of sail. Coastal brigs and the French onion-boats still came under sail to berth in the North Dock. The grain clippers were part of the Marieham fleet, based on the Aaland Islands and run on a shoestring by Captain Peterson. They did not survive the last war, but in the twenties they were very much a feature of the marine landscape. They seemed to have been manned mainly by tough young Scandinavians – Finns, Norwegians and Swedes – with a sprinkling of young Englishmen out for adventure. Years later, when I talked to Alan Burgess, who had sailed in one of them, I heard of the rough conditions on board, how the spars and sail area had been cut down for easier handling by smaller crews and of the deadly monotony of the diet. Captain Peterson was a hard businessman in the Onedin Line tradition and had to make his long out-of-date ships pay against the competition of steam and oil. We knew nothing of this in our Saturday afternoon rambles around the docks. We looked on the clippers as the heirs of the Swansea copper barques, which flourished almost up to 1914, bringing the copper ore from Chile to the works in the Hafod, after perilous voyages around Cape Horn.

Swansea, when I was young, seemed to be full of ancient mariners, the Cape Horners, who could 'hold you with a glittering eye' as they told you of mountainous seas off 'Cape Stiff' and of driving skippers fighting the gales under bare poles. Mr Williams, who came to do odd jobs around the house, had been a Cape Horner in his youth and we used to sit with him and demand his stories as he had his tea. Like Aunty Bess's, his yarns had a standardized start, 'We were three days south of the Plate and with a good wind when . . .' From there on everything happened as expected in sea yarns. The cook went mad with a butcher's cleaver, a man fell from the royals yardarm and was lost overboard in ice-crowded waves. 'He came from Tontine Street and he was on his first voyage. His father told me, "Look after him, Rhys." "As if he were my own brother," I said. Then he lost his footing because the sail we were trying to reef was frozen as hard as iron and thrashing like a shark's tail in the wind, and he'd forgotten the golden rule – never forget it when you go to sea, boys – one hand for the ship and one hand for yourself! I can still hear the shriek he gave as he plunged past me into the sea and I couldn't help shouting, "God, what shall I tell your father, Dai?" Yes, boys, he fell right past me to his watery grave off Cape Horn.'

At this point, Mr Williams had us all in tears – pleasurable tears, perhaps, for at twelve I was still a natural weeper. I could enjoy a good cry at every recitation of 'The Women of Mumbles Head', and I have a feeling that Mr Williams, like Coleridge's ancient mariner, secretly enjoyed the effect he was creating.

The geography of Swansea seemed designed to prevent me discovering how the town made its living. Our house looked

Coal-Tip Swansea

out to the sea; the works were tucked away out of our sight behind Town Hill in the Valley. There the tin-plate mills clanged and the colliery wheels turned and father's pupils came to him from strange places like Cwmllynfell and Rhydyfro. On Saturday nights the 'shonis' from the Valley took over Oxford Street, and Swansea Market and the shops stayed obligingly open to serve them. In Ben's – Ben Evans, where the 1890 building balanced on its plate glass windows and the change sang on wires – the wives spent their money on a new two-piece while the husbands patronized the Bush or The Three Lamps. On International days, when Wales played English at the St Helen's ground (and unbelievably, in those days England usually won), the crowd consoled themselves with a glorious Saturnalia through the Swansea streets. The miners and tin-plate workers took over the town. They wore cloth caps and white mufflers and had bottles of beer in their pockets. None of them, it was obvious, had ever attended the Misses Langdon's deportment classes!

When father took us deeper into the mining areas to watch him adjudicate at a local eisteddfod, I felt I was entering dangerous ground indeed. There was even one memorable weekend when we stayed with cousins and I was taken to a great political rally. It took place I think in the welfare hall at Treherbert at the top end of the Rhondda Valley and I left it convinced that the Revolution was about to break out immediately, that would sweep away Uncle Arthur, the National Eisteddfod and all the cosy world in which I lived so snugly in Walter Road. The hall was crowded again with the miners in their standardized wear of cloth caps, white mufflers and dark best suits. The band had played the 'Red Flag' three times and we had sung 'Calon Lan' until we were hoarse, when the chairman advanced to the centre of the stage and in a hushed voice, as if he was bringing us the first news of the Second Coming, announced, 'He's here'. The hall rocked with the cheering as the Leader came forward and held up his hand. The cheers changed into pin-drop silence as he held out his hand. A. J. Cook was, at the time, the undisputed master of the South Wales mining world. He seemed to me to be the reincarnation of every revolutionary leader I had read about – from

Robespierre to Trotsky. His speech could have been immediately translated into French and delivered to the crowds gathering to storm the Tuileries in 1791.

'Friends,' he began, 'no, more than friends, comrades – comrades in this final struggle with the bosses, the struggle which, with your support, we are bound to win. As I got into the train at Queen Street station in Cardiff, I thought, "What message can I bring to you here at Treherbert to strengthen your resolve – as if it needed strengthening! – in the battle before us." And as the train came out from Central Cardiff through the opulent suburb of Whitchurch, I looked out of the window and into the back gardens of the rich – you can only see them from the train. There was the washing on the line and what did it consist of? As far as the eye could see, of the finest crepe de Chine! The train moved on and we approached Pontypridd. Now we were entering the Valleys and I looked out of the window again! What did I see on the clotheslines? Ah, comrades, the crepe de Chine had gone. It was woollen underwear now, clean, spotlessly clean – the miners' wives are proud – but it was wool that was now waving in the wind! On again up into the Rhondda. Now we are coming to Porth. There stand the tips and winding gear under the dark, looming hills. And on the clotheslines? Yes, it is still wool, still spotlessly clean, but patched now – patched by the devoted needles of the noble women who stand behind every miner. On to the last stop, and as we entered Treherbert station, I looked out of the window again. And what did I see on the line? Ah, comrades, I have no need to tell you. It is clean, still spotlessly clean – but it is *cotton*! *Cotton*! Now, I knew what we are fighting for,' (and A.J.'s voice rose to a vibrating climax). 'IT IS TO BRING THE CREPE DE CHINE OF CARDIFF TO THE CLOTHES LINES OF TREHERBERT.'

The hall erupted into a tempest of cheering, and I felt ready myself to rush out and storm the Winter Palace or at least the Coal Exchange in Cardiff Docks. Years later I met the late Jim Griffiths on the train and listened spellbound to his stories of the Six Bells Stay Down and the clashes behind the scenes between the miners' leaders. I told him how impressed I'd been as a boy by A.J. Cook's speech. To my surprise, Jim said,

'You mean The Clothes Line Oration.' And he recalled it almost word for word. 'I should remember it,' he admitted, 'for I heard A.J. make it in the Ogmore Valley, then up the Garw, and up the Afan. He may have made it up half the mining valleys of Wales. Mind you, to be fair, he always changed the names of the stations!'

Once I was safely back from the valleys into the Swansea I knew, I must confess that I forgot the oratory; the Revolution did not seem so imminent and I slipped easily into the pleasant routine of bicycling off to Gower on Saturdays, and the desperate business of trying to stay top of the form in Latin or history. The scholarship to Oxford now loomed on the horizon. I spent laborious hours swotting up the dates of such vital events as the defeat and death of Totila the Ostrogoth as related by Procopius or discussing the implications of the Salisbury Oath for the government of William the Conqueror. I forgot or ignored the revolutionary advice of that explosive pamphlet *The Miner's Next Step*. Treherbert seemed a remote country on the other side of the moon as I sat in the Great Hall of Christ Church under the glorious hammerbeam roof and the portraits of splendidly periwigged eighteenth-century deans of the college and scribbled desperately to impress the examiners. By what seemed to me a miracle my scribblings produced a letter, a month later, informing me that I had become an Exhibitioner of Exeter College. I was to take up residence in the Michaelmas Term of 1927. I had reversed the demand of A.J. Cook. I was bringing the cotton of Swansea to hang side by side with the crepe de Chine of Oxford.

CHAPTER THREE

Oxford and the Hills

Looking back on it, I arrived at Oxford a total innocent and left it equally innocent as far as the harsh realities of the world were concerned. I went up in 1927, carrying in my mind a clear-cut picture of my father's Oxford; and indeed half the University still behaved as if 1891 was merely yesterday. Oxford was no longer Matthew Arnold's 'sweet city with its dreaming spires', but it was still Paul Pennyfeather's. There were still Bollinger Club Nights in certain of the grander colleges, when the quads echoed with the sound that Evelyn Waugh declared in *Decline and Fall* made everyone who heard it shrink, 'It is the sound of the English county families baying for broken glass'. Well, if they were not baying for broken glass, they were swimming in the Cherwell at Magdalen Bridge, clad in full evening dress and throwing bottles of bubbly to each other; or else dancing in their tails around the furniture of Trinity College Junior Common Room piled up in the quad and howling at the neighbouring college, 'Balliol, Balliol, bring out your white man'. I saw them at it during my first term and realized that I had come to live for a few years in a strange land.

I had already made forays into England from time to time. When I was ten, my eldest brother and I spent a week in London with friends. We marvelled at the underground, at the lights in Piccadilly sending up sky rockets advertising Bovril and at George Robey, with bowler hat and cane in the *Bing Boys on Broadway*. I think he was still bringing the house down with the catch phrase: 'I'm surprised at you, Ludendorf!'

We made a later pilgrimage for more cultural reasons. The British Empire Exhibition at Wembley introduced us to the great outside world, where we were delighted to receive free orange squash in the South African pavilion and ride on the hair-raising big dipper. There must have been a lot more besides, but these were the imperial achievements that impressed me most at the time. We were also taken to see the first production of *Saint Joan*. In the seats before us, a somewhat precious and middle-aged gentleman was escorting a young lady of dazzling exotic beauty – at any rate, I had seen no one dressed like her in Swansea! Just before the curtain rose, he fluted to his guest, 'Some people, my dear young lady, maintain that Shaw is greater than Shakespeare – including Mr Shaw. Tonight I am happy to agree with him.' I was deeply impressed, and even more so when the play began and Miss Sybil Thorndike started declaiming about 'Mer voices! Mer voices!' This, I felt, was the way the English should use their language. In 1924 the educated Englishman still spoke as if he owned the earth. In Oxford he behaved as if no one disputed it.

I entered the university at the very last moment when such an attitude was possible, when people didn't apologize about privilege and possessions, when eccentricity was expected from dons and confident government from Conservatives. Many – or perhaps not so many – years later I realized that there were serious cracks in that imposing façade. The First World War had tragically thinned the ranks of those who thought they were born to rule. Of the blazer-clad young men, photographed on the Exeter hall steps between 1908 and 1913, how many survived the Somme? The General Strike had split the country during the year in which I sat for my scholarship, but Honest Stan Baldwin had tactfully covered up the wounds. Two years later, in 1929, came the Great Crash to herald the Depression. In the meantime, there stood Oxford ready to welcome me, the Welsh Candide, who looked on this remarkable scene with the eyes of a fascinated outsider. I was as ignorant of the niceties of the English caste system as if I had been re-transported from Australia. I had never ventured into the strange mental labyrinth of English religion. I wasn't even

versed in the rituals of cricket and rugger. I simply looked at
the wonderful mishmash of peeling walls, Gothic spires,
tolling bells, surplice-clad processions marching into college
chapels, women undergraduates earnestly bicycling to lectures
in fluttering gowns, blond giants with trousers as wide as a
cowboy's chaps strolling towards the houseboats on the Isis,
aesthetes reading Proust in incense-filled rooms – I looked at it
all and delighted in it.

Somewhere offstage, the Cowley Motor Works were endlessly expanding, Ruskin College students were reading Marx,
and for all I knew, some Oxford Anthony Blunt was busy
sifting the year's crop of promising undergraduates with a
view to enlisting them in the KGB. I now feel a slight sense of
pique, of injured pride that no one bothered to recruit me!
They were right. I was never promising. At Oxford I continued the process I had begun at school of happily drifting
through life. After all, Oxford was simply an opulent version
of Swansea Grammar School on a national scale. Dr Trevor
Owen's dictum on education echoed through my mind as I
paid off the taxi and carried my bags through the open doorway to the head porter's lodge at Exeter College . . . 'if he has
anything in him we'll make certain he'll get a scholarship . . . if
he's got nothing in him . . . we'll make his passage through
school as pleasant as possible.' Secretly, I was planning to
choose the second alternative. From the very first moment I
arrived, Oxford started 'whispering to me the last enchant-
ment of the Middle Age'. I was at least twenty years out of
date, but it didn't seem to matter in that memorable Michaelmas Term of 1927. Others were arriving at the university to
move on, to get on, to mould the future. I happily sank back
into the past. In many respects I have been there ever since!

I do not know what happens at Oxford now. Then we still
dressed as traditional undergraduates. The wide, flapping
Oxford bags had been abandoned as vulgar (if indeed, anybody ever wore them at Oxford), but we all went to lectures in
gowns and mortarboards. We even wore them when we went
out after nine p.m. Young ladies could only visit men's rooms
at college in the afternoons. The proctors with their attendant,
bowlerhatted bulldogs patrolled the streets at night to make

Exeter College Chapel
"Jerryfied"

certain everyone still *in statu pupillari* behaved as gentlemen should.

We still chuckled at the story of the undergraduate caught by the proctors with a young lady of doubtful propriety on his arm. The head proctor raised his mortarboard and went through the prescribed ritual. 'Will you please introduce us to this lady?' Putting a bold face on it the undergraduate replied, 'Certainly, Mr Proctor – my sister.' The head proctor said sternly, 'Are you aware that this young lady, your sister, is the most notorious prostitute in Oxford?' 'Yes,' said the young gentleman, unabashed, 'Mother and I are quite worried about it.'

We still had to attend a certain number of compulsory chapels every week at seven a.m., when the scholar for the day had to read the lesson. Exeter Chapel was a replica of the Sainte Chapelle in Paris, built when in the middle of the nineteenth century a Gothic Revival madness fell on the dons. Its dizzily thin spire regularly invited the more daring of the Oxford climbing fraternity to crown it with a chamber pot. A rich Burne-Jones tapestry paid tribute to the fact that William Morris had once been an Exeter man. But the eye was immediately caught by the noble lectern, in the shape of a bronze eagle. A certain scholar was due to read the lesson after a night of gigantic potations. His friends managed to get him to the chapel by seven o'clock, and prompted him to rise when the time came for him to perform the duty laid down in 1362 by the pious founder of the college, Bishop Stapleton. The unhappy scholar staggered from the choir stalls, clung thankfully to the eagle and opened the Bible. He did his best to focus his dancing eyes on the text. 'And Jesus said . . .' he began. The text wobbled in his sight and he tried again. 'An Jesush shed . . .' Then he electrified the startled chapel with the despairing cry, 'If only this bloody bird would stop waggling its tail, I'd tell you what Jesus said.'

I had gained my Exhibition in history, so naturally this was the subject I proposed to study for the next three years. I was assigned two tutors. Professor Nevill Coghill was given the mysterious task of being my moral tutor. The very title was a pleasant survival from the medieval past. He later gained fame, and I hope fortune, with his version of Chaucer's *Canterbury Tales* in modern English. He also took Richard Burton under his wing, but wisely made no attempt to supervise my own morals, such as they were. He invited me once to tea and occasionally smiled and nodded to me in the quad. This was the full extent of his interest in my moral welfare. I was duly grateful.

My second tutor was C.T. Atkinson. He was a distinguished military historian but his charm and attraction rose from his being the very personification of those regal Oxford dons celebrated by Hilaire Belloc, 'with hearts of gold and lungs of bronze,' who sailed 'in amply billowing gown, Enormous through the Sacred Town.' He was staunchly Conservative and splendidly eccentric. Atters always received his freshmen in his rooms accompanied by his dog Pincher, an ageing and somewhat portly Sealyham. Pincher acted as a sort of test of your potential, a four-legged piece of litmus paper who turned blue and bit you if you were of no quality. I believe that Atters secretly credited Pincher with the power of foretelling the future. If he bit you, you were condemned to a Third at the Schools; if he growled, you might achieve a respectable

Second; and if as happened on rare occasions, he licked your hand, you were certain of a flying First. I got a surprising reception from Pincher. He simply went to sleep and snored, thus leaving my future in total confusion.

Atters was fiercely anti-feminist in university politics. He regarded the decision of Convocation in the 1900s to admit women to degrees as a disastrous betrayal of 'The Last Sanctuary for the Civilized Male in Western Europe'. He was compelled to yield to the monstrous regiment of women, but he was determined to scare them away from his own lectures. His tactics were legendary. When the keen feminists among them asserted their right to attend, he resorted to extreme measures. The story goes that after cycling in to college on a wet day, he calmly removed his trousers and put them to dry in front of the fire while he continued with his discourse. The outraged ladies fled in terror. Or else he punctuated his lectures with asides calculated to drive all self-respecting lady students from the room. On one occasion he was discussing the history of Newfoundland 'where', he added, 'even today men outnumber women by two to one, and even some of you ladies would have no difficulty in finding husbands.' The students all stood up in protest and started to walk out. Atters looked up and remarked pleasantly, 'Ladies, ladies, there's no hurry. The next boat doesn't leave until next week.'

In 1927, the course in modern history at Oxford extended officially to 1901, but few of our mentors ventured so far. Many of them felt that the Golden Jubilee of Queen Victoria was a more suitable closing point. One witty younger don explained to me with a disarming chuckle, 'At this university we feel that after 1887, history ends and polemics begin. Don't forget that there are still people teaching here who cannot discuss Mr Gladstone's 1893 oration on the Second Home Rule Bill except in terms of the utmost acidity. They were probably there to hear him.' 'And Lloyd George?' I asked. 'Ah, we do not speak of the unspeakable.' He was pulling my leg, of course, but there was some mature wisdom behind it all. Oxford set out to give you a Mandarin view of the past and a technique for studying it dispassionately. In its Olympian detachment, the university left it to your own inclination if you decided to use this technique to explore Marx or the Middle Ages.

Every student was invited to choose a special subject which he would study in depth, while he also covered the general movement of history. The idea was a sound one. It showed the beginner the sources from which the historian drew his basic material. It gave him an insight into the formidable discipline demanded of anyone who dares to write on any aspect of history. The medieval historian, to take one example, must be a master of paleography, an expert in the contractions employed by the scribes, a devourer of details from the Pipe Rolls, a sampler of charters and a lot more besides. The list of special subjects was a long one, but never went too far outside the boundaries of the west. We could immerse ourselves in the American Revolution, the Peninsular War, the Expansion of the Empire, or Le Siècle de Louis Quatorze, but we were not invited to study China under Sun Yat Sen, the Russian Revolution of 1917 or the Arabic World under the Abbasid califs. H.G. Wells had already published his invigorating scamper through the long story of mankind, and I still have the *Outline of History* in the parts I purchased in 1924. It is full of photographs of the great historic buildings of the world, and only one – 42nd St, New York – shows a motorcar. The map at the end shows Europe, Asia, Africa, and Australasia heavily overprinted with the optimistic caption United States of the World. Arnold Toynbee had begun his gigantic task of cataloguing, filing and eventually judging every one of the world's civilizations. Spengler was about to chill our souls with proof positive in his *Untergang des Abendlands*, that the west was doomed. I ignored them all. I was happy in my special subject, the third and fourth crusades. I ploughed through the long poem of the monk, Ambroise, on the trials of Richard the Lionheart in the Holy Land. I read the crabbed Latin of William of Tyre's account of the siege of Acre. I rejoiced with Villehardouin at the glittering sight of Byzantium as the Crusaders sailed into the waters of the Bosphorus in 1204. Invaluable preparation for my subsequent activities in giving grants to unemployed clubs in the Rhondda or landing in an assault craft on the beaches at Anzio!

But, come to think of it, would any other course of study have prepared me better for the strange troubled world of the 1930s that lay ahead? Would I have been better off reading classics or even mathematics? Oxford taught me one priceless thing – the art of enjoying life while you can – with or without money. Above all, without. I look back and see that strange, wistful young man – who must have been myself, although I find it almost impossible now to identify myself with him – listening to Myra Hess playing her piano arrangement of 'Jesu, Joy of Man's Desiring' at a Balliol concert; watching Lord Birkenhead walking down the centre of the Oxford Union debating chamber, in the middle of a debate, shocking everyone by still arrogantly smoking his cigar; standing in the crowd at dawn on May Day while the choir, high up on Magdalen tower, sang the May Morning Hymn; sitting embarrassed in a circle of earnest undergraduates at a Group confession of sins, in the presence of the plump pussy-cat of a prophet from America, Dr Frank Buchman.

The Oxford Group made their first assault on the souls of the anxious undergraduates during my early days at the university. Dr Buchman urged his neophytes to unburden their spiritual anxieties to each other. It was a sort of early Methodism for those with money. There were offers of weekends in country houses, for the good doctor had an eye for the well-connected convert. The authorities did not relish Dr Buchman's appropriation of the ancient name of Oxford for his new movement. No doubt it has gone on to higher and perhaps better things. I only saw its strange, rather hot-under-the-collar beinnings. But the memory of that one session in those rooms in Queen's College forces me to make my own confession – a rather surprising, almost unbelievable one for a Welshman of my generation. I had arrived at Oxford, not merely without strong religious convictions, but without any religion at all.

This was not the result of any sixth-form rebellion against parental discipline or of restless adolescent dissatisfaction with the orthodox doctrines of church or chapel. I became a religious drop-out very early on in life almost without realizing it. Midway through the First World War, my father, as they put it, 'began to lose his faith'. I wonder if he had ever firmly possessed it once he had glimpsed the intellectual delights of Oxford. After the war, I think that deep down he was a disappointed man. He had hopes of an appointment as one of the professors of music at the University of Wales. The advent of Sir Walford Davies, the bland, socially acceptable minstrel of the Establishment, with his microphone voice as soft as Mother Seigal's Soothing Syrup, ended all father's ambitions in that quarter. He retired from the field after the Swansea National Eisteddfod in 1925 and on the advice on his staunch friend, Sir Granville Bantock, left Wales to become an Overseas Examiner for Trinity College of Music. He felt that he had been rejected by Wales, and, in return, he rejected all the narrower aspects of chapel Christianity. The church might have tempted him, indeed it tried. A year after the Disestablishment, father found himself on one of those long train journeys that used to be a Welsh speciality – winding up through the valleys of Carmarthen and Cardigan or crawling around the wild coast of Merioneth, on to windy platforms on remote and now almost forgotten stations like Afon Wen, Moat Lane or Dovey Junction.

Dovey Junction is still there, the only station in Wales with no road to it. At periodic intervals the platforms used to sink slowly into the soft marshy ground of the estuary and a new platform was built over the old one. From the 1870s to the 1920s these junctions played a vital part in the social history of Wales. In the long waits between trains the Nonconformist ministers on their way to important preaching engagements, the MP's visiting their constituencies for the weekend, the administrators returning from conferences at Shrewsbury, would perforce meet and pace up and down in the fine weather or consume endless cups of tea in the waiting room when it rained. Here the youthful Lloyd George must have planned the opening moves of the Welsh Disestablishment battle and rising ministers angled for a 'call' to more important chapels in Cardiff, where the rich congregations were in dire need of spiritual refreshment. I once promoted a scheme for excavating the layers of sunken platforms at Dovey Junction. Keen archaeologists might be able to tell, by the layers of teacups or of the position of abandoned numbers of the *Liverpool Daily Post* and the *Western Mail* in the mud layer of Dovey V, the real reason for the clash between Chamberlain and Lloyd George over the Boer War. It must have been during the period of later Dovey X that father met a certain bishop at a critical junction of his affairs.

They paced up and down the platform under the shadow of the 2,500-foot summit of Taren Hendre. The bishop took my father confidently by the arm. 'Ah, my dear Vaughan-Thomas, why don't you join us? Now that we are disestablished in Wales we need some distinction in our clergy, especially on the musical side. There'll be no trouble about theological college; we'll make certain that it will be enjoyably short. Then a pleasant vicarage in the country with ample time for composing, eh?' They reached the end of the platform and turned. The bishop whispered his final temptation. 'Somewhere in the Towy valley is the ideal place. And, my dear boy, think – just think – of the fishing!'

Alas, father was no fisherman. He was already a regular subscriber to Chapman Cohen's rationalist weekly *The Freethinker*. *The Mistakes of Moses* by Col Robert Ingersol lay on his study table instead of Bishop Lightfoot's *Commentary on the Ephesians*. He was irretrievably lost to orthodox, conventional Christianity, and inevitably I got lost with him. In all fairness, he made no attempt to force his views on us. He never ordered his sons to stop listening to religion's siren song. We trooped into morning prayers with the rest of the small boys in Terrace Road School at Swansea. The classes stood in rows and we chanted verses from the Bible in unison. The headmaster gave the signal and a remarkable mumbling sound arose from the massed ranks, punctuated only by the need to draw breath. 'Erwaze, Erwaze. Offpleasurness. Anallerpassopeace. ShesateaofL IFEtallthatbeoldeather. Annappyizeveryonethat. Attainether.' Years later I was able to translate this mysterious rubric into the beautiful words about wisdom in Proverbs 3:17, 'Her ways are ways of pleasantness, and all her paths are peace. She is the tree of life to them that lay hold upon her: and happy is every one that retaineth her.'

Of course, I read the Bible when I went to the grammar

school, but only the bits that qualified as great literature. And I could hardly study history without delving into the story of the church, its ceremonies and its schisms – above all its schisms. But as I never attended a conventional religious service I had no real understanding of what Christianity was about. I saw everything from the outside.

There were some advantages in this when we were at school: we were even the envy of some of the boys. While they were marched to service in the long, well-dressed parade that passed our house in Walter Road every Sunday morning in summer, we were on our bikes pedalling towards the ungodly delights of bathing in the Gower bays. While they were learning their verses for Sunday school, we were playing the piano, or worse still, chess and draughts. While they were being urged to take care of their souls, we were blissfully unaware that we had any. We were never christened and never confirmed. We were never inculcated with a sense of sin. We knew a great deal about Voltaire and Plato but nothing at all about St Paul. Surprisingly, we were quite happy in our ignorance.

I therefore went up to Oxford as much an outsider in religion as I was to the class system. No one relishes being an outsider for long when he is young. One strives to be with it, which usually means with them, that is with whoever are the fashionable avant-garde of the time. I had arrived at the university in an intellectual interregnum. The hearties and aesthetes of the immediate postwar period had gone down; the intensely right- or left-wing politically-minded next generation had not yet arrived on the scene. For a brief few years, and maybe for the last time, we were invited to take a serious interest in religion as a sort of special subject. Naturally I complied. I felt that it was high time that I acquired a religion, especially as I had been deeply embarrassed during my first attendance at college chapel by the complex manoeuvres demanded by High Anglican ritual. I literally did not know which way to turn. I was even more embarrassed when people casually assumed that, because I came from Wales, I was bound to have emerged from a dark, narrow, hymn-singing, Nonconformist chapel prison. I was in the market for a healing creed.

I expressed my spiritual Odyssey in the sort of Popian light verse that I had been concocting ever since I was about fifteen. Again my Uncle Arthur was my inspirer. 'Everybody should write verse – occasional verse I mean. It's a consoling and gentlemanly occupation. But you must leave poetry alone. Never attempt it. It's for professionals only and invariably leads to disaster.' I think of Dylan Thomas and believe my uncle was right as usual. My verses made no pretensions at deep probing, but I was certainly in the market for a creed all right.

But what to buy? And how am I to tell
Eternal Truth in every salesman's yell?
The Group? They only save the Social Set.
They preach Predestination by Debrett.
The Comrades then? Ah, that way lies despair.
Chateau Yquem was never made to share.
Moscow, New York – machine-men either way!
USSR is just red USA.
The church of Rome? Of course, for you're in clover
If you're a well-known writer 'going over'.
Straight into Heaven you dive off Brighton Pier,
Even the 'Unloved One' scarce forbears a cheer.
Quick let me enter. Why do I delay,
Since Hilaire Belloc comes to show the way?
I push the door. Within the candles bloom,
Monseignors scuttle through religious gloom,
The bubbling kettles of consoling sound
Boil in each dark confession box around.
Voices through incense reach my secret ear;
'Cease, cease to struggle for your place is here.
Think of our thunder-call of noble names,
Xavier, Augustine, Mauriac, Merton, James,
And in the end we netted Baudelaire –
Can Wesley, Whitefield, Charles with these compare?'

But as I enter, swift there comes to me
A hymn in fruity, four-part harmony,
Sung in some Hebron on the mountain side,
Built all askew but never built with pride.
The Organ (not yet paid for) soars afar,
The voices follow chanting 'Crug-y-bar',
My place is here, so I go singing home;
The second tenors need me more than Rome.

Of course, they never did. And I never became a convert to
Rome either. I spurned the overtures of the Group. No one
recruited me for the Comrades. After all the turmoil I
remained precisely where I was when I first came to Oxford.
Given my background what more could I expect at twenty-
one? It would take many years of experience before I could
understand the desperate need felt by so many people for
certainty, for reassurance through 'the long littleness of Life'.
Or glimpse the deep spiritual anguish of a George Fox or a St
John of the Cross. Or realize the satisfaction given by the
beauty of noble ritual to men and women brought up in the
long traditions of church or chapel. I may still be an outsider
but I can now sympathize and certainly understand. At
twenty-one, all I did was to write another perky little poem as
I abandoned my superficial attempt to acquire a creed on the
cheap.

> The early Fathers of the Church
> Who praised the Lord with whip and birch,
> Tertullian, Origen and Co,
> Plus gloomy Bernard of Clairvaux.
> (And all those hairy, hoary sages
> Who bellowed down the Middle Ages
> That flesh is grass and Womankind
> The Devil's trick to make men blind)
> Warn us – for every hour we spend
> With a Delightful Female Friend,
> We forfeit that exact amount
> When casting up our Last Account.
> Sweet suicide if this were so,
> What a delightful way to go!
> No wonder sexy Christians sing
> 'O, Death, where is thy boasted sting?'
> Swift to my arms and quench the light,
> We'll squander ten more years tonight.

Which takes me naturally from sanctity to sex. I was brought
up in a period when sex was never spelt with a capital S. It was
a romantic private pleasure not a burdensome public duty. Sex
is delightful when you do it yourself, but infinitely depressing
to read about when done by others – unless those others are
gifted, witty and elegant. Of course in fact we are all only too

willing to lend an ear to any rich piece of gossip about our neighbours. And, when I was growing up, the *News of the World* was making a fortune from printing police court reports. But looking back on it, half the attraction lay in the wonderful verbal circumlocutions employed. 'He then made certain suggestions' sounds ten times more erotic than a detailed reprinting of the actual words spoken. Full-frontal nudity has destroyed the poetry of sex and left only the embarrassment and anguish. I have never needed a Freud to analyse my own sexual development. Again, I remember old Phil Tanner, in the Gower of my remote early youth, lifting his pint of ale and declaring 'There's nothing wrong with any man that a thousand pounds a year and a pretty girl won't cure immediately'. The basic problem of life, however, is how to get hold of both!

There was no such thing as sex education in schools when I was approaching adolescence. I got my first inkling about this absorbing subject from an older and more knowing fellow schoolboy. I received the news at first with incredulity and then with increasing curiosity. The means of gratifying that curiosity were, however, strictly limited in my Swansea of the early 1920s. Recently radio and television have implanted a picture of that period in the public mind – girls in cloche hats, with strings of pearls between their teeth, perpetually doing the charleston or the black bottom; wild parties in the back of flivvers, saxophones moaning and hip flasks at the ready; the bright young things off to a midnight bathing party; long cigarette-holders, straight-line dresses by Poirot; Gordon Selfridge flying out to Trouville with the Dolly Sisters, and the Blue Train taking Somerset Maugham down to his Riviera villa for best-selling scandal. For all we knew in Swansea, this was life as lived in opulent circles far beyond our ken in London, Paris, New York and other mysterious places. We could only say, in the immortal words of Dai from the Afan Valley after his first visit to Paris for the International match, 'Boys, it's in its infancy in Abercregan.'

The young ladies we met at parties or dances dressed in the style of the 20s. They could do the charleston if required but they were still not attuned to the permissive society. There

were daring handclasps, kisses and embraces, but neither we
nor they would have dreamed of going further. Of course we
young men sang bawdy songs and boasted of our secret pro-
wess together – half believing our own romantic lies. But
basically, in that age when contraceptives were available only
if you dared to visit Mr Black's dirty book shop in a back street
near the Grand Theatre, and when the pill was unheard of,
we behaved perforce like ladies and gentlemen. Or as Mr
George Thomas, now the distinguished Speaker of the House
of Commons, put it more vividly, 'The permissive society?
Wynford, in my day in the Rhondda you had to give a girl a
lick of sherbet before she'd give you a glimpse of her garters!'

In this atmosphere of public reticence and restraint about
sex, modern theories probably demand that we should all have
been tormented, unhappy, haunted by fears of impotence and
desperately in need of expert guidance from Dr Alex Comfort.
Perhaps some of us were, but I never came across them. I
certainly never felt unfairly frustrated myself. Welsh society
may have seemed narrow from the outside, but it always
insisted on an important, indeed an equal place for women.
There was no room for the machismo of the Latin world, that
dreary cult of male dominance that makes every male Spaniard
or Italian feel he is God's gift to womankind. Celtic women
never feel inferior. Boadicea of the Iceni was a Celt and we all
know what she did to the Roman machismo. Welsh women
also demanded a little poetry in the affair, and Welshmen were
expected to supply it.

But not the sort of poetry D.H. Lawrence was then attempting to create out of direct description of sexual activity. The
scandal of *Lady Chatterley's Lover* burst on us when I had just
gone to Oxford. Now Lawrence is a powerful writer of genius
and his book, in an Olympia Press edition smuggled in from
Paris, had the forbidden appeal to our generation of
Baudelaire's *Fleurs du Mal* on the students of the Sorbonne in
the 1860s or Swinburne on the Oxford of the 1870s. His
young disciple, Rhys Davies, who was with Lawrence when he
died on the Riviera in 1930, had also been busy shocking the
Welsh bourgeoisie with his Lawrencian novels of life in he
mining valleys of the Rhondda. They impressed me mightily at

the time and will, I am sure, bear revival. I think that he it was who carried Lady Chatterley to Wales, and produced the copy we passed from hand to hand. I read it but there was something lacking, a flaw that I couldn't quite place.

Some years later, I remember drinking with Dylan Thomas in a certain pub in Chelsea where the barmaid was a jovial bosomy lady with intellectual aspirations. He told me, 'She likes to be kind to poets.'

'What about this Lady Chatterley, then?' said the barmaid.

'It would complete your education,' said Dylan and produced a copy.

A few weeks later she returned it across the bar.

'What do you think of it?'

'Well, dear, very nice, I dare say, but there's not many laughs in it.' Ah! that was the flaw. Lawrence had made sex a duty, a religion, a service to humanity – anything but a pleasure.

Let me confess that there came a moment while I was at Oxford (as it comes to all of us) when I was at last shown 'the right true end of love'. My demonstrator was a Russian lady vastly more experienced than I was and kind into the bargain. When at last we lay

> All passion spent
> On the still lake of our content

I could not help, as a good Welshman, thanking her profusely. 'I know I'm not the most handsome or most brilliant man in the world.' I said. 'Why have you been so kind to me?'

She gave a low musical laugh. 'My dear, it was to improve my English.' After that, I knew that I would never be cast in the role of one of the world's great lovers. But at least she had put laughter back into love.

From that moment I never ceased to marvel at the kindness, the understanding and the forgiveness of women. So it has continued through my life.

> Time's Winged Chariot (poets say)
> Warns us to love while yet we may:
> Must I not hurry all the more
> Who find it parked outside my door?

For those who sipped Love in their prime
Must gulp it down at Closing Time.

In 1927, I was a long way yet from closing time. And I
didn't spend all my time theorizing about sex. I was seized
with another passion – rock climbing. I had already become
deeply committed to walking on the mountains, for the noble
and infrequented range of the Carmarthenshire Vans lifted its
2500-foot-high summits only twenty-five miles from my home
in Swansea. But one afternoon I went to work in the Oxford
Union Library and by accident came across a thick volume
entitled *Rock Climbing in the English Lake District*. It was full
of magnificent photographic plates of 1897 vintage, showing
climbers clad in knickerbockers, Norfolk jackets and cloth
caps festooned on astonishingly steep rock faces with strange
names like Moss Ghyll, Savage Gully and Kern Knotts Crack.
The name of the author was O.G. Jones – obviously a Welshman. But what was a Welshman doing on the steep rocks of

The Seconds
view of
the outer
Hebrides.
Sgurr
Alasdair

Cumberland? I started to read the book and went on to devour all similar volumes I could discover, from the Alpine Club journals to the Abraham brothers' opus on North Wales. In the next Long Vac. a group of us, all utter novices, purchased heavily-nailed boots, an alpine rope thick enough to moor a battleship and a tent, and bicycled our way to Snowdonia.

How lonely, withdrawn and secluded the hills seemed in those days, almost our own private property. Away from one or two well-known mountains, the whole landscape seemed deserted except for the sheep and occasional shepherd. If you met a walker on a peak like Yr Aran or Arenig Fawr you greeted him as Stanley greeted Livingstone. If he carried a rope, you knew he was a member of an exclusive club, almost a secret society. Most of the members of that secret society were

Oh. my poor feet.
The last of the Summer hikers
Wrynose Pass.

dons, professional men, high-grade civil servants, schoolmasters and undergraduates, who had all read their classics and Wordsworth, and who had taken to the hills almost as a secret religion. The pioneers of rock climbing in Britain were only two generations past, and the names of the second wave – men like Mallory, Winthrop Young, Herford and W.R. Reade – still seemed to echo among the misty crags. Fred Piggott and Jack Longland were about to tear the veil of mystery from the awesome cliffs of Clogwyn du'r Arddu and launch a new era in Welsh climbing, but, as usual, I was twenty years behind the times. I look at some of those early photographs we took of ourselves, in what we thought were desperately impressive stances on the central arête of Glyder Fawr or the Holly Tree Wall. There were are, poised over the precipices, clad in plus fours, old tweed jackets and trilbys, with boots heavily nailed with tricounis. In our rucksacks lay the first pocket guides to the Welsh cliffs issued by the Climbers Club in 1909 and 1910. They were mainly written by J.M. Archer Thompson, one of the greatest of the early rock climbers, who had led the exploration of the complicated rocks of Lliwedd and set new standards in the development of balance climbing. He was the classics master at Llandudno, and his guide books to Lliwedd and the climbs in the Ogwen Valley are liberally sprinkled with Latin quotations. As he prepared to tackle the cave pitch in the north gully of Tryfan the climber was helped on his way by a reference to Virgil:

> *Est specus ingens*
> *Intus se vesti legit obice saxi,*
> *Hic comitem in latebras aversum a lumine ducit*
> *Jam rapidus torrens . . .*

Presumably if the climber could not read Latin, he fell off!

Eventually those endless Long Vacations at Oxford – even my stay at the university – had come to an end. I descended from the mountain tops, took my degree and confidently looked to the Establishment to employ me in some interesting and lucrative fashion. My plan was simple and had the hearty approval of my college and my parents. I would sit the Civil Service examination – the one for the highest grades of course. Following the ancient example of the Chinese emperors, the Establishment, in Victorian times, decided to abandon the happy eighteenth-century practice of appointing indigenous relatives or ambitious young men to snug jobs on the recommendation of some political nobleman. Whitehall and the imperial mandarins were now – and still are – appointed by a strict public examination followed by an interview. My ambitions had already been fired by the success of one of my relatives, the son of a determined lady known in our family as Mrs The-Very-Best, from her oft-repeated declaration that nothing but the very best would do for herself and her son. Young Very-Best did very well indeed. He swept through Cambridge in triumph and almost topped the list in the Civil Service Examination. He had an air of quiet superiority when I went to him for advice. 'Take the Indian Civil as priority,' he said. 'You will have a better chance.' As we walked along it started to rain, and he opened his umbrella, an instrument which as a mountaineer I affected to despise. 'I advise you to carry one,' he said to me solemnly. 'In the upper echelons of the service it is a necessary concomitant.' I realized that he was already well on his way to his KCB and election to the Athenaeum!

My own attempt at becoming a mandarin ended in disaster – my first real failure in life. I did well enough in the written section. A specialized knowledge of the Hussite Revolution and a nodding acquaintance with the Pre-Conquest relations between England and Flanders seemed to be a distinct asset as I scribbled away in Burlington House. Once in front of the interviewers, my utter unsuitability as a candidate for sahib-dom was ruthlessly exposed. What could have possessed me to think that I could ever have governed Bengal or controlled a recalcitrant rajah in the Deccan? In truth the real reason I had fallen in with the idea of trying for the Indian Civil was the delicious vision of myself administering a mountainous district somewhere in the foothills of the Himalayas, with plenty of leave to be devoted to exploration in the Karakorum or the Kishtwar Himal. I saw myself leading a long line of porters up the long snow slopes towards a distant col with the savage glacier-covered peaks silhouetted against an icy-blue sky. What were those strange series of dents in the snow, far bigger than any bear tracks? Could they be . . . ? Was it possible . . . ? No, emphatically it was not! My marks for the interview put paid to my absurd attempt to become an empire builder-cum-explorer. I slunk back in shame to Swansea and gentlemanly unemployment.

CHAPTER FOUR

Struggling Through the Depression

My parents uttered no word of reproach but clearly they were sadly disappointed. Mrs The-Very-Best's brilliant son was rising rapidly through the grades of the Customs and Excise as if borne on a magic elevator. I was still on life's ground floor – or had I fallen into the basement? I looked around desperately for any sort of position. I had left it too late to try for a schoolmaster's vacancy, and, in any case, I knew in my heart of hearts that I was not cut out to be a pedagogue. I did make one half-hearted attempt to get the job of a temporary history master at Penarth High School, but I shuddered as I walked through the long corridors towards the headmaster's study. A faint aroma of unwashed boys hung in the air. The dull murmur of classes, ploughing unhappily through subjects in which they weren't interested, reached me as I passed the closed doors. I hesitated, then turned around and fled before I even reached the interview.

I wasn't the only one who fled in those extraordinary days of 1931. I remember the utter incredulity with which I heard the news of the formation of the National Government. I was sitting, feeling low, depressed and unwanted, on a seat under the verandah of the bowls pavilion in Cwmdonkin Park. It was a sunny August day and before me two pretty girls were playing tennis with a certain elegant languor, proper to pretty girls in those unregenerate days. A young reporter of my acquaintance on the local paper came hurrying up. He, too, had his eye on one of the pretty girls. With the conspiratorial air of someone in the know and close to the inner councils of the State that all reporters seem to adopt naturally as part of their profession, he said, 'Ramsay's gone and done it, with a vengeance at last.'

'Done what?' I asked.

'The most right-about turn in history! He's just back from the Palace. It was on the tape in the office when I looked in. Labour's out!'

'Good Heavens, why has he resigned?'

'He's not resigned. He's head of the new Government, mostly Tory with a dash of Liberal sauce. What a turn-up for the book!'

I walked slowly home, feeling the Great Depression already following my footsteps, but happily I was rescued from the dole queue – I wasn't qualified for it anyhow, as I had never worked – by luck, that little god who seemed to have watched over me with totally undeserved devotion. I found myself the next day on a walk in Gower. There was a general bewilderment in the air, for the morning papers were full of the formation of the National Government. I could see nothing ahead but endless unemployment for me, and as I walked the cliff path, below me the sea came creaming in over the rocks at the foot of the limestone crags beyond Horton. 'Break, break, break on thy gold grey stones, O sea,' I murmured to myself, for one of the by-products of the sort of education I received is a mind loaded with appropriate quotations that float up unbidden on all occasions. I had been pre-packaged for success in quiz programmes on the radio. It didn't seem to matter on that walk that the cold, grey rocks were bright limestone, and that warm sunlight bathed the whole scene. I was in the grip of the Depression, and Tennysonian mild melancholy seemed perfectly tuned to the Gower coast that afternoon.

Ahead of me I saw the unmistakable tall, slightly gangling figure of J.D. Williams, the editor of the local newspaper. I caught up with him, and we walked side by side as the gulls screamed and wheeled about a sack cast up on the shore. Just like myself, I thought. J.D.W. was a friend of my father, a man in his early fifties who had fought his way up in the brave old days of local journalism, when there were two Swansea evening papers each staunchly supporting its side of the two clashing causes of Liberalism and Conservatism. The *Cambrian Daily Leader* had its offices right in the centre of the ruins of the old Swansea castle, and the great presses thundered away, shaking the delicate medieval arches of Henry de Gower's square fourteenth-century keep. In these days of conservation, I can imagine the storm of protest – probably led by me – which would have followed the publication of any plan to build an office block within walls 600 years old. In 1910 no one turned a hair. Mr Asquith and his Liberals were riding high. Who would have dared question the right of the Swansea Liberal standard-bearer to fly the flag of progress high over the walls of ancient privilege? The *Leader* directors, who naturally included Sir Alfred Mond, commissioned the local architect to tack an odd tower or two onto the utilitarian structure that held the presses and the *Cambrian Daily Leader*, the heir to the old *Cambrian* newspaper of the 1820s, went on its way rejoicing in its championship of Lloyd George, Reggie McKenna, Lord Haldane and Sir Edward Grey.

The rival Conservative organ was the *South Wales Evening Post*, edited with considerable panache and a certain bucaneering unscrupulousness by Dai Davies the Post. Swansea divided itself into two camps. You either took the *Leader* and supported progress or you bought the *Post* and propped up the forces of black reaction. I need hardly say that we were *Cambrian Daily Leader* supporters. J.D.'s son Emlyn was with us at the Grammar School and took us on occasional visits to his father's office – an Aladdin's cave, full of the smell of printer's ink; of pieces of lead with your name on them still warm from the linotype machines; of the Creed, pouring out no Anglican doctrine in the classic prose of Cranmer, but crisp summaries of the day's news in the new language of journalese: 'Can conquer unemployment, L. George confident.' 'P.M. indicts M.P.s.' 'MacDonald bound NYorkwise.' The ghosts of the world-shaking events of my past look grinning over my shoulder as I write. J.D.W. presided over it all in the editor's sanctum.

He still believed in all the old and honourable traditions of the free press. To him it was the fourth estate, the guardian of the values in modern society, the enlightened encourager of local talent. He wasn't blind to certain disagreeable duties incumbent on the editor at election time. Until a Labour candidate appeared on the scene in the 1920s, the Liberals were assured of the workers' support but, apparently, at an agreed price. On the day before the election one of the staff of the *Leader* went for a walk along the foreshore in the quiet of the night. Halfway between the Slip and Brynmill, a figure loomed up in the darkness walking in the other direction, in a false beard and muffled in a coat. No words were spoken. The figure held out a hand and a bulky package was silently transferred. The muffled figure passed on into the night and a sizeable quota of the dockers' votes was also transferred to Sir Alfred Mond.

I heard such stories with a slight shudder and a secret delight. I was being given a privileged glimpse of the dark side of the moon. There came a day, however, when such innocent, naive and tiny pieces of corruption gave place to corruption on the grand scale, otherwise known as rationalization and reorganization. The Northcliffes, the Rothermeres and the rival tycoons of Fleet Street looked at the provincial press and saw a golden opportunity for moneymaking. Eliminate competition, supply the one paper left with syndicated articles from London, stuff the rest of the pages with adverts and a modicum of local news – and the trick was done. The directors of the rival local papers took Fleet Street's money, and the *Cambrian Daily Leader* disappeared from the scene. Dai the Post emerged with a satisfactory amount of cash, and poor J.D.W. was rather pushed to the sidelines. He still edited the weekly *Herald of Wales* but no longer sat in the seat of real power.

I think that this bitter experience drew him closer to my father, who had had his share of disappointment. It also made him generous of time and help to young men, especially those disappointed and despondent. He was a great walker on the hills and took me with him on fifteen-mile tramps over the Carmarthenshire Vans at weekends – consoling therapy to someone like myself who was all at sea in life. 'It will come right, somehow', was his constant message and somehow it came right for me that afternoon. J.D.W. was on his way to call on the Workers' Educational Association Summer School

9 *Right*: W. V.-T. with Field Marshal Alexander at Montegufoni, 1944

10 *Below*: A briefing on the Anzio beachhead by Major Pat Lort-Phillips, 1944

11 *Bottom*: Broadcasting from Lord Haw-Haw's microphone after the capture of Hamburg, 1945

12 Wedding day, January 1946, with the bridegroom's brother Vaughan and the bride's sister Catherine

13 David watching his father on the screen

being held in a hired house in Horton. Here earnest-minded workers, secretaries with intellectual aspirations, socially-conscious ministers of religion and a sprinkling of the unemployed met to spend their short few weeks of holiday listening to lectures on economics, European politics, modern English prose writing and other improving subjects. Presiding over it was kindly, earnest, slightly stammering Mansel Grenfell, the brother of David Grenfell who was then MP for Gower and one of the few Russian speakers in the House of Commons.

When I see the grim *apparatchiks* of the new trade union world or the Marxian professors and the ambitious Trotskyite young men of the New Left, I sigh over the memory of Mansel Grenfell, the man who gave me my first chance to earn money, actually to do something even if I couldn't do it well. He supported the Labour Party for purely religious reasons; it was the logical continuation of the work of the chapel. He didn't go as far as some party zealots who, in the wickedly witty words of Malcolm Muggeridge, seem to regard Jesus as the official Labour candidate for Galilee South, but Mansel, in all humility, would have welcomed Him as the ideal lecturer at the W.E.A. Gower Summer School. Mansel was that rare thing – a genuinely good man.

J.D.W. introduced me and I stayed for the evening session, which was inevitably followed by the discussion. I was distinctly shaken by the eloquence of all present. The tutors, the students, the unemployed, the secretaries, all seemed to be deeply versed in long quotations from R.W. Towney, Maynard Keynes, Karl Kautsky and a host of other names unknown to or perhaps deliberately unmentioned by my mentors at Oxford. After the discussion, we sat in the garden on the cliff edge under a full moon, drinking the obligatory and health-giving cups of cocoa. Mansel put his cup down and said firmly to me, 'You've had the privilege of going to a great university. You should pass on all you know to the under-privileged. Why not take on some of our unemployed groups. We can't pay much, the classes are weekly and at the end of the season the fee would work out – let me see – yes, we might get up to £20.' £20! Not much indeed! This was a fortune. Real money, actual banknotes being put into my hand! Passing on privilege? For that money, at that moment, I would have sold Exeter Chapel, the hall, the quadrangles, the rector and all!

In September Mansel introduced me to a whole series of little groups meeting in chapel vestries, small huts or spare rooms in welfare halls. I looked at them doubtfully and I think they looked back at me with equal doubt. They saw an anxious and uncertain young man who had the audacity to propose to lecture to them on economic history. I saw row upon row of shabbily-clad workers who were becoming part of the economic history themselves. I got to my feet and gave a carefully prepared outline of the course – starting with the Middle Ages, on to the rise of the new agriculture, a short scamper through the Industrial Revolution then swiftly into the safety of the technical developments of the future. It was the first time I had ever made a speech in public. I had read essays at undergraduate clubs and tried my hand at debates in the Junior Common Room at Exeter. I had appeared briefly 'on the boards' in school plays, but this was different. A public

The Welfare Hall. S. Wales Coalfield

speech is a form of verbal hypnotism. The speaker – the natural-born speaker not the carefully cultivated one – has to radiate an aura of complete confidence in what he is saying which enwraps the listener in a warm blanket of reassuring sound. In return the captured audience radiates back a continual encouragement, so that the whole thing becomes a joint performance. Some great orators – Lloyd George was certainly one of them – planned ahead for the exact point at which this juncture would take place. From there on the speaker, as it were, had them in the hollow of his hand. Winston Churchill carefully prepared his effects. Later on I was fortunate enough to be given a copy of his speech every time I broadcast the commentary at the public functions he attended. I was fascinated to see the way he had pointed and marked almost every word on the small, easily handled cards on which they were typed. The pauses were carefully indicated, the words to be emphasized underlined in red, and the exact strength of the emphasis measured by the number of the red lines employed. The manuscript was as carefully orchestrated as a Beethoven symphony. I wish I could have preserved one of these masterpieces but a polite secretary always appeared at my elbow at the end of the show and after murmuring, 'Mr Churchill hopes you have found his notes helpful' held out his hand and put them safely out of my reach into his pocket.

These refinements were far from my mind when I stood up in the wooden hut behind Seion Chapel in Llansamlet with rows of blank faces before me and the rain beating against the windows – rain laced with the fumes from the nearby spelter works. I took a deep breath and plunged in. I talked as vividly as I could about the Peasants' Revolt, the Renaissance, the development of the steam engine and anything I could remember about the economic side of history – which frankly was not very much. My audience had just returned from standing in a queue at the Labour Exchange to collect the tiny dole of those unhappy days. One elderly man in the front row near the stove gently closed his eyes and went quietly to sleep. I hurriedly plunged into my last quotation from Professor Bury (I wonder how he would have gone down on a wet morning in that wooden hut in Llansamlet). 'To comprehend the significance of the present we must be acquainted with the history of the past.' I gave a sigh of relief and sat down. There was a dead silence. I felt a cold chill of anxiety as the class secretary rose to speak.

He was a man of long experience in the trade union world, a veteran of Labour Party conferences, a master of the technique of committee meetings, a stickler for the correct form of procedure. He rose, cleared his throat impressively, and gave his verdict. 'Well, friends. We've heard a most interesting address and I'm sure we will hear many more in the future and I now put it to your vote, democratically exercised, that we have Mr Thomas here as our lecturer. After all, he hasn't any other job and therefore he is one of us. I ask you now to raise your hands in the usual manner. William, wake up Dai Griffiths by the stove there to make it unanimous. Mr Thomas, don't worry, last week Dai slept through a speech by Aneurin Bevan himself. All in favour?' The secretary didn't bother to count but beamed at me, 'Carried unanimously'. At last I was launched on my career of talk that has hardly been interrupted for the last fifty years.

On four mornings a week I took a bus or a tram to the industrial suburbs of Swansea or Port Talbot and delivered my oration to my classes. I suppose I used them to practise on and they forgave all my experimental stumbles and mistakes. I felt honoured to be one of them. I was beginning my real education. Where was Oxford now? Oxford with its sounding bells; its long walks across the shining water meadows as the eights went upriver with flashing oars and the cox shouting 'Give her ten'; Oxford of the hushed silence among the books under the dome of the Radcliffe Camera; of the procession of dons in scarlet robes and velvet caps escorting the Distinguished Statesman to his Latin oration in the Sheldonian; Oxford, far-off unreal city of endless leisure, talk, punts trailing under the willows along the Cherwell; Matthew Arnold's city of unrealized, unrealizable dreams! And here I was on the day after my Llansamlet debut in a decayed warehouse in the shadow of Landore viaduct, with a little cluster of men before me who may have been thrown on the scrapheap but who knew far more about life, its trials and triumphs and tragedies than ever I discovered at Oxford. In every class there was always someone who also knew far more than I did about economic history, about one aspect of it, anyhow.

I began to dread the moment in the discussion when the expert rose gently above the cloth caps and white mufflers, and ignoring the sound of the trains that always seemed to run overhead, began. 'Once again we've had a most interesting account of the three field system but I wonder if the lecturer can tell us how it squares with Marx's theory of surplus value.' Of course, this particular lecturer couldn't square the three field system with anything, leave alone Karl Marx. I had to retire leaving the three fields wide open to the expert, who thereupon delivered a complicated address himself with long quotations from Engels, 'Anti-Düring' and the 'Critique of the Gotha Programme'. I came to a quiet arrangement offstage with the expert. He should always have his say as long as he prefaced it with a sentence or two paying tribute to the remarkable knowledge displayed by the lecturer. I don't think I turned my classes into recruitment centres for the Communist Party, for the secretary always took me – or perhaps I

An Afan Valley Viaduct. S Wales Coalfield.

should say, I took him for I was the only one who had any money – around the corner to the Collier's Arms where he reassured me. 'Don't worry, Mr Thomas. The boys aren't really listening to either of you. You are both a wonderful way of passing the time.'

I left the Collier's Arms and returned to that other Swansea only three miles away, where I had been born and where the middle-class business and professional men, the university professors, the churchmen and the bank managers carried on with their golf and Rotary clubs and other activities as if the Landore Unemployed Club was on another planet, as indeed it was. I began to lead a double life. In the mornings I was deeply immersed with my new unemployed friends, my new comrades in adversity. In the afternoons and evenings I became a young man about Swansea. A group of young men, all a few years younger than myself, had just emerged from the Grammar School and were the pure product of the permissive atmosphere of that remarkable educational establishment. Dylan Thomas, naturally, had declared his intention of becoming a great poet as soon as possible but his friend Daniel Jones was equally impressive. He had won a Mendelssohn Scholarship to the Royal College of Music and eventually became Wales' finest composer. He was in my view the real inspirer of Dylan's early verse, besides being a polymath who had an impressive array of literary talents. I used to see him at his table in the Kardomah café on Saturday mornings and imagined him to be the Dr Johnson of the small circle of aspiring poets, painters and novelists around him. He was a little portly, with glasses that gave him an air of authority, and his *obita dicta* were relished by Fred Janes the painter, Vernon Watkins the poet, and Tom Pritchard, who was always about to write the great novel which would do for Swansea what Joyce's *Ulysses* had done for Dublin. All this was over forty-five years ago and we had a right to our illusions.

Alongside Daniel Jones Dylan seemed absurdly young. He had just left the Grammar School at the age of sixteen and, through the influence of J.D. Williams, had been taken on as a junior reporter on the *Swansea Evening Post*. He dressed the part in the style of the tough American reporters on *The Front*

Page, with a wide-brimmed trilby hat and a cigarette always in his lips. In the bar of the Three Lamps he manfully drank his pint with his hard-bitten colleagues and hinted at harrowing knowledge of the secret life of Swansea.

I met him there one evening when he said to me confidentially, 'Care to meet an actress tonight? I've got the entrée backstage.' He spoke the words with studied unconcern, but he made it sound as if he was making me free of the whole romantic world of greasepaint, dazzling young stars, stage-door johnnies and champagne suppers.

We arrived, breathless, at the dressing room. A voice as cracked as the paint on the door called out, 'Come in, dearie', and we found ourselves in the presence of none other than dear old Nellie Wallace.

Dylan rose to the occasion. 'Miss Wallace, we bring you the homage of the artists of the future to the artists of the past.'

Miss Wallace gave him a rather old-fashioned look and enquired, 'Variety or legit?'

'Legit,' we replied. We didn't know what it meant, but it sounded better.

'In that case boys, you've got a hell of a road to travel. Have some gin?' Miss Wallace produced a bottle from behind a pile of cosmetics and poured out the strongest gin I've ever tasted in my life. It exploded in Dylan and myself with devastating effect.

'Take it easy, boys, take it easy,' Miss Wallace chuckled. 'Here's one thing at any rate in which the artists of the past can wipe the floor with the artists of the future.' And she dealt with the gin in one quick gulp, put on her famous black bonnet, and left us to fairly bounce onto the stage. We heard the roar of applause and that fruity voice singing:

> Next Monday morning is my wedding day . . .
> With little Percy-worcy, he's promised to be mine
> We're going to blow the candle out at half-past nine

'This,' said the youthful Dylan afterwards with solemn emphasis, 'will be an incident for our memoirs.'

Dylan never wrote memoirs, but no man depended more completely for his inspiration on his own town, his early

memories and upon the green unsullied landscape of Carmarthenshire. He used to return to them like a homing pigeon
every time he had work to do. Come to think of it, I never saw
him write a poem in London. He needed the seclusion of the
little summerhouse annexe of the Boat House at Laugharne
where he sat polishing and repolishing every word, and covering the floor with rejected drafts. He didn't care what became
of them. All his friends have endless versions of his poems, and
only Dr Daniel Jones, with his intimate knowledge of Dylan's
creative process, can decide between them. Still, these continually altered drafts with their long lists of alternative words,
show what a hard-working craftsman Dylan was when it came
to his poetry. The Roaring Boy disappeared and the dedicated
craftsman took his place.

He drank in those early days, but not in the sad, compulsive,
escapist and exhibitionist way of his later period. He was a
melodious, companionable drinker with a gift of almost spontaneous humorous verse. I only wish I had kept half the
lampoons and limericks that he scattered around with a lavish
hand; but I do remember a singing party in which I was
involved with Dylan, Daniel Jones, Vernon Watkins and
Professor Thomas Taig, then Lecturer in English at Swansea
University College, in the inn at Merton on the edge of Gower.
With us was a delightful man of the law, then beginning his
career as a solicitor, named Stuart Thomas. Stuart was no
artist but he had an understanding sympathy for the oddities
of artists. He, too, had emerged from the mould of the grammar school with a glint of freedom in his eyes but had immediately been clamped into another, sterner mould by his father –
as gaunt a specimen of late Victorian rectitude as it was
possible to find. Thomas, père, had discouraged his gifted wife
from playing the piano as soon as they were married, and all
through his married life ate his breakfast in silence with the
newspaper propped up before him, to hide the sight of his
family – especially his son, Stuart. Whenever possible Stuart
fled to more acceptable company. We were lucky to have him,
for he was the only man among us with any grasp of practical
affairs. In later years he continually saved his artist friends
from the consequences of their follies. But for him, Dylan

would have been bankrupt long before his death, and his widow and children would never have received the steady income that they now enjoy.

All this was far off in the future as we sat drinking after hours in the inn at Merton. The song was in full blast and we were all improvising on a theme suggested by Dylan – the unexpected interruption, by a Welsh vampire, of a session of the Swansea Town Council. We took it in turn to contribute a line each and roared out the chorus:

> At the corner of Pell Street a vampire appears,
> Singing 'Garlic, sweet garlic' – it's sung there for years.
> See, it taps at the window of Councillor Rees
> And it sings, as it taps, a most sinister piece.

Chorus. Councillors' jugulars suck I with glee.
> Oh ho, for the taste of a scrumptious J.P.
> Tremble, ye aldermen! Town Clerks beware!
> As I hoover the veins of your succulent Mayor!

> In the Guildhall Bloodorium the Council's convened,
> The motion, Re Pell Street and Bloodsucking Fiend;
> Proposer, Rev Samuel (Labour), Landore –
> When Whoop through the window the Vampire's roar.

Singing – 'Councillors' jugulars . . .' and so on for twenty more verses.

'Who's that singing?' the landlord enquired with awe.

'The greatest poet in Wales,' I announced.

'I don't know about the greatest,' said the landlord, 'but I'm sure of one thing though, he's by far the loudest.'

That is how I will always remember Dylan – being natural with people he knew and liked and not acting the great Bohemian. I once talked about Dylan to Dame Edith Sitwell. It was in the year she died and although she was ill and lay on her bed to talk, she looked like a splendid medieval queen still receiving her courtiers in her chamber of state, clad in black gloves extended upon a coverlet of red velvet. Dylan rated his meeting with her, when he first came to London, as the beginning of his career as a poet. 'I've seen her,' he told me in triumph. 'A marvellous talking missal from the Middle Ages, and she positively gloats over my poems.'

'How did he behave when he first met you?' I asked Dame Edith.

'Beautifully.' And then she gave a slow smile. 'Beautifully, but I've never seen him behave anything but beautifully with me. He always behaved with me like a son with his mother.'

'Did he ever overstep the mark?'

'Well, one day he came to lunch with me – that was the only time when I have seen him a little – perhaps a little over, do you see? And he said, "I'm sorry to smell so awful, Edith, it's Margate." "Ah," I said, "Yes of course, my dear boy, naturally it's Margate. I quite understand *that*!" '

Dylan frankly was a little afraid of Edith Sitwell. He was delighted to have her approval, but frightened of the disaster of misbehaving in her presence. He need not have worried. She had a savage tongue but she employed it with an aristocratic discrimination. She would have soothed over his wildest social disasters with splendid tact. Others were not so kind or understanding. And now the Dylan we knew has been swallowed by the legend. I have to keep reminding myself that public Dylan wasn't the real Dylan.

Swansea, like any town with pretensions to culture in the 1930s, had a Little Theatre. It was run by amateurs under the inspiration of Professor Thomas Taig and prided itself on keeping abreast of the times. Shaw was mingled with Auden and Isherwood, and Barrie was tempered with Euripides and a touch of Eugene O'Neill. I joined, not with any ambitions as an actor but as a sort of solace to my still-stranded career. The theatre itself was a converted gospel hall, tucked against a limestone cliff behind the seafront of Mumbles and approached up a sort of steep ski slope which left the more elderly patrons panting. I never played any outstanding role but, to my surprise, was once invited to perform as Lorenzo in *The Merchant of Venice*. Dylan, to his equal surprise, was cast as Stephano, servant to Portia.

Now Stephano hasn't a great deal to do, and Dylan found that he had plenty of chances to slip down to the nearby pub of Fulton's Vaults, where he happily refreshed himself at regular intervals. My big moment came in Act Five, when I arrived with Jessica at Portia's garden at night and together we declaimed that magical verbal duet which begins, 'The moon shines bright. In such a night as this . . .' I flattered myself that Shakespeare would have approved of the way I brought out the singing poetry of the lines. I turned to give Dylan his cue, 'Who comes so fast in silence of the night?' The answer was no one! Dylan was still wrapped in the silence of Fulton's Vaults. I had no option but to soldier on and invite Jessica to have a restful sit-down while I launched myself into the famous description of the heavens echoing to the music of the spheres. Still, I had to get back to the plot and surely Dylan must have returned by now! Boldly I cried again, 'I hear a sound. Here comes the messenger!' Shakespeare never wrote such words but I was desperate. Again no sound offstage. I looked around wildly and then gasped out to Jessica:

'Dids't hear not what I said about the heavens?
Then sit once more, fair Jessica. Pay more attention.'

On I went through the speech again with special emphasis on the lines that declare our inability to listen to the music of the spheres because 'this muddy vesture of decay, Doth grossly close it in, we cannot hear it.' This time, I vowed, Dylan would hear me through whatever muddy vesture of decay he possessed, even if I had to blow the scenery down. I fairly bellowed, 'Come on, come on, thou sluggish messenger.' There was a slight shuffle backstage. I hissed through my teeth, 'Who comes — at last — in silence of the night?'

On came a wobbling and distinctly happy Dylan who slapped me on the back and announced to the astonished audience, 'It's me, old boy. Don't you recognize me? Sorry I'm late. What do I say next?'

What I said was, 'Let's get out of this,' and seizing Dylan and Jessica, whipped them offstage in double-quick time, adding as I went as a last concession to the plot, 'Portia shall hear of this.'

This, very properly, was my last appearance in any dramatic performance for the rest of my life. A few days later I received a note from my kindly tutor at Oxford saying that there was a vacancy for a Junior Keeper of Manuscripts and Records at the National Library of Wales at Aberystwyth. Salary £160 per annum. Why not apply? Here, at last, was one place where knowledge of William of Tyre or the Albigensian Crusade might come in useful. I could not go on much longer living on my parents with only £20 in my pocket. I went to the interview and came away with the appointment. Within a few weeks I was metamorphosed. The little friend of all the unemployed, the drinking companion of Dylan, the Irving of Swansea became the learned and studious librarian, seated at his desk in a long silent gallery, surrounded by a vast array of volumes and papers to be meticulously catalogued. I was delighted to get the money but soon began to wonder if I was the right man in the right job. This was not the fault of the librarian, the library staff or even of Aberystwyth. If I had been a genuine student, a man with real scholarship in his bones, I would have rejoiced exceedingly in my new position and settled down happily at the library for life.

Aberystwyth was then the perfect town for the unambitious man. It had a ruined medieval castle, a small harbour which dried out at low tide, a little Regency square around the parish church and a mid-Victorian seafront stretching in an elegant bow-windowed curve between two high hills. In the centre of the curve rose a marvellously turreted piece of Victoriana, a Betjeman dream of architectural delight, which is now part of

Educational Ice-cream Cones.
University College, Aberystwyth.
1929.

the university college but which started life as a giant hotel. Thomas Savin was a railway tycoon with a brilliant idea for promoting tourism which was far ahead of his time. In fact, he invented the package tour. You paid for a first-class ticket at Euston, which entitled you to a free week's holiday at Aberystwyth's new caravanserai. It was too good to last. Savin's hotel went bankrupt just in time to become the nucleus of the first Welsh University College. In my day, the college had not yet suffered the effects of the modern education explosion which has now sprayed new concrete and glass slabs over the hillside at the back of the town. The students were happy in their spiky neo-Gothic castle. I was happy, too, for I attended palaeography classes under its pointed arches.

Behind Aberystwyth spread the glorious wilderness of Plynlimon, with its waterfalls, lonely lakes and miles of windswept moorlands. I marked it down immediately as my escape hatch for Sundays. I bicycled on the lonely deserted roads of those days up to Ponterwyd, then on up the track that led into the heart of the wilderness, past the little cottage where Sir John Rhys, the great Celtic scholar, was born. I always stopped and took off my hat to Sir John's memory, not only because he was a scholar of European fame but because he retained his peasant simplicity and wit even in the most distinguished company. He became principal of Jesus College, Oxford and the story goes that the young gentlemen of the college called on him to ask him to instal baths. 'Baths! Baths!' said Sir John. 'What do you want baths for? You are only up for eight weeks!'

As I reached the inner fastness of Plynlimon, I trod in the footsteps of another remarkable scholar who was still a power in the land when I came to Aberystwyth. Professor H.J. Fleure was a distinguished geographer and archaeologist who, with his collaborator H.J.E. Peake, was publishing a series of influential books on the prehistory of man under the intriguing title of *The Corridors of Time*. One of these corridors had led him up to the lonely farm of Nant-y-Moch where the river Rheidol tumbled down in foaming cascades from the great hollow under the very summit of Plynlimon. In 1932 this must have been one of the remotest of the inhabited places of Wales. Now the professor, as all good professors should, had a theory. He believed that the shape of a man's head indicated the racial origin of its possessor. This is putting it rather crudely, for the theory made great play with cephalic indices and the difference between brachycephalic and dolicho- cephalic skulls.

The professor wandered happily through the landscape, callipers in hand, measuring heads in all directions. His jour- neys eventually brought him to Nant-y-Moch where the brothers Evans were quite willing to oblige. To his delight John Evans possessed the most perfect brachycephalic – or was it dolichocephalic – skull yet measured. It was proof positive that here, in the secret fastness of Plynlimon there yet lingered on the original stock of those dark, short little Welshmen who long preceded the tall, fair-haired Celts and whose modern descendants are the main source of supply for scrum halves in Welsh rugby teams. The professor persuaded John, in return for a small annuity paid by the college to bequeath his head to him when the moment came for him to 'pass over'.

There was a slight feeling among the scattered community in the hills that John had rather let them down. He had signed the agreement in all innocence as a gesture to science and here he was being branded as Plynlimon Man. As one farmer's wife said to me, 'What about the funeral then! They'll have to saw his head off before they bury him. Well I can't see our minister praying over a headless body, can you?' The dilemma solved itself. The professor died before the farmer and, alas, his theory died with him. John Evans went to his Maker intact and today the waters of the vast new dam have drowned Nant-y- Moch, the home of Plynlimon Man, the professor's theory and all memories of the hills of forty-five years ago.

But my expeditions to Plynlimon and my acts of homage to Sir John Rhys, in a curious way, forced me to take a new, close look at myself. Here was John Evans walking about with a valuable head on his shoulders because he was a very special sort of Welshman; but what sort of a Welshman was I? To tell the truth I couldn't speak the language. When father made his break with the world of the chapel, I lost my only chance of being brought up as a Welsh speaker, since the part of Swansea in which we lived was entirely anglicized. Welsh-speaking Swansea lay on the other side of the Town Hill – a mystery land into which we never went when we were young. Our playmates and teachers all spoke English to us. We heard mother and father speaking Welsh at home but we could not join in.

At Aberystwyth I found myself for the first time living in a true Welsh-speaking community where I felt cut off and an outsider with only English at my command. I set myself to acquire the language. Let me admit, straight away, that Welsh is not an easy language to learn – especially if you have been brought up entirely on English. The pronunciation difficulties have been exaggerated. Englishmen have mastered Portuguese where vowels and consonants slip all over the place; and have no trouble with the Spanish 'll' although they draw the line at the similar Welsh 'll'. Welsh 'ch' is exactly like that in Scottish 'loch' and 'dd' is virtually the same as the 'th' in 'the'. So what's the problem, say the keen Welsh nationalists, who were born Welsh-speaking and demand that the language should be used by everyone living in Wales. The problem comes when you run all these linguistically strong sounds together in a place name like Machynlleth and add to pronunciation complexities the rules for mutating certain consonants at the beginnings of words. I was lucky. I had heard Welsh spoken since my earliest days, so had no difficulty over pronunciation. I am glad I made the extra effort to read and speak the language as well, for Welsh has a rich and exciting literature and one that is being continually renewed in our own day. Do I want the Welsh language to survive? Emphatically yes. Something of infinite value to my own country, and Britain too, would go from our national life with the death of an ancient language; but I think I learnt Welsh above all because I did not want to become a mass-produced, standardized man.

I certainly didn't feel like one as I sat at my long table in the National Library, that remarkable neo-classical palace of books set on the high hill behind Aberystwyth so that it dominated the whole landscape. You felt, as you looked at it, that the long flight of steps and the balanced wings of the shining structure were proudly proclaiming, 'Look well on us.

We are the proof that Wales is genuinely cultured'. The library had alighted on this particular hill as a result of the usual struggle between North and South Wales over the siting of all important national buildings. Bangor fought Cardiff so that for years the National Library hovered like Mohammed's coffin between heaven and – well wherever you locate the other place. Eventually it came to earth halfway between, in Aberystwyth, the place predestined by geography for happy compromise.

I enjoyed the knowledge that, as I sorted out papers in my long gallery, I was close to the historic and literary treasures of Wales. Just along the corridor were the special fireproof rooms where reposed the great collection of manuscripts brought together by Sir John Williams, the royal physician, to form the nucleus of the library. Nearly every manuscript of importance for Welsh historians lay within a few yards of where I sat every day at work. I rejoiced in their romantic names – the Black Book of Carmarthen, the White Book of Rhydderch, the Book of Taliesin! Under the Copyright Act of 1911, Aberystwyth was one of the six libraries in Britain that had to receive a copy of nearly every book published in the country. I began to read avidly and haphazardly the cornucopia of literature that poured on the dizzy heads of the librarians. Let me admit that I did not neglect to sample what used to be described as 'the more curious' volumes in the library, and this laid the foundations of a knowledge of the more classical works of restrained pornography, proper – or perhaps improper – to a true student of social history. I must have been the only man in Wales who was reading Voltaire's *La Pucelle* alongside Jeremy Taylor's *Holy Living and Holy Dying*.

The work I was actually paid to do consisted of cataloguing the papers of the Ocean Colliery Company which had been deposited in the library by Lord Davies of Llandinam. They turned out to be far more entertaining than I had expected. They told the story of the titanic industrial battle between the thrusting Victorian capitalist, David Davies, who was making millions out of developing the steam coal of the Rhondda Valley, and the Marquis of Bute, the head of the Bute interests, who controlled the outlet of David Davies' coal through Cardiff docks. David Davies was known as Top Sawyer because as a young man in the saw pits of mid-Wales, where he began, he was always the man on top. He continued all his life to be the man on top. He became a powerful railway contractor and was one of the first to put his money into exploiting the steam coal of the Rhondda. The stories about him are legion. As he sank the new Ocean pit, he saw his money ebbing away when the rich seams he sought failed to appear. At last he had to call the workmen together and tell them he'd reached the end of his resources. 'I've not a penny left,' he told them, 'except this half crown in my pocket. You've had it all.'

'We'll have that too,' shouted a voice at the back.

'It's yours,' said Davies. He tossed them the coin and walked away. The workmen were so impressed with this gesture that they voted to give him a final week's work free.

David Davies had gone away despondently to try to save the wreckage of his fortunes by completing the new railway to West Wales. He was standing on the embankment beyond Whitland when he saw his manager running excitedly towards him waving a telegram. Davies read it and said soberly, 'I will not exchange this scrap of paper for forty thousand pounds.' He was right. His new shaft had struck the richest seam in the Rhondda. He was on his way to becoming Davies the Ocean, king of the steam coal for which the world's navies and shipping lines were clamouring.

A totally contrasting figure, the Marquis of Bute had inherited his estates in Cardiff from his enterprising father and grandfather who had virtually created industrial Cardiff. He was enormously wealthy and enormously cultured – an authority on Coptic Church symbolism and Scottish heraldry, a convert to the Roman Catholic Church, a leading investigator of psychical phenomena and the translator of Turgenev. Like all rich Victorian romantics, he fell to building and naturally in the Gothic style. He demanded towers, battlements, crenellations, balustrades and all the architectural *bric-a-brac* of the Middle Ages – anything, one feels, to shut out the Victorian view of Cardiff. He got full measure from his architect, William Burges. Together they converted Cardiff Castle into a Roman fort with a Welsh carcassonne gaily stuck onto the western wall. They rebuilt Castell Coch, the Red Castle in the hills behind Cardiff, as one of those castles you see on hock labels, complete with a drawbridge that really worked – so well indeed that it once shot half a Sunday school treat into the dry moat. Castell Coch now looked so like a Rhineland stronghold that the Marquis decided to plant a vineyard at its foot. He spent money lavishly and actually put his Welsh white wine onto the market in 1875. *Punch* was unkind about the result and predicted that it would take four men to drink the wine – one to swallow it, two to hold the victim down and one to pour it down his throat. This was unfair. The wine eventually became good, a worthy forerunner of the renaissance of wine-making in Britain today. The Marquis was finally defeated by the First World War and a run of bad seasons. 'Never forget,' one old Glamorgan farmer told me, 'never forget that Welsh weather is teetotal!'

While the Marquis was planning new vineyards or thinking of a better phrase for 'virgin soil' in English, Davies the Ocean was starting to fret and fume in his Welsh Klondike of the Rhondda. The more coal he produced the more money he seemed to be paying in tolls to the Bute interests. At all costs he had to sidestep Cardiff. The battle lines were drawn up with the protagonists both, as it were, ready made for a Victorian novel. On one side, Top Sawyer, Welsh-speaking Methodist, a self-made Samuel Smiles hero intent on money, power and industrial progress. On the other, the great nobleman in his Gothic tower with his mind on Coptic rituals, new castles, and his next speech in the House of Lords on the position of the British chargé d'affaires at the Vatican. As I turned the thick files of letters, engineers' reports, plans of new buildings and bills of costs I became absorbed in the struggle. What David Davies proposed was a bold scheme to divert the Rhondda coal completely from Cardiff to big new docks he planned to build at Barry, about eight miles further down the Bristol Channel. Huge sums of money were involved. MPs had to be lobbied, landowners secretly sweetened, wagonloads counted by spies, newspaper editors flattered and briefed. I was reading a superb and yet unshot film script which ended with the inevitable victory of Davies the Ocean. Today his statue stands at the entrance to Barry docks – stocky, confident, with the plans of the docks in his hands and an air of being ready to face the future whatever may come. The bronze face of Top Sawyer can now no longer alter its expression of sturdy optimism, but today it looks out on a vast expanse of empty water which mirrors the outline of idle coal hoists. The sidings are full of rusting railway engines. Barry, which rose to glory on David Davies's steam coal, has now become the graveyard of steam.

There is a painful irony in all this – hardly softened by the curious fact that it was the heirs of the fortune created by David Davies who took over the role of the Marquis of Bute as patrons of the arts. To the Misses Davies of Gregynog, Wales owes one of the finest collections of Impressionist paintings outside France. Renoir's deliciously nubile Parisienne under her umbrella looks smilingly at you out of her gilded frame in the National Museum at Cardiff. I wonder if she can see the coal mines, the dark tips and lines of slate-roofed cottages in the rain of the Rhondda, whence came the money that brought her to Wales. Oddly, I began to see the Rhondda vividly as I neatly filed away the last papers of the David Davies collection. The poet Gray had sung:

> Full many a gem of purest ray serene
> The dark unfathomed caves of Ocean bear.

I have now explored those caves and found them full of black diamonds and uneasy thoughts. I could see my old friends in the unemployed clubs waiting for the dole in the very valleys where David Davies had first set his miners to work. Even the winding gear at the top of the Ocean coal shaft was turning more slowly. Had I the right to be sitting in cultured comfort in my warm gallery in Aberystwyth? At this distance of time, I admit that I can see now my real motive behind all the high-minded thoughts of service that occurred to me as I completed my cataloguing. I knew in my heart of hearts that I wasn't a genuine scholar. I wasn't really cut out to be a researcher, sitting happily among his manuscripts, busy chasing an obscure point in a disputed interpretation of an interpolated passage in the thirty-eighth MS of the *Historia Regum Britanniae*. I take my hat off to those who have the skill and patience to seek the truth through years of detective work. At twenty-three I wanted a whole lot of things that didn't seem to be on tap in Aberystwyth, from travel in romantic places to drinking with poets and dazzling love affairs with rising film stars. My mind was a jumble of half-baked, unrealized plans, ideas, ambitions. In short, I was exactly like everyone else at twenty-three. I pulled out a crumpled newspaper from my pocket. It contained an advertisement for the post of Area Officer in the South Wales and Monmouthshire Council of Social Service, an organization newly set up to help the unemployed in the mining valleys. I saw myself as the perfect man for the job. I placed the David Davies papers in a neat pile and wrote out my application.

A few weeks later I found myself in Cardiff for the interview. What is life but an endless succession of interviews? It starts with the school examinations, then on you go to the interviews for your first job, your subsequent jobs and your promotions. After forty-five you are still attending interviews, although probably on the other side of the table. Even death does not free you from the interview incubus. If you are a Christian you believe – or used to believe, for I have no doubt that modern theologians have soothed the whole thing over – in the most vital interview of them all, the Last Judgement.

I count my Cardiff interview as my most Vital Judgement. I faced a row of men of goodwill, the leaders of the community. But did they have goodwill towards me? The chairman, Captain Geoffrey Crawshay, certainly did. He was the heir to the remains of the great fortune amassed by the famous iron-masters of Merthyr: a tall handsome man, with a distinguished war record and a heart of gold. He was in the forefront of every good cause, from funding the Crawshay Rugby Fifteen for aspiring young players to riding his white horse in his white robes, as the Herald Bard, leading the long procession of the poets and musicians in the Gorsedd ceremony. Other bards might allow their trousers to come peeping out from under the bardic nightdress, but never Captain Crawshay! He rode in immaculate white, gallantly but hopelessly setting a sartorial standard to the pipe-smoking poets who shambled happily along in his wake.

Sir Percy Watkins sat at Captain Crawshay's side. He was small, precise, an admirable civil servant who had just retired from the Welsh Board of Education and had come back to Wales as the representative of the National Council of Social Service, charged with the duty of supervising the money voted to the council by the government for establishing clubs for the unemployed. In these clubs it was hoped men, and women too, might be able to help themselves in all sorts of ways from boot-repairing to allotments. Here was a place where they could hold their Workers' Educational Association classes, keep fit with PT and try to supplement the meagre dole of those degenerate days. The area officers were being appointed to encourage these clubs and assess the grants they needed. Sir Percy certainly assessed me. He saw, with the same clarity of the examiners at my Civil Service interview, that by no stretch of the imagination was I a heaven-born administrator. He wrote one word alongside my name: 'Immature'. Of course he was right, and I am still immature as I pass the seventy mark – but how his comment rankled at the time!

How did I come to know about Sir Percy's comment? Quite simple! Sitting at the board to take the official minutes was Miss Charlotte Rowlands, a girl from Caernarvon in North Wales. She it was who had been left with the responsibility of sorting out the applications for the job in the absence of Sir Percy. He had insisted, 'The entry closes on Monday morning. If any applications arrive after that date, put them in the wastepaper basket. If they can't write in on time, they can't be much good anyway.' My application arrived on Thursday! But Sir Percy's secretary read it, and – as she said afterwards – felt it had something. She placed it at the top of the pile with the result that I got the job. Many years later I married the secretary as well.

I now entered a strange period of my life in which I spent my time amid scenes of the utmost depression – dole queues, closed coal pits, men demoralized by the means test – and yet I look back on it as a period of great personal happiness. The answer to this paradox lies in the remarkable quality of life in the mining valleys. W.H. Auden had just published his poem with the lines:

and Glamorgan hid a life
Grim as a tidal rock-pool in its glove-shaped valleys.

How utterly wrong he was. He was simply reflecting the outsider's view of the Valleys as a wilderness of slate-roofed houses leaning against coal tips wedged into slots amongst black mountains. Every man was supposed to be an out-of-work Communist who also sang melancholy hymns at rugby matches. Occasionally, as light relief, the funeral of Dai the Bookie passed the welfare hall (not yet paid for) and Capel Zion looked down in stern disapproval. Always the rain fell with the persistence of an endless sermon.

Parts of this have some elements of truth but the picture left out one vital factor that made every valley misery bearable – the heart-warming comradeship of the people and the humour that ran through it all. Gwyn Thomas, the most brilliant Welsh talker of our times, has caught the tone perfectly in those memorable novels of his about life in the Rhondda during the Great Depression. This comradeship and laughter made the Depression un-depressing. The miners knew that, in a small way, you were sharing their anguish – you were their 'butty', one of the boys.

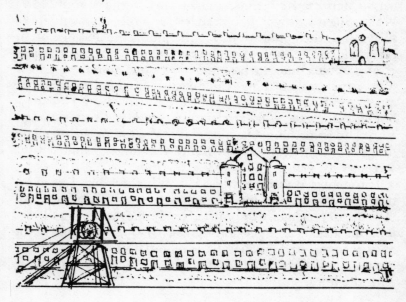

I settled myself in rooms in Cardiff, got on my second-hand motorbike and chugged up and down the valleys in response to the stream of appeals which now descended on our headquarters. I used to sit with the committee and make out careful lists of the club's requirements to be submitted later to the grants committee of the Council. The limit of the money available was the princely sum of £25. It was also possible to give money to the clubs to put up their own huts by voluntary labour. I found myself being taken to a fantastic variety of curious sites, and spending long hours trying to find out who actually owned some patch of scruffy ground that had been covered with rotting tin cans for the previous thirty years. I had no idea that the earth of Britain had been so tangled up by the law. Or else I would arrive at some dead end in the mountains in pouring rain, with the members of the committee ready to lead me down the gully, the unpaved alley that led down between the houses where the sheep wandered in and out of tiny front gardens, to some hut or converted decayed warehouse clinging desperately to the steep hillside. I remember entering one such club where the chairman had written a moving letting saying that, if a grant was received, the club would immediately expand its programme of 'psychical training'. What could this be? New WEA classes? PT? I went to find out on the usual rainy afternoon. The chairman led me down the gully, saying, 'Have you brought the money with you, Mr Thomas?' I explained that I had to see the club in action first before we filled in the form. 'Oh, that's easy. We've got the best psychical training in all the valleys.' He flung the club door open dramatically. The room was packed with men in the regulation cloth caps and mufflers all grouped around a square in the centre. The chairman escorted me to the only two chairs visible, both set beside the square. We sat down and the chairman gave the order. 'Dai Williams get ready.' Out walked a big hulk of a man in running shorts, with 'I love you, Marged' tattooed on his left arm. 'Rhys Bach,' the chairman called. Rhys appeared, a spry little man with boxing gloves which he kept darting up to his nose and snorting as he did a sort of ritual dance in the middle of the ring. 'Dai Williams,' the chairman ordered, 'knock hell out of Rhys Bach, here, to please Mr Thomas from Cardiff.'

Never has there been such an unequal contest. Rhys Bach did his best. He gave a marvellous display of fancy footwork at a safe distance, but all the time Dai Williams was coiling back that formidable Marged-tattooed left. Incautiously Rhys Bach came in closer. Dai unloosed his left with shattering effect. Rhys staggered back, tripped and fell into my lap with a fine cascade of blood and loose teeth and an incipient black eye. The chairman leant over the prostrate hero and beamed cheerfully at me. 'Lovely boys, Mr Thomas! Lovely boys! Now, you are bound to give us a grant.' Indeed I did. For to me they were indeed lovely boys.

For three years I went happily up and down the valleys scattering my £25s with a lavish hand. Not everyone viewed my activities with favour. The men of the Left regarded the whole business of unemployed clubs with total disapproval. Up in the Communist stronghold of Maerdy, the Little Moscow where Arthur Horner ruled, memories were still vivid of the great strikes, the clarion call of *The Miner's Next Step*, the oratory of A. J. Cook. Even the Labour Party felt that there was a danger that our unemployed clubs were mere palliatives, designed to keep the out-of-work quiet and half-contented. I cannot think they did any harm at all. They were no cure for the industrial ills of South Wales but they did help some people I grew to value through a period of intense misery.

They helped me, too. I used to sit and listen to the stories of the work underground, the technique of cutting the coal, the rockfalls, the strikes – a whole new, dramatic and tragic world opened before me. This was the reality behind the David Davies papers I had so carefully catalogued in Aberystwyth. I went out with the women and boys in winter onto the Cilfynydd tip to scrabble for the little bits of coal left after the washeries had taken all the valuable lumps. I crawled down the small levels that some companies allowed the out-of-work miners to open in narrow and unproductive seams to get enough coal for the winter. The old hands initiated me into the art of pillar and stall working and how to make the roof 'sing' as a safeguard against rock falls. On rare occasions we went off on Unemployed Outings to Porthcawl or Port Eynon which rivalled those immortalized by Dylan Thomas. In other words, these were the three years in which I grew up – or at least ceased to be quite as immature as Sir Percy Watkins had judged me.

As time went on, it became increasingly clear that I would eventually have to find another sphere of activity. I had become aware of the subtle South Wales doctrine of the unfortunate lapse. There were some occasions – very rare, I must make clear – when the grants I had made seemed to suddenly disappear. I would enter a club and the chairman would hurriedly take me aside. 'Glad you've come, Mr Thomas. Come into my room for a moment.' Then the inevitable admission. 'Mr Thomas, to tell you the truth – no, you're one of us now – to tell you the honest truth, we've had an unfortunate lapse. The treasurer! Last seen in Porthcawl. His wife's in a pitiful state, poor dab. It's the temptation, you know. It could have happened to any one of us.' Then followed the meeting with the committee, and – to tell the honest truth – a new application for a grant to cover the deficit, strongly supported by me. How could anyone blame the poor treasurer?

But there came a time when I was on the verge of the most unfortunate lapse of all. I had given a certain club the regulation grant of £25 and had gone up to see how they were getting on. The chairman had promised me that the money was going to be used to launch a splendidly adventurous educational programme – lectures on foreign affairs, on English and Welsh literature, on Bible criticism – in fact, on every subject which was held by the authorities in 1933 to be of vital importance to the welfare of the unemployed miner. The local headmaster – universally known for his interest in philosophy as Evans the Elevated Mind – was standing by, ready to start the classes as soon as the ink was dry on the cheque. I had anticipated a murmur of happy intellectual activity as I entered the bleak lower regions of the decayed store which served as the club premises. They were deserted. I went up the rickety stairs to the next floor. No sign of life. Then on up to the third floor, where I was astonished to find the club members in a tight knot around the window, like bees swarming around their queen. The chairman spun round, gave a start, then advanced upon me with a hurriedly assumed smile of welcome.

'Mr Thomas bach, what a surprise! We were only saying yesterday that we hoped you would turn up today. In fact, the committee were unanimous about it.'

'But what's going on here, Mr Phillips?'

'Now I'm glad you've put that very question, Mr Thomas bach. As a matter of fact – and I wouldn't conceal it from you for a moment – we've put some money on the dogs. We can see the track from the upper window here. The next race begins in a few minutes, so the boys, very naturally, want to see how their money goes.'

'But, Mr Phillips, how could you have got the money to put on the dogs?'

'Mr Thomas, I'd better tell you the honest truth – no, the real honest truth. It's your money we've put on, the twenty-five pounds you gave us.'

'Good heavens, Mr Phillips, but that's Government money!'

'Don't worry, Mr Thomas, we're on a certain winner, and once it romps home we'll be meeting Evans the Elevated Mind tonight, and I'll promise you one thing, we'll cascade culture round this place.'

'Oh, Mr Phillips, what on earth made you do this?'

'Mr Thomas, to be honest with you again, we had to.' And Mr Phillips lowered his voice with the air of an old friend breaking the news of a sudden death in the family, 'We've had an unfortunate lapse.'

It was a classic case; the temptation, the inevitable hurried departure of the treasurer for somewhere like Porthcawl after 'a little confusion between the red and black figures'. 'Could have happened to any one of us; and he's sent us a most apologetic letter!' But Mr Phillips offered me immediate comfort.

'Don't worry Mr Thomas. We can't go wrong. Dai Williams's brother is letting them out of the trap. And even if we lose, we're still on a winner because we've got you, haven't we. You'll never let us down. After all, it *was* a genuine unfortunate lapse.'

Suddenly a rousing cheer from the crowd at the window interrupted us. As forecast – or perhaps as aided by Dai

Williams's brother – Pontlottyn Patsy had raced in a certain winner. The chairman was exultant.

'Ah, wait 'til I see Evans the Elevated tonight! And who knows, Mr Thomas, we ourselves may be able to take a trip to Porthcawl.'

I rode home thoughtfully. I could see a distinct and perhaps a dramatic ending to my period of usefulness to the unemployed. Government auditors might not be quite as sympathetic as I had been to the difficulties of distinguishing between black and red figures on balance sheets. I, myself, might have to take a trip to Porthcawl and send that apologetic letter. That evening I poured out my anxieties to my future wife, who had now left the world of social service to become the secretary to the new programme controller of BBC Welsh radio. Once again she guided my career in a new direction.

The BBC had begun developing its regional stations and was in the process of setting up a new, separate organization for Welsh broadcasting. The corporation was anxious to recruit Welshmen to head the various departments and one such department had the intriguing title of Outside Broadcasts. It conjured up visions of commentaries on historic occasions, thrilling sporting events, interviews around the world with the famous and notorious. I must admit that, up to this moment, I had not been a constant listener. I had been singing in pubs, racing up to North Wales on my motorbike for climbing weekends, listening to the stories of the unemployed, arguing with poets and painters – doing everything, in fact, but listen to the radio. Charlotte set me a crash course and together we sat down to sample the cornucopia of culture which the BBC was providing for the British public under the stern guidance of John Reith. Strange names swam into my ken – Christopher Stone, A.J. Alan, Mr Middleton, now perhaps consigned to undeserved oblivion, for nothing faded more rapidly than a radio reputation made in the days before the universal use of recording. In spite of myself I was impressed. The BBC was, after all, an opulent extension of the WEA! With a young man's impudence, I decided the corporation would suit me. More surprisingly, the mandarins of the corporation decided that I would suit them. Early in 1936, I became an Outside Broadcasts Assistant at a salary of £250 a year. This was the only title I ever possessed during my twenty happy years with the BBC.

I left the mining valleys with a slight feeling of deserting a battlefield. For years afterwards my mind kept returning to them whenever I felt depressed far away from South Wales – like a soldier in the First World War recalling the heart-warming comradeship of the trenches. I put it all down in light verse:

> The sight of the English is getting me down.
> Fly westward, my heart, from this festering town
> On the Wings of a Dove – and a First Class Return –
> To the front room of 'Cartref' at Ynys-y-Wern.
>
> Swift through the dark flies the 5.59,
> Past Slough and past Didcot and derelict mine,
> Past pubs and Lucanias and adverts for ales
> Till the back-sides of chapels cry 'Welcome to Wales'.
>
> The light of the chip-shop shines bright through the dark,
> The couples lie laced in the asphalted park;
> In the vestry of Carmel (conductor, Seth Hughes)
> The iron-clad Gleemen are raping the Muse.
>
> They're 'Comrades', they're 'Martyrs', they're 'Crossing
>   the plain'.
> They're roaring of Love in a three-part refrain,
> But what hymns from Novello's, at threepence a part,
> Can mirror the music I feel in my heart?
>
> Glorious welcome that's waiting for me,
> Hymns on the Harmonium and Welsh-cake for tea,
> A lecture on Marx, his importance today,
> All the raptures of love from a Bangor B.A!

CHAPTER FIVE

Learning the Trade at the BBC

Joining the BBC in 1936 was rather like becoming a novice in a Jesuit seminary. The disciplines had been firmly laid down by the Blessed John Reith. The corporation had perforce to amuse the masses from time to time, but its aims were constantly directed towards higher things. The government had surely not given the BBC a monopoly over the most powerful medium of mass communication ever invented for it to become simply a substitute for the cinema or the music hall in the home. The director general put it in a crisp sentence, soon after my appointment, on the only occasion he ever spoke to me. 'Welcome on board, Mr Thomas; but never forget that the BBC is not an organ of mere entertainment.' He rolled the word mere over his tongue with a rich Scots accent and a contemptuous relish that came straight from John Knox.

Reith left the corporation a year or so after I joined, but the BBC retained the stamp he put on it until the advent of Sir Hugh Greene nearly thirty years later. At the start of my broadcasting career, I was always aware of that gaunt, immensely tall, heavily-eyebrowed figure brooding in his third floor office in the great white palace of culture that he had built at the corner of Portland Place. You approached his desk across a carpet which seemed, to those who had to walk over it, as large as that of Mussolini's in the Palazzo Venezia. Here he sat – in his favourite image – like the captain on the bridge, guiding his great ship towards the wider horizons of art, music, religion, indeed towards all the higher things of the mind. In the heart of Broadcasting House lay the powerhouse, the chapel. It had been specially consecrated by the Bishop of London and, according to the story whispered to me as soon as I became a member of the staff, had been reconsecrated following a certain incident after the morning service which involved the chorus master and an attractive female chorister.

Perhaps I am a little starry-eyed about the old BBC, because I never rose high in the hierarchy; I operated in the delightful radio Arcadia of Outside Broadcasts and, in any case, I had entered the corporation by the back door. I had joined the BBC at Cardiff. Wales was always a rather special place when it came to radio and television and indeed it has remained so to the present day. It was the perpetual problem on the agenda, a nuisance to all the centralized organizations that had to deal with it. As one BBC high-up put it to me, 'Your country, my dear boy, is administratively untidy.' It didn't fit into any pattern, it threw out all careful budgetary calculations and ruined every engineering programme. For Wales, like Caesar's Gaul, had divided itself into three parts. There were, first of all, the Welsh-speaking Welsh, most of whom had the inconvenient habit of living in beautiful but deep mountain valleys distinctly hostile to radio and TV waves. Then came the people of Welsh descent who, for a whole series of reasons, had lost the language, while retaining their pride in being Welsh. Finally, there were the English people who had settled in Wales, including those who had conquered South Pembrokeshire and West Gower seven hundred years ago to make it 'a Little England beyond Wales'. These Welsh complexities were certainly beyond England!

The Welsh-speaking Welsh, especially the intelligentsia, wanted an independent corporation which would put out most of its programmes in the Welsh language. The non-Welsh-speaking Welsh wanted programmes about Wales but in a language they could understand. The English living in Wales wanted the general output of the BBC, with a minimum content of Welsh interest. No one, to this day, has solved the problem. Whoever is appointed to a position of power in Welsh broadcasting finds himself sitting on a pincushion whch inevitably turns into a bed of nails. When I came to Cardiff, the occupant of this uncomfortable, almost impossible office was Sir Rhys Hopkin Morris. He couldn't solve the insoluble problem but he was the only man in Wales capable of turning a bed of nails into a comfortable armchair.

He was a Cardiganshire man who seemed to be made to order to please everyone. He was a Welsh-speaking Welshman who was a keen Methodist and a teetotaller, which pleased Welsh Wales; he was a lawyer of scrupulous honesty, determined to give a fair deal to all sides, which pleased the non-Welsh-speaking Welsh, and he had once been a Liberal MP who had fallen out with Lloyd George, and that pleased the English. For fifteen years, until he decided to return to politics, he kept Wales convinced it was happy with the BBC even when it wasn't.

I'm not sure if he was profoundly interested in broadcasting techniques, or even the arts. He simply found the artists, the musicians, and the commentators too, endlessly amusing – odd fish, and as refreshingly human as any of his clients at the bar. He was at his best when he sat back in his office at the end of the day with all his tiresome administrative duties safely completed, dressed in the formal legal garb he still enjoyed wearing together with the old-fashioned wing collar, known in those days as a 'come to Jesus'. The smoke from his pipe coiled up to the ceiling as he regaled us with the gossip, the scandals and stories about his old friends at the bar. I regret – as I so often do in similar circumstances – that I never wrote it all down, for the Welsh bar in the old days must have been as full of good stories as that legal classic, *The Old South Munster Circuit*.

Hopkin relished the florid eloquence of the great practitioners of both the pulpit and the bar, although he occasionally felt that they went too far in the Marshall Hall line. Llewellyn Williams, in particular, had an emotional set piece, guaranteed to bring the jury to tears and immediate acquittal, which he unleashed at the end of his final address. Like Marshall Hall he passed down the jury box with the accusing, pointing finger. 'Search your hearts, each one of you, and when the time comes, as come it must to all of us, and you stand before the Great White Throne, how will you answer that terrible question? Have you – yes, you – said of an innocent man, "This man is guilty"'? Guilty! Guilty! The one word that can destroy a man body and soul. Would you dare to utter it before that Great White Throne? Will you dare pronounce this word – in this court – about this man – Now!'

Usually the jury did not dare, but on one occasion Llewellyn Williams was working up towards his final peroration and the jury remained impassive. Hopkin was then acting as junior counsel. Llewellyn muttered to him, 'What on earth can I do to move them?' Hopkin rose and whispered in his ear, 'Why not give a new coat of whitewash to the Great White Throne?' Llewellyn Williams lost the case and Hopkin Morris was never forgiven.

So the talk went on. I revelled in it. After all, I had now entered the new kingdom of talk, for what is radio but endless talk with a little added music? My own department of Outside Broadcasts was deeply concerned with the art of talk. My job was to organize running commentaries on sporting events and great public occasions, and to arrange street interviews where needed. Everything was live, for in those days recording had not got into its stride, so every outside broadcast was a wild adventure. I had joined OBs at a fascinating time. No one had, as yet, made a careful study or a meticulous analysis of the whole business of the running commentary. Describing an event as it actually happened and simultaneously transmitting that description to the wide world was a totally new thing in the history of mankind, only made possible by the invention of 'the wireless'. There had, it is true, been some hints of the shape of things to come even in late Victorian days. The telephone was an instrument for immediate transmission, and Sullivan delighted the Prince of Wales and his guests by relaying a Gilbert and Sullivan opera, *Iolanthe*, from the Savoy Theatre to Marlborough House; but this was still a long way from broadcasting as we understand it today, from the bringing of sound continuously into the actual houses of the people. After the invention of printing, the printed word had reigned supreme in the home for over four hundred years. True, people left their houses to hear the spoken word at church and chapel, at political meetings and music halls. Even the cinema, when it arrived, demanded a weekly trip out of the home. But news,

14 The flat in
Hampstead

15 With David at the
Palace after the
presentation of the O B E

16 Walking the Roof of Wales, 1958

17 With Alun Williams of the BBC, received into the Gorsedd at the Eisteddfod at Ammanford, 1974

gossip, advice, fiction all came to a family through the medium of print. By the 1890s the newspapers and the popular magazines reigned supreme in the family circles of Britain.

Then, almost overnight, came the revolution. In an astonishingly small period of time, the wireless became the very centre of family life. Father, mother and the kids clustered in worship around the primitive loudspeakers. Even my Aunty Bess acquired one of the early crystal sets and sat, with headphones on, trying to find the right spot on the little chunk of bright rock that brought her into nightly contact with the Savoy Orpheans. The spoken word had returned to power in a rush, and the BBC, as its appointed guardian, had carefully to assess its dangerous potential. How would broadcasting affect religion? Would it empty the churches? Would it ruin attendances at sporting events? What about the threat to newspapers? Were there dangerous legal implications? With all these unsolved questions in the air, the BBC had perforce to play for safety. As much as possible of the spoken word had best be written down before it was uttered. Only certain carefully selected and eminently safe speakers on safe subjects could be safely let loose on the public. Music hall comics were a special risk in the early non-recording days. Max Miller's patter looked innocent on paper, but richly bawdy once he had put in the winks, the pauses, the 'Now, listen ladies! It's not what you think!'

Running commentaries on sporting events and public occasions were not in the same class as Max Miller as public risks, but they had best be entrusted to highly-respected and long-established experts in the sport or the event, irrespective of their descriptive powers. To help the listener, and even more the commentator, at rugby matches, the BBC printed the plan of the field in the *Radio Times* as a sort of grid, and many a broadcaster made a reputation out of the way he was able to interject 'Square Four' at the appropriate time.

I joined Outside Broadcasts department at the moment when it was undergoing a revolution and when Square Four was about to be banished into outer darkness. The unlikely Lenin of the commentary revolution was an old Etonian, Seymour Joly de Lotbinière, who rivalled his own name for sheer length, and was inevitably known affectionately as Lobby. The story went the round of OBs, that after a broadcast at Windsor, King George V invited Lobby to stay behind while he introduced him to all the other members of the Royal Family. Afterwards, Lobby confessed to the King's secreatry that he had been flattered but rather at a loss to understand why he had been accorded the honour. Said the secretary, 'My dear fellow, the King called them all in to look at you in case they didn't believe his story that he'd just met the tallest man in Britain.'

Like many exceptionally tall men, Lobby was unfailingly courteous and considerate, with a cool analytic mind which he may have inherited from his remarkable father. In 1915 Colonel Joly de Lotbinière was an engineer officer attached to the Gallipoli landing force. He designed and built eight floating piers. The piers could be locked together and anchored, and they were also ballasted with 4,000 sealed tins of water in each. The army would thus have had fresh water and an adequate landing stage within a few hours of going ashore. Colonel de Lotbinière had made a brilliant anticipation of Mulberry, the great prefabricated harbour in Normandy during the Second World War. To the anguish of Lotbinière, the Navy gave his vital invention no priority and not one of his piers reached the peninsula. I, myself, only came across this interesting piece of family history when I happened to pick up Robert Rhodes James's book on Gallipoli a few years ago. It was characteristic of Lobby that he never once mentioned it during our long association. But the story may explain from whence came Lobby's calm determination to do the right thing as he saw it, come what may.

And the right thing, at the moment I joined the department, was the radical reform of sound commentary. In the beginning, the corporation had naturally selected its commentators from the ranks of well-known journalists or from long-established figures in particular sports. These men were certainly expert but were they eloquent? Some of them knew everything about the event they were attending except how to describe it. Lobby decided to reverse the order of priority. Eloquence and facility of expression should come first and the expert would become number two, giving the inside information at the intervals or when the action required it. Even before Isherwood, Lobby invited every commentator to make a brave declaration, 'I am a camera.' This verbal cameraman had been sent to the event to be the eyes of the listener. Therefore he had to translate immediate visual impressions into arresting sound; and, I should add, continuous sound. A pause of ten seconds brings death a to commentary.

There should also be a pattern and a rhythm to a good commentary. In sport the score should be announced at regular intervals and the exact position of the players indicated as they move. All this may sound obvious, even elementary, but it is surprisingly difficult to execute when you are wearing headphones and are confronted with a live microphone which is conveying your voice to millions as you speak. No wonder the early commentators littered their commentaries with long pauses, and sentences like, 'I can't quite see from here', or 'Yes, yes, I think it is – yes, it must be. . .' and that old standby, 'and any moment now the procession will be in sight!' You still encounter them in parodies of commentaries written by playwrights and novelists, but Lobby banished them forever from the BBC scene. He also demanded careful preparation before each important commentary – doing your homework was his term for it. When long pauses occurred in ceremonies and processions – as inevitably they do – the commentator had to be prepared in advance to fill them with interesting material. Lobby himself had given an example of how to do this brilliantly when he kept listeners interested for two hours during a ghastly delay in the wedding ceremony of Prince Bernhardt and Princess Juliana. As he admitted himself, he dragged in every known fact of Dutch history except the death of William the Silent!

Lobby gathered around him a notable band of commentators such as John Snagge, Michael Standing, Howard Marshall and Thomas Woodruff. After each broadcast he conducted full postmortems which became a memorable part of the OB scene. Lobby would never make a harsh unjustified criticism. He prefaced every point with a gentle, 'I confess I was a little puzzled to hear you begin with no reference to the change in the weather . . .' or any other mistake you had made in those vital opening minutes of a broadcast. Then he would pace gently around the room, making a masterly analysis of your performance and emphasizing every point by vigorously striking his left fist into the palm of his right hand. On one memorable occasion, while Stewart Macpherson was being submitted to the full Lobby analytic treatment, he was moved to shout, 'OK Lobby. I agree – before you beat yourself to death!'

I, too, underwent the postmortems from time to time. I never contradicted Lobby. Instead, I followed my Uncle Arthur's precept and retired to write a light-hearted jingle about the Perfect Commentator.

> The Commentator is, we know.
> The Whitest Man on radio!
> Handsome and sober, highly paid,
> Napoleon of the Talking Trade.
> Stern guardian of the Spoken Word,
> From him the voice of Truth is heard.
> The honest Truth? Well, I'll admit
> He's got to hot it up a bit:
> With cunning adjectival skill
> He guilds the lily, coats the pill.
> 'A glorious patch of colour' throws
> O'er knock-kneed limping public shows!
> He turns our darkness into light,
> For him alone our boxers fight;
> Enraptured listeners declare
> 'He's better far than being there!'
>
> But sometimes when I take my stand,
> A member of this glorious band,
> On shaky balcony, or street,
> A cold wind blowing round my feet,
> My notes all wet with dripping rain,
> The damned procession late again.
> Oh, how temptation seizes me
> To say exactly what I see!
>
> This very month when I was sent
> To see them open Parliament.
> This was my almost-spoken word,
> And this was what you nearly heard.

'Well, here at the House of Commons door,
It's just the mixture as before –
Same old crowd and same old street,
Same old policeman, same old feet,
And if it's all the same you.
The same old commentary, too!'

The five minutes, background stuff,
Then when the public's had enough,
Switch on to old historic lore
To keep them quiet a minute more.
No sign? Right, try the human touch,
A note of pathos; not *too* much;
That Chelsea Pensioner's about it
(No commentary complete without it!)
Keep on padding – any hope?
(There goes my final 'background' dope!)

At last, thank Heaven, they come! They come!
(Quick – in effects! Pep up that drum!)
Oh, glorious vision, what a sight!
All men and parties now unite
To show our Island's history
Mirrored in pomp and pageantry
Trades Union leaders try, poor dears,
To masquerade as noble peers,
With bulging Tory peeresses,
Shoe-horned into whale-boned dresses.
Don't notice all that peeling painting,
Or count the pimply guardsmen fainting,
Lay on the colour, for we know
Moss Bros. and moth-balls save the show!
State Trumpeters, you wretched men,
Look out – you're blowing flat again!
Quick, quick, back to the studio!
Too late! Too late. They blow! They B-blow!

I look at that light-hearted picture of Lobby's perfect commentator, and remember that there was one man who would
never have been shaken by off-key state trumpeters or processions running half an hour late. In truth, on the one occasion
when this Napoleon of the talking trade got shaken, he shook
the whole broadcasting world as well!

Tommy Woodruff was, I think, the most remarkable of

the new-style commentators inspired by de Lotbinière. He was an ex-navy commander, dashing, optimistic, who didn't always suffer fools gladly, but was gifted with a fine command of words. He was equally at home in sport and ceremony and I owed him a debt of gratitude for the way he had nursed me through my first big commentary test. I had sat at his side in the commentary box on Constitution Hill in that memorable summer of 1937, when he described the great procession returning from Westminster Abbey at the Coronation of King George VI.

It was the last splendid parade of the sartorial glories of the *ancien régime*, with all the uniforms outlined in gold braid, medals galore glittering on every breast, generals in plumed hats riding on their chargers as if they were off to Omdurman, a whole bevy of bedecked and now obsolete royalty preceding the royal coach. Tremblingly I contributed my five minutes as the Welsh regiments marched past, and the engineers panicked as I slipped into Welsh – they thought that they had got the main commentary crossed with a feed to the Urdu section. Then Tommy erupted as the coach itself appeared. His adjectives cascaded over it – 'this dazzling, scintillating, coruscating fairy tale of a coach'. Ah! this, I felt, was how commentary should be; the great occasion matched with great eloquence, sentences sky-rocketing with confident splendour over the scene!

Naturally we were both dressed in morning coats, stiff collars and grey waistcoats. No one could see us, and we had to walk in our full fig at dawn through the assembling crowds, but we were the BBC and had standards to maintain. In 1937, announcers still wore dinner jackets when they read the news or introduced speakers in the evening. After all, as Stuart Hibberd once explained, 'a lot of our talkers looked in on their way to dine at their clubs and we had to receive them properly'. The BBC represented style and national dignity. Any deviation from the accepted conduct of gentlemanly behaviour was unthinkable – even impossible. Yet, only a few days after Tommy Woodruff's triumph on Constitution Hill, the Unthinkable, the Impossible occurred.

His commentary on the Coronation procession was to be followed by a description – which everyone anticipated would be as brilliant as his evocation of the army on ceremonial parade – of the illumination of the fleet at Portsmouth. I had gone down to Cardiff to make preliminary arrangements for the forthcoming royal tour of Wales, and had an appointment to discuss them with Tommy on the morning after his Portsmouth broadcast. As a result, I did not hear his performance, since I was in the night sleeper to Paddington. I was therefore distinctly puzzled, as I left the station in the early morning, to find London plastered with mysterious newspaper posters. 'The Fleet's Lit Up', they proclaimed. 'Remarkable Description by Naval Commander.' 'Fairy Lights over the Royal Navy.' When I entered Broadcasting House I found an atmosphere of hushed disaster, as if a rich uncle had suddenly died and had then been found to be bankrupt. I passed Recorded Programmes. 'What's up?' I asked. 'Didn't you hear it?' 'I was in a sleeper on the train at the time.' 'Well, don't say anything but listen to this.' And they lured me into a cubicle where I had a private audition of the first earthquake to hit the solid structure of the British Broadcasting Corporation.

Tommy had apparently done himself rather well in the wardroom of his old ship, HMS *Nelson*. As he climbed to his commentary point high up on the fighting top, the sea air had its inevitable effect. The sober, steady voice of Stuart Hibberd cued over to Portsmouth, and the not so sober and distinctly unsteady voice of Thomas Woodruff took up the story in phrases that have now passed into broadcasting history.

'The fleet's lit up . . . dozens of fairy lights . . . there's nothing between me but sea and sky . . .' Again and again the delighted listeners were assured that the fleet, like the commentator, was well and truly illuminated, until the announcer on duty tactfully faded out the whole delicious fantasia.

Clearly my pleasant session with Tommy for arrangements of a royal visit to Wales was off. I tiptoed tactfully away from the stricken purlieus of B H and walked down Upper Regent Street. Coming towards me was a well-known bowler-hatted figure with an elegant rolled umbrella. By heavens, it was Tommy himself! He had almost been flung ashore from HMS *Nelson* and now he was coming in to face the music. He stopped and gave me a brave, disarming grin.

'What will you do, Tommy?' I asked.

'Well, you know what I always say. Never look back, never apologize, keep on talking. I'll have to look back, but, by heavens, I'm going to keep on talking.'

'Good luck,' I said.

'I'll need it,' he replied. He squared his shoulders, set his bowler at the jaunty angle popularized by Admiral Beatty, put his umbrella to his shoulder and strode boldly towards the wrath of Sir John Reith that awaited him on the third floor of Broadcasting House.

The row was tremendous. Sir John was all for sacking him on the spot. Lobby fought valiantly for his best commentator but Tommy was saved by the universal roar of delight that arose from the whole nation. At last the BBC had shown it could be human. After a suitable three months retirement – 'due to strain' – Woodruff returned as a commentator and carried on successfully until he was recalled to the navy at the beginning of the Second World War. The Fleet's Lit Up affair, however, proved to me that life in the Reithian BBC was not to be taken too seriously as long as I stayed in Outside Broadcasts and remained in my twenties. There was something extraordinarily pleasant about learning an art from friendly experts in exciting surroundings. It must have been the same for the lucky beginner in Caxton's press in Westminster or luckier still in the studio of some great painter of the Italian Renaissance. For sound commentary was both an art and a craft. A minor art, perhaps, that did not last long – twenty years at the most, until television came to alter the rules and technique – but a most rewarding art for those who practised it.

Behind the commentator stood the sound engineers, checking his headphones, nursing him, bringing him up to the starting post like trainers making certain the favourite was at the top of his form. In those days, all outside broadcasters formed a close-knit team. They were all operating outside the safety of the studio and anything could happen – and did. The doyen of sound engineers was a genial Yorkshire man, who could do anything with valves and transmitters and also with the English language. He was the last master of malapropism, and also had a delightful habit of coining or re-coining proverbs.

To this day, I am uncertain about certain pieces of prover-
bial wisdom after R.H. had worked them over. How utterly
reasonable sounds his statement, 'You can't find a needle if
you haven't got a haystack!' How vivid his explanation of a
certain commentator in difficulty. 'He's buttered his bed, he
must lie in it.' How reassuring to me his reply over the phone to
Lobby's enquiry as to how I was doing at an important broadcast. 'Don't worry. He's getting on like a horse on fire.' A
whole library of his better expressions was lovingly collected
by his subordinates. 'Chickery pokery' – defined by the com-
pilers of *Drawn from the Wood* as 'evil intentions at morning
coffee'. Or 'cast your octopus over this' for 'have a look at the
script'. I admit I was a bit disconcerted when R.H. gave me
instructions on how to cue an important service at St Paul's
from one of the upper galleries. 'Vaughnie, when I tip you the
wink, just skip up the spirella staircase, give the old padre the
flick and he's off.' The 'old padre' was the Archbishop of
Canterbury! This was an example which rivalled the memorable exhortation of a certain Guards Colonel who assembled
all his officers after the rehearsal, on the day before the funeral
of King George VI at St George's Chapel, Windsor. 'Not bad.
Now tomorrow' – and he paused – 'remember I want everything to be tickety-boo on the day of the race.'

R.H.'s masterpiece was his reply to a certain distinguished
royal lady who was trying to persuade him to arrange a further
rehearsal. 'What can I say to persuade you,' she pleaded. 'Eh
Ma'am, you don't have to persuade me. You are talking to the
perverted.'

Perhaps, in a curious way we were all 'the perverted' – those
of us who were drifting happily and unheedingly through
those strange sleepwalking years that preceded the outbreak of
the Second World War. While I was busy learning my craft as
a commentator and driving through Wales describing everything from boxing matches to the ceremony of Crowning the
Bard at the National Eisteddfod, the Nazis were equally busy
turning Germany into the most formidable war machine the
world had yet known. There is always a temptation for those
who look back on the course of history to wonder why on
earth those who were living at a time of approaching disaster

didn't take active steps to prevent it. What were those Anglo-Saxons thinking about while William the Conqueror was obviously preparing to invade them? Surely anyone could have seen that Germany was bound to march through Belgium in 1914. And now here was Hitler publishing in *Mein Kampf* the exact blueprint of his plans for world conquest, and we simply didn't believe him. We went on going to dances, falling on climbing holidays in the Alps, contributing poems to short-lived little magazines, doing all the things that young people who considered themselves intelligent and progressive should do, and all the time the Germans were tearing up the treaty of Versailles, eliminating the Jews, marching into the Rhineland, doubling their armaments, and listening to the raucous, hypnotic, compelling voice of Hitler threatening new violations of the international structure of peace, usually on a Saturday afternoon. Why didn't we drop everything and campaign vociferously for early intervention in Germany as soon as the Nazi menace became obvious? Well, there are a hundred reasons – some of them selfish and cowardly, others idealistic and high-minded – why Europe sat dazed and inactive while Hitler prepared his gigantic smash and grab raid, but underlying them all was one over-riding feeling that, maybe, prevented any realistic appreciation of events. We just couldn't believe that anyone, for any reason whatever, would willingly, deliberately start a Second World War.

When I was growing up, we were all talking of the Locarno Spirit, we were reading *Good-bye to All That*. The film of *All Quiet on the Western Front* was about to make screen history. 'Never, never again', was the overwhelming message of everything we read about war. Never, under any circumstances. Even if we had read *Mein Kampf* – which we hadn't – we would still never have believed Hitler would be mad enough to start another world war. Every one of his agressions arrived as a Saturday shock which our mentors in the press carefully explained away. We were avid readers of the column of Madame Tabouis – 'the greatest living journalist. She *knows* what's going on!' But did she? I remember reading in her column that Mussolini had just remarked to Hitler, 'After all, the French army is still the greatest in Europe.' This was a great

comfort to us all on the week Hitler annexed Austria! For final enlightenment we turned to the John Gunther best seller *Inside Europe*, where we were assured that the Führer, in spite of some awkward appearances to the contrary, was still a man who desired a peaceful resettlement of the boundaries of Europe, once he had united all his Germans to their Fatherland.

I began to have my own doubts after a trip I took across Europe in 1937 with Dr Geraint Dyfnallt-Owen, who was a new colleague at the BBC in Cardiff. I was now the proud possessor of a Hillman Minx, and decided to drive across Europe to the Black Sea in August and early September. These were the days, long before mass tourism had scattered holiday hordes into the most secret places of the earth, when you still planned a holiday yourself and the roads beyond the Austrian border were completely unknown to the average motorist. I like to remember that drive as bathed in endless sunshine, as all the memoir writers assure us were the August days of 1914, for I, too, had a feeling that I would never again see the old Europe intact, with its cities still standing, its peasants still dressed as peasants, its aristocrats still maintaining a certain state and style.

When we crossed the German border near Aachen we found ourselves straight away in the hothouse world of the Nazis. The time was approaching for the annual Nuremberg Rally. Every street and public building was hung with swastika banners – that formidable yet superbly decorative black hooked cross in its white circle on a flaming red background. The Brown Shirts were on the march and the whole country seemed to be echoing with the tramp of booted feet and the blare of brass bands. When the great day came, Hitler mounted the podium and stood surrounded by his henchmen, an obscene but overwhelmingly powerful parody of Charlemagne amid his paladins. A storm of regimented *'Sieg Heils'* had accompanied his march towards the platform. In 1937 we, in Britain, had no experience of this mass manipulation of an audience. Our cheering, even at soccer matches, was still spontaneous and undrilled. This chanting of a single slogan by thousands of male voices struck a chill of fear into me. The chanting gave way to a sudden silence and Hitler stepped forward to the microphone. He raised his arm and spoke one word, *'Deutsche'* – Germans! Again a deep hoarse sound erupted from the vast crowd. Not a drilled sound this time but a vast bellow, almost torn from the throats of his audience, a sheer gut reaction which had nothing to do with reason or logic or eloquence. This man with his Charlie Chaplin moustache no longer looked the mountebank we were portraying in our newspaper cartoons. He was a leader of incomparable power who held a willing nation in his grip to do as he liked with it. We drove thoughtfully eastwards into the lands of the Danube plain and on to the Balkans, which at this time could still deserve the title of exotic.

Hitler's voice and the thunder of his aircraft flying low over Nuremberg seemed to pursue us. How could little Austria, Hungary and Rumania stand up to him if he decided to push

Hungary. Village Scene 1937.

towards the Black Sea? But the further we moved from the borders of Germany the more peaceful seemed the political landscape. Again we said to ourselves, Hitler may threaten but he'll never start that world war. We looked up at the windows of the chancellery in Vienna where only a few years before Dollfuss had been murdered by the Nazis, and then went off to drink coffee and eat rich cakes at Sachers. Well, we reflected, little Austria is still here. The Nazis didn't take over after all.

On into Hungary, where normality seemed even more pronounced. We listened to the gipsy fiddlers and the cimbalom players in the cafés on Margarit Island beside the not-so-blue Danube, and went on a regulation tour of the Hungarian House of Parliament – a glorious Gothic gasholder of a building, where the guide in equally spiky English addressed us at the bottom of the vast ornamental staircase. ' 'Ere we stand at cradle of Ungar liberty. 'Ere the Emperor Franz Josef old his balls. Picture to yourself the scene – the gentlemen in their "fracs" waiting for the ladies in the toilets.' What, alas, has happened to the cradle of Ungar liberty since those days? And does Rumania under its communistic totalitarian dress retain any trace of that Merry Widow country I saw in 1937? The peasants wore their costumes, as vividly coloured as butterflies, because they were the only ones they had and not because they had been ordered to wear them on May Day by the Ministry of National Culture.

Rumania, we knew, was militarily strong in spite of the fact that the officer corps of the royal guards were the last officers in Europe to lace themselves in the old Prussian-style corsets. Hadn't we read, probably in that infallible column of Madame Tabouis, that in the event of attack Rumania would surround itself with a ditch of fire fuelled by the Ploesti oilfields. We chuckled over the limerick circulating in the British Embassy about King Carol and his gloriously red-headed Madame Lupescu, the last European Pompadour:

> In Rumania there came to the rescue
> A red-head named Magda Lupescu.
> It's a far better thing
> To live under a King.
> Could democracy do better – I ask you?

Unfortunately, in the year following that European trip, democracy did a great deal worse! When Chamberlain flew to Munich I was no longer among those who cheered him on. In fact I happened to be in Downing Street when Premier Daladier and his foreign minister, George Bonnet, came across for an eleventh-hour consultation before they flew out for those fateful meetings with the Führer which eventually ended at Munich. The air was already alive with rumours of a sellout. My future wife, Charlotte, had moved to London where she was in touch with senior members of the Civil Service. She regaled me with all the gossip that never reached Cardiff — about splits in the Cabinet, what Sir Horace Wilson had said to Sir Samuel Hoare in a corridor in the Athenaeum, why Ribbentrop had quarrelled with Göring. For a brief moment I felt I was 'Inside Europe'. Of course I knew nothing about the real military strength of the various nations, least of all that of Britain. The same went for everyone in the crowd with me in Downing Street. The black limousine drove into the street and I caught a brief glimpse of the occupants. Daladier looked broad, bluff and slightly bewildered, Bonnet sharp and slightly foxy. Both had their hats drawn down to give them the air of two shady financiers sneaking into their office through a back door to avoid a stormy meeting with their shareholders. As soon as the car appeared, a steady chanting began. 'Stand by the Czechs! Stand by the Czechs! Stand by the Czechs!' I joined in, involuntarily, and shouted with the rest. The two Frenchmen scuttled hurriedly into Number Ten. The shouting died away, and France and England settled down to their task of working out a deal with Hitler. So ended my heroic, last-minute attempt to avert the Second World War!

CHAPTER SIX

War Report

It is a strange but powerful exercise in nostalgia to try to recall exactly where you were when you first heard that a world-shattering event had taken place. My position, as Outside Broadcasts assistant to BBC (Wales) was not exactly in the centre of world affairs on the morning of 3 September 1939. Britain's ultimatum to Germany was due to expire at eleven a.m. while we were in the middle of one of those 'Seaside Nights' programmes, beloved of prewar broadcasters, where you took the microphone on an elaborate tour of all the places of entertainment in the town. Llandudno was the holiday town we had selected for glorification by radio. We had an elaborate setup of broadcasts from concert parties to an interview with the mayor, and presiding over the arrangements was the genial figure of Wyndham Lewis, who also exercised his wizardry on the giant Wurlitzer that rose and sank into the pit of the Odeon Cinema, like some genie of music conjured out of a bottle at regular intervals. I was to do a commentary in the evening at the Pier Pavilion where we were inviting volunteers from the audience to 'Be your own conductor', which always ended in happy, harmonic chaos. Hanging over our official gaiety, like an uncovered overdraft at a bank, was the knowledge that Chamberlain had at last screwed up his resolution to honour his pledge to Poland, and that Ambassador Henderson would soon be on his way to the German Foreign Office at Berlin. The Prime Minister was due to broadcast to the nation at 11.15 a.m. Naturally I ceased worrying about 'Be your own conductor', and we all gathered at the appointed hour around the hotel wireless set. We listened in glum silence to the sad, depressed and depressing tones of the PM's voice. It was hardly a clarion call to action. 'Commence hostilities' was not the message. Rather was it 'Stop broadcasting', for the BBC's war plans, based on the best possible forecasts, demanded an immediate cut to a skeleton service, with a few gallant announcers bravely sticking it out in Broadcasting House to reassure the public and maintain morale as a hurricane of bombs fell upon London Town. We limply returned to base, all except Wyndham who, with irrepressible showman's optimism, dashed off to commission a large notice to be placed outside the cinema, 'Be Patriotic. Come inside and learn the new war songs.'

My own war song was distinctly muted! I drove back to Cardiff through a countryside of still, quiet beauty and tried to imagine what the German tanks were doing to the Polish countryside. Outside Merthyr a policeman stepped out from the side of the road and signalled us down in the gathering dusk. 'All lights dimmed from now on,' he said. He saw the BBC sign on the car and added, 'Pity they've stopped that programme from Llandudno, though. I wanted to hear it because my wife's there. Oh, well, perhaps they'll repeat it next week when the present troubles are over.' Unfortunately, we never got around to it!

I had been classified for some months as being in a reserved occupation, so my first reaction to the war was to wait and see what the BBC was going to do about it. I was thirty-one so not liable for immediate call up, even had I been unreserved. I sat twiddling my thumbs while Poland collapsed and Europe relapsed into that strange period of sleepwalking known as the phoney war. Luckily for me, this first immobile period came quickly to an end. No bombs fell on London. Europe and the war were held in what Churchill has aptly called a sinister trance. Cautiously the BBC crept back into action. Even Outside Broadcasts began to sneak out on morale-building visits to training camps and factories. I felt better still when I was asked to join OBs in London as a replacement for some of the younger members who had been called up.

I found a profoundly changed BBC, a Corporation which

had started to gear itself seriously for war. The old formality was rapidly disappearing. The announcers had given up their dinner jackets 'for the duration' and the corporation had hurriedly changed its idealistic prewar motto of 'Nation shall speak peace unto Nation' for the enigmatic '*Quicunque*'. 'What does it mean?' one anxious listener enquired, only to receive the translation, 'Anything goes'. Which prompted the wits to the following verse:

> Ah, how I feel the deep disgrace
> Of lechery at Portland Place,
> Where, hugger-mugger underground,
> Announcers, typists all are found
> Locked in a deep embrace of lust,
> Their creed '*Quicunque*' – love or bust!
> Ah, where are now our Reithian glories?
> O *tempora*, O stinking *mores*!

But when the blitz broke over our startled heads our Reithian *mores* were still seen to be undamaged. The BBC, like the nation, stood up to the ordeal with courage and skill.

Living through the blitz was my first serious exercise in the art of survival. We all became expert at sleeping in basements and carting our few possessions out of houses where all the windows had been blown in over our heads; at steeling ourselves against that terrifying crescendo whine of a falling bomb with the earth shaking around you as a terrier shakes a rat. There were evenings when we broadcast from tube stations crowded with sleepers in Henry Moore attitudes and permeated with the sour smell of unwashed clothes, or waited in fire stations while houses burned fiercely around us. Then came the walk home through streets littered with the snake writhings of hoses, to find the local publican busy nailing a notice, 'Business as Usual', on the wrecked four-ale bar. In memory, the whole period takes on the form of a stylized ballet, with all of us playing, with noble intensity, our predestined parts. People ran away from London, and I was there only because I had to be. Yet because we remained, we felt a certain pride in staying in a city burning around us. We behaved as we did because we expected posterity to approve of

our behaviour. Churchill had told us that this was our finest
hour, and we very sensibly made the most of it.

After the blitz came the Home Guard. We went off to our
statutory rifle firing at Bisley and our grenade throwing at a
range on a South London racecourse. 'Pull the pin, count three
and throw.' Until then this was the most dangerous thing I had
done in the war. I look at the diary I kept at the time and come
across an entry dated 6 January 1942 which takes me back
vividly to the days I spent in 'Dad's Army'. Here we all are in
the basement of Dickins and Jones in Regent Street at a lecture
on anti-tank tactics delivered by a tough, utterly competent
sergeant of the Tank Regiment named Cliffe. No possible
doubt, the British Army is saved by its NCOs. He held us in
the hollow of hand.

'Gentlemen, here is the first principle of anti-tank warfare. A
German tank is built for only one purpose – to be knocked out
by us. And here are the tricks that will do the job for you. The
68 grenade – it's a lovely weapon, gentlemen, a lovely weapon,
there's no getting away from it. Next the STP – the grenade
that's got everything, positively everything. And the Blacker
bombard – what a gun, gentlemen, what a gun! Quiet as a
lamb to handle – if you know how! The 73 grenade – dig
yourself a pit, gentlemen, and as the tank goes over, plant it in
his wheel-tracks as a tiny seed of love. Just to encourage you,
you can stop a tank with your bare hands, provided it's driven
by an Eyetie. Pal of mine in Libya sees a tank coming and he's
got damn all to stop it (excuse the language gentlemen). He lies
down and the tank comes lumbering past him. He hops out of
his little hidy-hole and hangs his beret over the driver's peri-
scope, cool as you like. Inside the driver suddenly discovers
day has turned into night. My pal hops on. Soon the commander opens his tin lid. My pal heaves in a brick. As soon as these
ice-cream merchants hear it tinkling around inside, they don't
wait to see if it's a bomb. They hop out, PDQ, same as I
would. And presto – there's your tank knocked out.'

Luckily I was never called upon to plant a tiny seed of love in
the track of a German tank as it lumbered up Regent Street.
Instead there were night manoeuvres when we lay in the
gutters around the Langham Hotel ready to pick off imaginary

parachutists creeping around the corner, while behind us a rival Home Guard unit, playing the part of the enemy, had succeeded in getting two of their men into Broadcasting House with fake passes marked A. Hitler and H. Göring. How strangely beautiful those half-ruined streets of London seemed on a blitz-free moonlit night. No sound except the steady tread of a policeman checking the blackout. The Regency façades of Portland Place stretched away in silvered, diminishing perspective, as empty and mysterious and silent as a Chirico painting. For the last time, London showed herself in her ruin as a city where a man might still live with civilized pleasure. We came home to tune in to 'Germany Calling' and hear the strident tones of Lord Haw-Haw, William Joyce, promising us even more terrible reprisals in the coming days, but somehow we never believed in them.

Michael Standing had now replaced de Lotbinière as the Head of Outside Broadcasts, for Lobby had been called to higher things. Michael had gathered a new group of commentators around him, for Tommy Woodruff had gone back to the navy and John Snagge to direct the panel of announcers. There had been a desperate need, during the days of threatened invasion, for each announcer to be identified by his well-known voice. A new cast therefore took the stage in Outside Broadcasts. There was Raymond Glendenning with his impressive moustache and his gift for brilliant description of sporting events. He was the fastest commentator who ever took to the air and the only one who could keep pace with a greyhound race. There, too, was John Ellison, with his flair for the world of stage and variety, and Henry Riddell, who was the man of solid organization in the department. Two notable additions occurred, one before and one after the blitz.

Stewart Macpherson was a quick-witted Canadian, fast-talking in transatlantic style with a great zest for life and a buoyant curiosity about the more recondite aspects of British society. I think that there were moments, as he once told me, when he thought we were all taking part in some out-of-date 1910 movie. Gilbert Harding joined us later and he certainly would have been delighted to have kept the whole world in a perpetual playback of 1910 vintage. We made a close-knit group to which it was both a privilege and fun to belong. Together we travelled in those overcrowded wartime trains to report on everything from anti-E-boat patrols out of Felixstowe to potato growing on the Isle of Arran. We described what little sport went on in those days. We kept an allotment at the top of Portland Place where we dug for victory. We flew with the air crews in training or shivered at Scapa Flow on board the *King George V* at anchor, but through it all we were worried by one over-riding thought. Were we bringing the microphone close enough to the actual fighting? Surely it ought now to be possible to take the technique of the running commentary into battle? Providing, of course, that the running was in the right direction!

By 1942 the whole business of reporting the war was starting to change. The War Office had begun in 1939 where it had left off in 1918, and old attitudes to the press may have lingered on in some military quarters, relics of those far-off days when Kitchener could emerge from his tent during the Omdurman campaign and scatter the waiting correspondents with the snarl, 'Out of my way, you drunken swabs'. The story goes that the original badge issued to the press in 1939 consisted of the initials W C, surrounded by a symbolic chain. This was hurriedly changed to a simple C after vigorous protest. A select body of correspondents was accredited to the army under the careful guidance of press officers. The BBC radio recording cars loaded with equipment were awkward new additions to the correspondents' armoury and much more inconvenient than the journalist's typewriters. Discs were difficult to censor and the recording machinery cumbersome to get anywhere near the front. The running commentary could only occur when the front obliged by coming near the commentator, as it did for Charles Gardiner when he stood on the cliffs of Dover and watched the first aerial dogfights over the Channel. The result was immensely exciting but certain old-style pundits in the services were worried. 'Makes war sound too much like a cricket match.'

The war was not exactly flowing in our favour in the first few years and there was not much inducement to expand the original establishment of the press corps. But after El Alamein and the landings in North Africa the whole climate of war reporting changed. New fronts were being opened up, and the press corps and its attached radio section had to be expanded. The members of Outside Broadcasts were naturally among the first to be selected, thanks to the enthusiasm of Michael Standing and the persuasive influence of Lobby.

The armed services had learnt a great deal about press and radio since the early days of their association in 1939. They realized to the full the importance of reporting the war on the most extensive scale and made themselves available to reporters in a way that would have shocked Kitchener and surprised Haig. Correspondents were invited into the front line on every possible occasion, and they had only themselves to blame if they did not take advantage of the invitation.

All through the first war years the recording equipment available to the war reporter had remained unchanged. Everything depended upon discs, cut by an engineer. The Germans started to experiment with tape, but we stayed with disc recording until the end of the war. We did make the disc method more flexible, and when I landed on the Anzio beachhead I carried a type of portable gramophone on which I could record a short despatch after carefully cranking up the motor. For top level broadcastable quality, however, you still had to have the full scale disc-cutting battery-driven equipment, with engineer attached. The problem about doing a running commentary on a battle thus remained unsolved in 1943. We had tried carrying the equipment on anti-E-boat patrols out of Felixstowe, but the vibration of the racing motorboats made disc-cutting impossible. Then, suddenly, the RAF came forward with an offer. Their bombers had been steadily growing in size and range as the war progressed. The Lancaster could not only carry a greater bomb load but could accommodate two extra passengers if need be. Bomber Command was now willing to send a BBC team on an air raid over Germany. At last, we had found the ideal method of transporting recording gear into battle. Even more important for me – Michael Standing broke the news that I had been selected as the commentator. My engineer would be Reg Pidsley. He had volunteered for the job, as he told me afterwards, 'just to give my two youngsters something to talk about.'

From the moment of our appointment, we seemed to be carried along by a preordained ritual. We were being put into a machine that would not stop until we were delivered high over some burning city – to return in triumph or to drop down into the flames. I admit I kept thinking about that last eventuality all the time we went through the preparatory stages of the ritual, but the closer we came to takeoff the less it loomed in my mind. This feeling was at its strongest when we reported to Imperial House, Kingsway, for our medical examination. We sat waiting with a group of Free Frenchmen who had just escaped from occupied France and a couple of young parsons who were volunteering as chaplains. We were stripped and prodded and ticketed like carcasses of prize meat. 'Don't worry,' a cheerful sergeant in charge reassured us. 'If you're for aircrew you've got to have a double rupture or a wooden leg before they fail you these days.' We emerged clutching our certificates and drove off next day to the north to report to area HQ at Grantham.

In the mellow warm sunlight we stopped for early lunch at Biggleswade. I remember looking at the people around us eating and drinking and going about their everyday business and feeling that Reg and I were already beings set apart, going towards a secret and strange experience in which they would never share. At Grantham the Air Officer Commanding, a man in his early forties, keen-faced and incisive, simply said to us, 'All we ask you is to describe exactly what you see. No window dressing.' We dutifully promised, and drove on to our designated aerodrome. From the top of a low hill beyond Belvoir – where now they are fighting over the plan to mine coal over the lush landscape – I looked down on a miscellaneous collection of huts, hangars and concrete runways, with an old cement works tucked into one corner. Its name was Langar. It has long since been abandoned but back in 1943 I felt how strange it was that I had arrived to bomb Germany from this somewhat undistinguished part of the English Midlands of which I had never heard before in my life.

We went into the officers' mess, where the Wing Commander

called out, 'Ken, come over and meet your BBC men.'
Flight Lieutenant Ken Letford came across. He was about
twenty-five, handsome, quiet, completely master of himself, a
veteran of fifty-two operational trips over occupied Europe
which had given him a faraway look in his eyes. As soon as I
saw him I felt total confidence. We settled down to a merry
RAF evening. The whole station seemed to be interested in our
job and anxious to nurse us out to Germany and safely back
again. Beer flowed. We sang at the piano – RAF songs with no
holds barred. I remember thinking, at one moment, that singing fifteen verses of 'Barnacle Bill' was perhaps not the best
way of spending what might turn out to be my last night on
earth. Yet all the lads were getting pleasure out of it and their
pleasure gave me a queer sense of comfort. We went singing to
bed at midnight and as we stumbled through the blackout
towards our Nissen huts, Ken whispered to me, 'I've had the
buzz. We're operating tomorrow.'

Next morning on 3 September 1943 – and I can write the
date without looking up any reference book because everything that happened that day and night is still crystal clear in
my mind – we installed our gear in the aircraft F for Freddie,
which was painted black and spread out its protective wings
over the bomb trollies and the fuel trucks fussing around it.
The inside had a faint acid drop smell. We had to crawl and
wriggle past tables, seats, instrument panels and lines of wire.
Our gear went on to the sorbo-rubber bed amidships where
they laid wounded men. I was to stand beside the pilot looking
down through the Perspex blister – a sort of small side dome.

We met the rest of the team: Bill Bray, young, shy, tall – the
bombardier; Jock from Glasgow – he used to be a cinema
operator and kept on telling me, 'Ye'll enjoy it all. It's worth
seeing the lights. You can't describe it. It's worth seeing with
your own eyes.' Then Con, the Australian, our navigator, and
Sparkie, the wireless op. We had two gunners, the bounding,
confident Jimmy in the mid-upper turret and Dev, a Sussex
farmworker, in the rear turret. It was strange to hear a voice
out of a Thomas Hardy novel announcing, 'Night fighter
attacking, sir'. It made the whole event as easy and warm as if
William Dewey was tuning in his bass viol in *Far from the*

Madding Crowd. They were a group who had gone through a lot together. You felt that they acted as a crew even when they were apart, and it was quite obvious that Ken was the mainspring from which they drew their confidence. They accepted Reg Pidsley and me into their secret circle and we felt honoured. They were all just over twenty and we were in our thirties. They nursed us as if we were old men, creaking in every limb.

We test flighted in the afternoon. Then back in time for tea, eggs and chips – the Operational Egg, as it was known in the RAF, in those days of strict rationing. I said to Bill Bray, 'This egg is a bit of a rare treat.' Bill replied, 'Wait till you see what you've got to go through to earn it.' Then we strolled across to the briefing room to learn our fate. Right in front of us was a huge map mounted on rollers. The sergeant pulled down the sections. The Dutch coast. The Ruhr, (and then to a general groan) Berlin! I felt frightened.

The crews were sitting at their tables in little groups checking their weather reports and navigating gen. The atmosphere was that of a boys' boarding school busily engaged in their prep. There was a general murmur. The headmaster entered – the AOC of the group. He spoke briefly. We were to be part of a force of 300 bombers. Our tactics were new ones. The first raid had been a success but the second had, as he put it, gone astray. Now Air Marshal Harris himself had designed the new plan. The whole raid would be concentrated into ten minutes over the target and Harris was confident that this would outwit the German night fighters ('Wish I was,' muttered a pilot behind me). The AOC wished us a rousing good luck and then we filed out into the crew changing room.

Mike Standing and Ronnie Pelletier had arrived from the BBC. They kept on asking me if I felt all right, rather like Mayan high priests reassuring one of their sacrificial victims. In the crew room we were now footballers preparing for the big game, or knights being accoutred by their squires before Agincourt. The boys helped Pidsley and me into our Mae Wests and our parachute harness. I dangled my oxygen mask in my hand with my flying helmet and checked that I had my escape packet, complete with Dutch, French and Danish money, safely stuffed into one of my pockets. I also carried a little broken ring that Vic Moody, our second in command of OB engineers, had lent me. It had seen him through the First World War. Most of the crew had their ritualist superstitions. Jimmy carried a little white doll. Ken always put his right hand first into the sleeve of his jacket. Con did a complicated wave with his left hand. So we propitiated the Gods.

I looked across at the crew next to us. They too were wrapping themselves up in the modern flyer's armour. Their pilot seemed to be dressing slowly. Bill Bray whispered to me, 'They won't make it. They turned back last time.' Everybody knew the pilot had lost his nerve. His crew knew it. They would go through the motions of takeoff and somehow – somewhere – there would be a problem with the engines and then a return to base. What then? An enquiry? Court martial? I turned away and followed Ken Letford out into the waiting dusk.

That white face of the man who had lost his nerve seemed to go with me as we walked to the lorry that took us down the long line of waiting aircraft to F for Freddie. I knew now exactly what the feeling was that churned away inside him. But once we were inside our Lancaster it was pushed to the back of my mind. We were caught up in the ritual of testing our equipment. I plugged in my oxygen mask but I must have done so imperfectly. When we recorded the commentary, I unconsciously slowed down. Val Gielgud told me afterwards, 'Splendid, my dear boy, but splendidly operatic?' He was right; the whole raid had an operatic feel about it, starting with the thunderous prelude of the takeoff.

The signal flashed. We taxied on to the runway. No delay. A stream of Lancasters, all heavily bomb-laden, had to be flung up into the darkening sky in a matter of half an hour. Suddenly we went pounding down the long length of the flare path, lifted and were up into the dangers of the wartime sky. We were operational a second after liftoff, for the Germans sometimes sent over intruders to catch a Lanc. or two in that vulnerable moment when the heavy bombers lumbered into the air. We circled and climbed. From all over the darkening Midlands and East Anglia other aircraft were rising to join us, with their navigation lights still on as they slipped into formation. We moved seawards like a swarm of fireflies. A single searchlight stabbed up into the sky from somewhere in Norfolk to give us a last guide mark. Then all lights went out. I could see the outline shape of the Lancaster behind us – a huge black condor soaring towards its prey, with a legion of others in the deepening night behind it. Jock nudged me and pointed eastwards. Right across our path a strange white moving fence had suddenly leapt up from the sea. The Dutch coast. The prelude was over.

The first act consisted of penetrating the screen of ack-ack batteries and searchlights that the Germans had laid along the coast of Holland. Behind it the night fighters, the ME 110s, would come swarming up to pursue the bombers across Germany itself until we reached Berlin. As we neared the coast the fence resolved itself into dangerous white fingers feeling up into the sky to clutch us and almost pull us down of their own accord. We were in the centre of the raid and the forerunners had already stirred up the hornets' nest. Bursting shells twinkled amongst the swinging searchlights. Suddenly, right ahead of us, the dazzling bright arms swept together to clutch an unhappy Lancaster. It twisted and turned like a moth impaled alive on a deadly sharp pin. Then the flak twinkled around it. A glow appeared in the cockpit and spread back along the fuselage. It gave a sudden lurch and dropped into the darkness. My stomach went down with it. I had no more time for pity for now we were in amongst the searchlights ourselves.

With our heavy load we were flying at about 19,000 feet and the searchlights shot up far, far higher. They waved around us, and I suddenly thought that they were exactly like luminous seaweed in some Gower rock pool and we were a shrimp darting through its dangers. We darted out successfully. True to the forecast, cloud lay over the mainland of Holland and the sky darkened as we moved away from the searchlights. The first act was successfully over and the cloud cover would help us until we neared Berlin.

We droned steadily on, hour after hour. Ken kept instructing his boys to watch for the night fighters, but we were in luck. The darkened sky gave us our cover, helping us deeper and deeper into Germany. Then Bill Bray came up to my side. 'The Big City,' he said. Below us the clouds had now rolled back, and lights started to wink on the ground. The ack-ack had sprung into life, but it was the eastern sky that riveted our sight. Right across the horizon it seemed as if a great fountain of light was rising into the heavens and this fountain was surrounded by a moving palisade of searchlights, a bullring into which we were being remorselessly pushed towards the matadors waiting for us in their ME 110s. The second act had begun, an act of terrifying Wagnerian splendour.

Again we threaded our way between the stems of the search-light beams. Again I felt that I should try to push them away with my bare hands, and again that awful moment when a beam rested on us and lit up the whole cockpit: Ken at the controls, Bill Bray now lying forward in the bomb-aiming position in the nose, Jock and myself all frozen at our posts – and then passed on to grip the Lancaster behind us. Again the fierce uprush of flak. The Lancaster shuddered and suddenly seemed to disintegrate. The wings seemed to split apart but now I had to look away for we had entered the bullring. The sky above us was full of lights; burning chandeliers falling down on us, bursting rosettes of flak everywhere. I pressed my face as close to the Perspex as I could and looked down. Below me was the awe-inspiring and beautiful yet macabre spectacle of Berlin burning in its death agony. Reg Pidsley's voice came to me over the headphones, 'Cutting, skipper.' I set myself to find the phrase that would crystallize the sight of the dying city. Yes, that was it. The ground far below looked as if someone had been throwing jewellery down on black velvet. The bombs burst like glowing rubies. There were emeralds flashing fire and sapphires of dangerous delight. Horrible but beautiful!

The crew were carefully going through their duty to add to the fury below. The bomb aimer ordered, 'Left, left, steady. Left again. Hold her.' Then the quiet chant. 'Bombs going. Bombs going.' We lifted as the 'big cookie', the 4000-pounder, dropped, and then came that slow country voice of Dev in the rear turret. 'Night fighter attacking, sir.' They say that fear clutches at your very bowels. It does! There was a furious rattle of gunfire, a reek of cordite through the cockpit and an exultant shout from Con, 'He's down. He's going down.' The crisp voice of Ken cut in, 'Don't all speak at once. Can you see him?' 'Yes, yes, there he goes ... doesn't he look lovely?' 'Bloody good show.' Men speak like that in the middle of the stress of war. Reg went on steadily recording and got the whole thing on disc.

The ME 110 went tumbling down under our wing, falling like a flaming oily rag into the mess below. I was – we all were – still alive. The flares falling out of the sky, the tracers that flew up towards us so slowly at first and then whipped by, the bursting flowers of the ack-ack – they surely couldn't touch us now. 'Keep weaving.' The bullring of searchlights was ahead of us again. We seemed to float among them and miraculously they turned away. We were out safely on the other side and again cloud floated in below us to blanket the ack-ack. Every minute we were drawing away to the security of the north. I ceased talking and got Reg to come out and look back on Berlin through the blister. From fifty miles away, we could still see the great volcano in full eruption. 'Coo,' said Reg, thoughtfully, and went back to nurse his recording gear in the darkness. The second act was over.

The third act turned from Wagner almost into Mozart. We had no hesitation in swinging away from the danger of night fighters over southern Sweden. The Swedes perforce had to fire on us since the Germans were watching from across the water. 'Neutrality!' said Ken. 'Doesn't it make you sick.' Other aircraft had a more practical way of showing their disapproval. They dropped on Sweden the propaganda leaflets designed with such laborious but pointless care by Richard Crossman's department to convince the Germans that war does not pay. 'Never drop 'em over the Big City, old boy,' said one pilot after we got back. 'I'm not going to lay a fluttering paper trail for some bloody Hun night fighter to follow and shoot me up the backside. Besides, I can't exactly imagine the folk in Berlin rushing to pick 'em up, after we'd just blown their houses down about their ears, can you?' Indeed, I could not.

But now the tension was relaxed. We came down to 9000 feet above the North Sea. An irresistible flood of relief swept over us. We took off our oxygen masks. Jock started to sing softly that celebrated RAF version of the universal services anthem, 'Bless 'em All':

> There's many a Lancaster back from Berlin
> Bound for old Blighty's shore,
> Carrying its cargo of terrified men
> Shit-scared and prone on the floor.

And on to the derisive finale:

> For we're showing our ass to them all
> As back to our billets we crawl,
> For Christ's sake, give Margate
> As our next target,
> And as for Berlin – Bless 'em all!

Or at least, words to that effect.

We came home as the dawn broke clear and calm. We received our signal to land and that gentle bump on the tarmac was the sweetest sound I ever heard. It didn't seem to matter that another Lanc. had landed on the wrong runway and went right across our bows. We were down intact. I didn't exactly kiss the ground as we got into the truck to go to the debriefing but I felt like it. Ken and the lads patted us on the back, and Jimmy said, 'I was right, wasn't I? I told you you'd enjoy it!'

Now we had to race back to London with our precious loot to get the discs censored and put them on the air in the one o'clock news. I fell asleep in the car and Michael and Ronnie did all the preliminaries at Broadcasting House. I drank black coffee and recovered to get in front of the microphone in time. But the honours really went to Reg Pidsley. In that weaving, bucking aircraft he had stayed in the darkness cutting perfect discs, above all the one covering our shooting down of the night fighter. At last we had carried the microphone into the front line of the war.

It has to be said that I also gained personally from that raid. It gave me my first real lift, my first taste of the adulation that can come to a successful radio or TV performer. It was all on a much smaller scale than the instant glory that besets a pop or film star but I admit it was sweet. I was in danger of slightly losing touch with reality in those days that followed my return from Berlin. In the corridors of the BBC they actually looked on me as a hero!

I was brought down to earth by a call on the office phone. At the other end was the unmistakable voice of Dylan Thomas. 'Hullo, Hero,' he intoned. 'I'm in the King's Road and I've reached the last pub before the end. I need you, boy.' I was sure he did. Just before I left for Langar I had received a letter from him. 'I'm whimpering in the bed with mumps and gout, the music-hall duo . . . my face is a sad bladder and my big toe full of teeth. And tradesmen bludgeon the house all day and summonses fall like grouse. Do your best and do not think too hardly of your mumpish, Gehennatoed, Dylan.' I put an ungrudged £5 in my pocket and set out for the pub.

It was a good hour before I got there and much had happened since that phone call − five large beers to be precise. Dylan was in full flight in his Roaring Boy from Wales role. He was reciting a poem describing the strange and totally imaginary goings-on in a little West Wales seaside town on Saturday night. The whole thing was splendidly bawdy and richly comic. He had begun to copy it out when he rang me, and the first four lines are clear enough. Then the beer started to flow more freely, and the last two lines only come back to me through Dylan's remembered voice. As we left, he crumpled the poem into my pocket, and I thought I had dropped it in the reeling King's Road. But when I sat down to write this chapter I turned out the old suitcase containing my souvenirs of the raid. I picked up one of the propaganda pamphlets − and out dropped Dylan's poem. I must have taken the pamphlet to show him and forgotten it was in my pocket. It was like discovering that an incendiary had been left in the bomb bay when we returned to base. While I was dropping bombs on Berlin, Dylan had been concocting the big cookie to drop on Cardiganshire:

> Sooner than you can water milk or cry Amen
> Darkness comes, psalming, over Cards. again;
> Some lights go on; some men go out; some men slip in;
> Some girls lie down, calling the beer-brown bulls to sin
> And boom among their fishy fields; some elders stand
> With thermoses and telescopes and spy the land

Where farmers plough by night and sailors rock and rise
Tattooed with texts, between the Atlantic thighs
Of Mrs Rosser Tea and little Nell the Knock:
One pulls out Pam in Paris from his money sock
One from the mothy darkness of his black back house
Drinks vinegar and paraffin and blinds a mouse;
One reads his cheque-book in the dark and eats fish heads;
One creeps into the Cross Inn and fouls the beds;
One in the rubbered hedges rolls with a bald Liz
Who's old enough to be his mother (and she is);
Customers in the snugbar by the gobgreen logs
Tell other customers what they do with dogs;
The chemist is performing an unnatural act
In the organ loft; and the lavatory is packed.

A slightly bawdy poem by Dylan Thomas closely linked with a
pamphlet designed to be dropped over burning Berlin – one of
the mad juxtapositions of war! But whoever claimed that war
was a rational occupation? The soldiers themselves had a crisp
word for it which any old sweat will obligingly translate:
SNAFU. Or as Clausewitz, the great philosopher of the obvious, put it with characteristic Germanic precision in his mighty
three volumes *On War*: 'We see, therefore, how, from the
commencement, the absolute, the mathematical as it is called,
nowhere finds any sure basis in the calculations in the Art of
War; and that from the outset, there is a play of possibilities,
probabilities, good and bad luck, which spreads about with all
the coarse and fine threads of the web, and makes War of all
branches of human activity the most like a gambling game.'
Yes, sir, you can say that again! My war memories after that
raid over Berlin are a weird mix-up of comedy and tragedy, of
fear and horror, of cheering on victories and of racing rapidly
to the rear. The nearer I got to the fighting the less certain I was
that I knew what was happening. After a war, historians put a
pattern on it. I've done it myself when I wrote the story of the
Anzio Beachhead. And that air raid over Berlin really did have
an operatic shape and rhythm to it.

It was after Berlin that the real chaos of war came home to me.
That broadcast had given my career its liftoff. Within weeks, I

was on my way to Italy, where the British Eighth Army of General Montgomery and the American Fifth Army of General Mark Clark were stuck in the mountains north of Naples. General Montgomery was about to leave, and rain was falling with Welsh persistence. The high mountains were deep in snow and the Germans had built a formidable barrier between Naples and Rome in the Gustav Line. Clearly the front was stuck, and morale far from high. General Fuller summed up the campaign as a five-hundred-mile steeplechase, with each fence a river, a ridge, a ravine. 'In such a campaign of what use are your tanks, your guns, your men, for what you want is an army of bullet-proof kangaroos!' The chief kangaroo, Monty, was preparing to hop back to Britain. 'Where I shall be in command of the Second Front. Therefore it will be a success,' he insisted to a distinguished American correspondent. 'I'm leaving, but don't forget. The men of my Eighth Army have got their tails up. Well up!' 'Excuse me, general,' said the American. 'Up what?'

In the centre of this stymied campaign I found a BBC team of reporters already well established. Their names had become household words, for they had all seen service in the desert and had followed the fortunes of Monty's Eighth Army up to the present stalemate north of Naples. Richard Dimbleby had already returned to England and Frank Gillard – 'a tiger in chase of a story' as Howard Marshall described him to me – was getting ready to follow him to cover the Second Front. Godfrey Talbot, balanced and judicious, was coming out to replace him at the centre of affairs at Naples, so it fell to Dennis Johnston, covering the front from Vasto, over on the Adriatic coast, to initiate me into the mystery of war reporting.

I had first met Dennis in the heady days when we had both newly joined the BBC. We sat together at the first BBC training school in Hallam Street and I was enchanted by his wit and by the slightly sardonic way he observed the English social ballet dance. He, too, was an outsider from that remarkable Anglo-Irish society which has contributed so much to the British literary and military scene. He had already made his name as a playwright with *The Moon in the Yellow River*. He received the solemn lectures we attended on certain aspects of broadcasting technique with the same surprised detachment he had devoted to Irish politics. He had once described a distinguished Irish politician as 'still hanging on to life by the rings under his eyes'. He brought this same surprised detachment to the strange business of war reporting.

Sitting in a decayed holiday villa overlooking a wintry, distinctly non-holiday-looking sea, Dennis instructed me in cable-ese, the strange code-language used by generations of foreign correspondents who had to pay so much per word in their communications to their editors in distant London. Anything, even Shakespeare, can be reduced to cable-ese, maintained Dennis. Take these celebrated lines of Omar Khayyam about penetrating the mystery of life in this strange world, 'Think, in this battered caravanserai, Whose portals are alternate night and day'. They can be swiftly and economically reduced to 'Pondering blitzed pub a.m. p.m.-wise'. I duly practised this economical trick but wondered if I would ever have an occasion to use it, since our front had now frozen into numbed silence in the snow.

'My dear Vaughan,' said Dennis – pouring out a glass of wine referred to by those enlightened connoisseurs, the American GIs, as dago red – 'no editor at home will believe there is no news. Arthur Barker will be pacing around the news room enquiring, "What, no cable from Johnston? Must be asleep out there." I'll scrape up something from this morning's briefing. Ah. Here's the very thing! A report that a dog came over from the German positions north of Lanciano. The Canadians have adopted it.'

'But Dennis, a dog sniffing around our front line! That's not news.'

'Wait and see,' smiled Dennis.

Sure enough, when we switched on the evening news from London, the dog had made it. Frank Phillips announced, 'Reports from the Eighth Army Front indicate that the Germans are now using trained dogs in an ingenious attempt to penetrate the Canadian defences.'

'You see,' said Dennis, 'lesson number two. Never neglect dogs in warfare. Especially if you are also fighting your editor!'

But within weeks of my arrival in Italy, the so-called static

front erupted violently. I embarked on the invasion Armada at
Naples which was to slip us ashore at Anzio, with the
confident slogan, 'Rome in ten days'.

At 01.53, in the small cold hours after midnight on 22
January 1944, I stood on the deck of the control craft of the
Senior Naval Officer Landing (SNOL for short) and looked
anxiously to the vague black line of the shore to the eastward.
The night started to fill with little sounds: the faint creak of the
derricks as the assault craft swung out, the quiet thud of
the screws of the LCTs moving close inshore. All around me,
the first wave was preparing for the landing. It seemed impossible that this huge concentration of Allied shipping – cruisers,
transports, hospital ships, minesweepers, assault craft – could
be lying off this hostile coast undiscovered by the enemy. Then
the uncanny silence of the night was torn apart with staggering
brutality and a crashing explosion rocked the anchorage as if
an ammunition ship had exploded. It was the rocket ship
going into action – 792 five-inch rockets bursting on the beach
to smash every minefield and defence post. In the glare the
long line of assault craft seemed poised like racehorses at the
starting gate.

A muffled figure on the bridge at my side muttered, 'That's
shaken them. Now we're in for it.' I braced myself for the
shock of the searchlights stabbing out from the shore followed
by the tracers pouring over the waters. But again a silence
more intense than ever held the whole area as the assault craft
crept in.

02.00 Zero Hour itself, and suddenly the radio on board
began to crackle. The first wave had touched down and not a
shot had been fired. The incredible had happened. We had got
the one thing we never bargained for, utter and complete
surprise. There were mines still on the beaches. 'We must take
a risk,' a helpful officer declared, 'We must order the troops to
push on.'

As the first light of dawn spread over the horizon, it was now
our turn to land. SNOL himself came on the bridge to see us
off. He looked down on the little group in khaki huddled in the
well of his ship. 'Goodbye,' he shouted, 'and good . . .' but his
farewell stopped in mid-career. The steersman of the small

landing craft we were about to board had allowed it to scrape against the immaculate topsides of the headquarters ship. SNOL seized his loud-hailer and roared. 'You there! Don't stand about like a half-plucked fowl! Cast off!'

Propelled by the force of SNOL's farewell we made for the shore. Some yards out we stuck on a sandbank. 'Forward brigade,' ordered the brigadier and immediately we stepped off into the chill water. The rest of our company were tall Guardsmen who went in up to their waists. I went in up to my armpits, holding high my only defensive weapon – the new portable BBC gramophone-type recorder. I was towed on to the sands by a kindly sergeant. A voice with a familiar accent came to me out of the semi-darkness ahead. 'Mind the mines, boyo.' 'South Wales,' I shouted. Back came the voice, 'Yes, how did you guess?' However there was no need to guess about the astonishing success of our landing. As the light increased we could see the long lines of marching troops entering the woodlands behind Anzio, the first guns coming ashore, the tanks lumbering after them. The sun strengthened and by midday we pushed on to the main road running out of Anzio towards Rome. We could see the smiling countryside ahead untouched by war and, in the distance, the welcoming outline of the Alban Hills. 'Bliss was it at that dawn to be alive.' The peasants crowded excitedly around our jeep and pointed down the road. 'Niente Tedeschi?' We asked in our broken Italian. 'Nobody. Nothing. A Roma pronto!' came the reply.

Time for a quick brew-up and then, surely, the orders would arrive to push on at all speed, to occupy the Alban Hills and reconnoitre to the very gates of Rome. We held the whole world in our hands on that clear morning of January 1944.

So we waited for the orders to advance.

We went on waiting . . . the hours passed . . . the sun became warm . . . the road stretched invitingly ahead . . . but still no instructions reached us to get into our jeeps. 'Well,' said the sergeant who was with us, 'that's it lads. We won't be moving before nightfall. Better kip down here and be ready for an early start tomorrow morning. They'll be pushing us fast up that road.'

Four months later, I stood – or rather lay crouched in a ditch

– to find British soldiers still halted in the same spot, but the landscape around them had undergone a violent change. The farmhouses were heaps of rubble, the trees mere shell-torn skeletons, and the fields churned by tanks into a sodden morass. A complicated trench system zigzagged across the tortured countryside. At night the star shells soared up over shell holes and barbed wire while the guns flashed and rumbled in the rear. Our bold stroke for freeing the front south of Rome had gone badly astray. General Lucas had sat down in our beachhead to await the German counterattack. Inevitably the Germans had obliged. They had raced troops to the landing site and sealed it off. When at last Lucas had tried to advance, Field Marshal Kesselring had easily blunted his spearhead and then counterattacked with such skill and fury that the Anglo-American force was almost flung into the sea. Almost but not quite. By a supreme effort the Germans were held and the Allies settled down for the next three months to live in what Goebbels contemptuously called the largest voluntary concentration camp in Europe, where every part remained within range of the long-range German guns and an old-style, 1914-type trench warfare bickered endlessly around the perimeter. At last, at the end of May, almost exactly four months after the landing came the breakout. On 5 June, the Fifth Army entered Rome. I stayed on the beachhead from the day it began to that blissful day when it ceased to exist.

Anzio memories: a mix-up of horror, laughter, misery and farce. In a curious way I felt they belonged personally to me and those who shared the beachhead experience. This was our private war. What right had 'Cassandra' to describe it as 'All Hell let loose in a band-box' when he had never set foot in the place. When the hordes of pressmen from Naples crammed into Anzio a few days before the breakout, all jostling to be the first into Rome, I regarded them with amused contempt. We were the real people who deserved that title. I almost regretted the moment when we saw the first troops coming towards us across a ditch of the Pontine Marshes from the south and we realized that our Anzio was a beachhead no more. In the perverse way of men who never know when they are happy, we almost lamented our freedom.

So at last we got to Rome. What a liberation! This was the
first great European city we had captured intact, un-bombed,
with cafes and theatres and cheering crowds and beautiful
women in the streets. We raced to St Peter's Square. The Holy
Father came out on to the traditional balcony to bless a million
people who had crowded the vast neutral piazza encircled by
the glorious arms of Bernini's colonnade. We held up our
microphones to record the cheering, the singing, the wild
shouts of relief. The bands played in the streets. Vino flowed
like water. Everyone in the Allied uniform was an instant hero.
The whole BBC team was on the spot, recording all day,
rushing back to the press camp, filing despatches, interviewing

St Maria di Cosmedin.

everyone of importance in sight. Tired but happy we sank late to rest. This had been our finest journalistic hour. We were in the very centre of world news.

We were there for exactly twenty-four hours. On the night of 5 June 1944, we were basking in the limelight. On the morning of 6 June we were cast in the outer darkness of journalistic oblivion. Godfrey Talbot met me in the corridor of the press centre, now no longer established in some bombed windowless half-ruined villa but in the comparative lush Albergo Citta above the baroque splendour of the Spanish Steps. 'Look at this.' A cable from London. 'Allied troops landed in Normandy 6 a.m. this morning.' Said Godfrey, 'Well, at least we can all take the morning off.' I felt a flood of delight sweep through me. No duty despatches. Complete freedom to relax in liberated Rome. This was, after all, what we had fought for so long at Anzio. I had laid my plans for this moment all through the dark days of the beachhead. I knew exactly what I was going to do first. I was going to give myself the unparalleled luxury of a real Roman haircut.

In Naples, just before the Anzio landing, I had purchased the only phrase-book available, the incomparable Dr Alfano's *Modern Polyglot Conversational Italian*. The ingenious Dr Alfano had realized that the first need of the keen liberator was a handy little volume telling him what to liberate. The Doctor hurriedly ransacked all available dictionaries and produced the greatest piece of joyous mistranslation I have ever come across. It became an immediate best seller with the troops. The soldiery were instructed in the correct conversation to use in every difficult situation. No doubt the Italian was impeccable, but the wild glory of the *Modern Polyglot* lay in its English sentences. Here is the conversation you were supposed to hold with your barber from the section, 'Al Barbiere':

Customer: Be quick and put on my wrapper and a white napkin and strap your razors when you have lathered me . . . Ah! you have put the brush in my mouth.

Barber: It was because you spoke when I did not expect it. The young bride's hair was black, thick, coarse, her forehead broad and square. An ordinary hairdresser would not have been able to hide the sternness of her features, but I have given her head a gentle and languishing expression.

Customer: Truly I am struck with admiration. But, Mister Artist, for all your talent, you have cut me. I am bleeding. You have been shaving against the grain.

Barber: No, sir, I have only taken off a little pimple. With a bit of court plaster, it will not be seen.

Customer: Doesn't my hair need to be freshened up a little?

Barber: I will cut a little off behind, but I will not touch the tuft on the forehead or about the ears.

Customer: Why ever not?

Barber: Because, sir, you would then appear to have too low a forehead and ears too long. Do you wish me to give you a touch of the curling irons?

Customer: It is unnecessary. My hair curls naturally.

Barber: Shall I put on a little oil or pomatum?

Customer: Put on a little scented oil.

Barber: Look in the glass.

When I did so after a luxurious half hour of hair washing, skin soothing and careful trimming of the little moustache I then sported, I got a pleasant surprise. I looked almost human again. I turned with pleasure to read the last sentence recommended by Dr Alfano, as I handed over a generous tip in Amgot money. '*Va, benissimo*. I see you are an artist worthy to shave and trim your contemporaries.'

The armies soon moved out of Rome to pursue the retreating Germans, who were fighting a steady rearguard action as they retired up Italy to their next defensive line along the Apennines, 200 miles to the north. Ahead of us lay names of honour and glory in the world of art – Siena, Pisa, Florence itself. Who would forgive the generals if their war brought destruction to cities and towns which were rare monuments to man's achievement over long centuries? Driving an army through this country was like driving a tank through the British Museum. Our generals were no Philistines and they did their best in most difficult circumstances to save what they could without too great a sacrifice of their men, but there was irony in the wit of General de Montsabert of the French Army as he contemplated the problem.

'This campaign is becoming difficult. It is not the Art of War any more but the War of Art. The fifteenth century? I must not attack but make an outflanking movement. The sixteenth?

Then I permit myself a little machine-gun fire. The seventeenth? Ah! now we can have artillery support. The eighteenth means tanks and for the nineteenth, monsieur, I have no hesitation in calling in the air. If only Italy had all been built in the twentieth century we should be on the Alps by now.'

The problem came home vividly as I watched the French capture the enchanting Sienese hill-town of San Gimignano, with its forest of defensive towers left over from the feuds of the Middle Ages. De Montsabert, true to his principles, had outflanked the little town, and the Goumiers, from North Africa, were moving up in their dark robes through the vineyards around it as a few Tiger tanks threw delaying shells at them. No one was in sight as I entered through the great gateway in the encircling wall, but every narrow street was littered with broken tiles. Suddenly an enthusiastic Italian fairly leapt on me from the Collegiate Church doorway. 'At last,' he shouted, 'the tourists – they have come back. I am the best guide. I show everybody round. I take the Tedeschi on their visits. I am now to take you. First we visit the Academia.' There was a loud crack overhead, and another cascade of tiles fell into the street. My guide regarded this as no more than a passing shower. 'Courage,' he said to me, 'I have treasures to show you.' But I had already dived for safety into the corridors of the Collegiate Church.

My guide followed and stopped me. 'Here we must pause. A supreme delight now awaits you. The Annunciation by Ghirlandaio. See the colours. See the expression on the face of the Virgin. Ah, Carina!' A further bang outside, and I scuttled still further down the corridor to emerge in the great church itself. I stood before the noble fresco of the crucifixion by Barna da Siena, which had won the admiration of my friend, the late Michael Ayrton. He said of it, 'Nowhere is Barna's ferocious dramatic power more in evidence.' I had no time to appreciate this nice point. A louder bang than usual seemed to rock the outside wall. I felt a sting on my cheek and put my hand up to find blood on it. A small piece of the great Barna fresco was missing from the painting of the Gamblers for Christ's Raiment. No question about it. I had become one of the few people ever to be wounded by an Old Master!

The Goumiers had by now completely outflanked the town. The Tiger tank retired. San Gimignano emerged relatively safe. But the whole incident sent me northwards with a sinking heart. I had joined a small party consisting of Eric Linklater and Sy Korman of the *Chicago Tribune*. I drove my jeep through the heart of June to find out exactly where the front had got to.

We made a strange jeep-load. Eric Linklater was short, slightly bald, wore glasses, and was the last man in the world whom you would immediately recognize for what he was – a brilliant novelist, a distinguished military historian and a soldier with a heroic record in the First World War. Sy Korman was tall, gaunt, raw-boned, and his uniform looked as if it had been issued to him by a relief organization during a famine. He was brave and untiring in pursuit of a story. As for myself, I was a red-faced roly-poly sort of soldier, a fugitive from Falstaff's army.

We came to the high ridges that guard Florence, and reported to the HQ of the hospitable 8th Indian Division. Captain Uni Nayar, their press officer, did us proud. He produced a curry of epic proportions and we tucked in; so heartily that when the time came to move poor Sy Korman had tummy trouble on a big scale.

'Stay where you are,' I reassured him. 'I'll tell you if there's anything happening.' Nayar, Linklater and Quereshi, the Reuter correspondent with the 8th Indians, now joined me in my jeep and we drove north through a landscape of cypress trees, white-walled Renaissance villas and vine-clad hillsides. The war had erupted over a painting by Fra Lippo Lippi.

The silence of fear held the countryside. The guns thudded here and there and a stray shell whistled overhead on a pointless mission across a powdery-blue sky. On the brow of the ridge before us stood a medieval castle, complete with towers, turrets, battlements and a view towards the distant domes of Florence. We raced up through the dust to avoid giving an easy target to snipers and machine-gunners – for the front was all around us and no old soldier takes any risks he can conveniently dodge.

We shot into the safety of a small courtyard. Indian soldiers were everywhere, some squatting in the corners clapping their hands over the circular *chapattis* that seemed so strange in Renaissance Italy. We had come to the HQ company of the Mahratta Light Infantry. The colonel was upstairs asleep after being up all night dealing with a Tiger tank at the bottom of the garden.

We went into the castle itself. Two great golden crucifixes leant against the walls of the entrance, alongside them a Virgin and Child on a dark, wooden panel. 'They are very good,' said Linklater. 'Too good,' said I. 'They must be copies.'

We went into the drawing room. Cases were stacked against the wall, and a few British soldiers from the signals company attached to the Mahrattas were rummaging amongst the shelves. A pile of invitation cards was still on a table near the door. I picked one up and read that Lady Ida Sitwell would be at home at Montegufoni and that there would be dancing.

Montegufoni! Of course, it was Sir George Sitwell's castle we were in. Sitwell on gardens littered the shelves. Everywhere were books, photographs and *objets d'art* which bore the hallmark of the marvellous and terrifying eccentric who was the father of Osbert, Edith and Sacheverell. Linklater, as a friend of the family, felt he ought gently to expostulate with the sergeant. 'We were only looking for something like an Agatha Christie, sir,' he explained, 'but there's damn all here.'

How wrong he was! At that moment I felt myself being tugged on the arm. I was surrounded by a group of Italian refugees, papa, mamma and all the garlic-perfumed bambinos. They shouted, '*Capolavori degli Uffizi. E vero, è vero*', and propelled me towards the main hall. As they opened the doors I could see stacks of dark frames inside the gloom. Then papa shouted, '*Moment*', *aspett*'.' He raced around the hall, opening the huge shutters. As he opened each shutter a shaft of sunlight shot down, like the spots in a theatre, and lit up the frames. Down shot the first shaft – and I gave a gasp of delight and astonishment. There before me was one of the world's greatest paintings, Botticelli's 'Primavera'. Down came the second shaft: again a glorious revelation – Uccello's 'Battle of San Romano'. On through the hall, with shaft after shaft of the sun lighting up picture after picture. Giottos, Cimabues,

Andrea del Sartos, Lippo Lippis – the greatest concentration of superb painting I had ever seen. And all at my mercy! For a moment I was overcome with a wild temptation. Not even the Great Train Robbers had been given such an opportunity. I could have put an assorted pair of masterpieces in my jeep, whipped them back via the BBC and spent the rest of my life enjoying bootlegged Botticelli in the bathroom.

But at that moment a triumphant cry of '*Il professore*' echoed around the hall and my 'moment of truth' ended. Il professore entered at the run, one of the librarians of the Uffizi. These were indeed the masterpieces of the gallery. The Allies had bombed the marshalling yards and in panic the Fascists had ordered the paintings to be scattered around Florence. The war rolled north, the Germans had no transport to spare and there was the anguished Professore bicycling from castle to castle appealing to unheeding soldiers, on both sides, who had a battle on their hands, to stop shooting in the cause of the Renaissance! He didn't get far.

Now, at last, he had hopes. He turned to Linklater. 'You are a colonel. Quick, you must stop the war.'

We did our best. We roused the CO from sleep. He'd noticed some paintings about, but he had a Tiger tank to deal with and painting wasn't exactly his line, though the wife did a certain amount of watercolours. But once we'd explained the position, he acted promptly. He cleared out the refugees eating their salami and drinking their Chianti amongst the Fra Angelicos. Dark Mahratta soldiers stood on guard over the Uccellos. As for the Botticelli – Eric Linklater adjusted his glasses to make sure he'd got the right woman and, on our behalf, imprinted a kiss on the lips of Primavera.

Later, led by the professore, we ducked and dodged our way along the skyline to the two neighbouring castles of Montagnana and Poppino. The professore made light of the odd bullets that whistled over. 'I, Cesare Fasola, was an ancient Alpini'; and away he bounded with his green pork-pie hat decorated with a small feather.

More pictures, some damaged, some hidden in wine vats for safety and which to the end of time will exude a slight perfume of Chianti into the exclusive air of art galleries on warm days.

'Now, you have seen with your own eyes, you must stop the war!'

We decided that Linklater as senior man had more chance of stopping the war than I had. He would stay at divisional HQ; I would race back and send a discreetly worded despatch to the BBC. We pondered carefully how we would describe Montegufoni so that there would be no danger of bringing down German gunfire on it. 'An old Italian farmhouse' was our best effort. Alas, when they heard it in England, the Sitwells were naturally indignant at hearing the lordly castle on which their family had lavished so much care demoted to a decrepit old farmhouse. But later Edith Sitwell forgave me in the same way as she forgave Dylan for Margate.

I never entered Florence. Like Moses I only glimpsed the promised land from without, with my despatch on the Primavera. I was called back to Rome, and immediately a new chapter opened in my personal experience of war. Berlin had been drama 19,000 feet up. Anzio had been four months of fear and agony, saved by courage and comradeship. The advance to Florence had been a walk over cultural eggshells. I was now invited to take part in the most joyful liberation of all time. At least as far as I was concerned.

The name of the operation was Anvil. The Allies had broken out of the Normany beachhead and were sweeping eastward to the Seine. Now was the time, maintained the American high command, to put the Italian operation into cold storage and land seven of its divisions in the south of France. These would sweep up the Rhone Valley and unite with the Normandy advance to form an irresistible force along the Rhine – a dagger ready to plunge into the heart of Germany. Not so, pleaded Churchill, let us strike north-eastwards out of Italy, link with Tito's partisans and advance into southern Germany and Austria. We would have an added bonus. We could anticipate the Russians' westward onrush, with incalculable results for the future of Europe. For better or for worse, it was the American view which prevailed. In accordance with the plans of General Marshall and General Eisenhower, and with the enthusiastic support of President Roosevelt, I found myself, as dawn broke on the warm 15th day of August, 1944

– my birthday – crouching against the steel sides of a packed
L C T with recording gear festooned all over my ill-fitting
battle dress.

We raced for the shore in the approved style for well-
conducted amphibious assaults. The shells from the fleet
whistled overhead and burst with a roar on the enemy
defences. Or we hoped they did. The G Is around me swore
like Norman Mailer heroes and looked as if they had been
signed up for Darrell Zanuck's *Longest Day*. Our objective, of
all places, was the sands of St Raphael in the south of
France.

A thick smoke screen drifted across the beach ahead. Our
L C T grounded in lukewarm water, down came the ramp and
we splashed through the smoke to the shore. The G Is prepared
to sell their lives dearly and I prepared to record them doing it.
A whistle shrilled somewhere in the murk and we ran forward.
At any moment the machine-guns would be opening up. The
light was increasing in spite of the smoke screen. Suddenly we
were out of the smoke and blinking in the first sunshine of the
day. Ahead of us, no German strongpoint but a Riviera villa
which had escaped all our shells. The door opened, and an
immaculately dressed Frenchman appeared. He carried a tray
on which were ten glasses and a bottle of Veuve Clicquot '34.
We stopped the war immediately and crowded around. Carefully he poured out the wine and handed glasses to the sweat-
ing and astonished G Is.

'*Messieurs les Américains*,' he said, '*soyez les bienvenus*,'
and then added, gently, 'even if you are four years late.'

He set the keynote for the stern days that followed. The
experts still argue learnedly and acidly about the point of
the champagne campaign. But time softens controversy, and
the history of distant wars grows mellow like '49 burgundy.
At last we can see Anvil in its true perspective. It wasn't fought
for military motives at all. One glance at the map and the route
taken by the invading armies makes the *raison d'être* of the
champagne campaign crystal clear.

Ahead of the advancing troops was grouped such a collection of noble names that the mouth waters as the hand types
them: Châteauneuf du Pape, Tavel, Tain-l'Hermitage,

Château Canon
The Tower of the Church over the
vineyard.

Château Grillet, Côte Rotie. And beyond, the greatest objective of them all – Burgundy and the Côte d'Or!

On the surface all was going well, with the Germans on the run and the Americans racing through the Jura towards Besançon. But when a few days later I dropped into American HQ for a briefing on the general situation I detected a slight lack of the usual buoyancy in the air. General Patch was clearly uncertain about the position of his French allies. After the briefing, a colonel on the staff – an old comrade-in-arms of Anzio days – took me aside.

'You're going across to see the Frogs this afternoon, I hear?' I had, indeed, intended to go scouting through the vague no-man's-land of fifty miles which now separated the two armies.

'Well,' said the colonel thoughtfully, 'I wonder if you'd give me your private opinion, while you're there, on a little problem that's got us kinda worried. I've got a feeling that the Frogs are doing a little bit of a "go slow" on us. I've got no proof. On paper, all's well. But in this game I've found that it's sometimes wise to back a hunch, and right now I've a hunch that our friends are staying a little too long at this place Chalon something or other. Not like them, either. Those babies can move all right when they want to.'

Chalon something or other! Obviously this was Chalon-sur-Saône. I felt that I already had a shrewd idea why the 'Frogs were dragging their feet'.

That evening I presented myself at the field HQ of Montsabert and received the usual warm welcome. The intelligence officer took me to the map tent and we reviewed the situation.

There was no doubt that the enemy was retreating, but the point was – how fast was he moving? Was he prepared to fight a strong rearguard action before Dijon? 'I need hardly tell you,' said my friend, 'the terrible consequences of such a decision. It would mean war, mechanized war, among the grands crus! Would France forgive us if we allowed such a thing to happen? We must not forget 1870.'

We both looked thoughtfully at the colonel's private map of the German positions. They were – quite properly – marked with care on the relevant sheet of Larmat's *Atlas Vinicole de la France*. There had been reports of a Tiger tank at Meursault and of demolitions prepared at Chassagne-Montrachet. There might even be a strong German rearguard assembled behind Beaune. A picture immediately leapt into my mind of air attacks on Chambolle-Musigny, of tanks rolling forward over the carefully tended vines of Vosne-Romanée, of smoke rising from the burnt-out château of Clos de Vougeot.

Then occurred one of those dramatic strokes that are the speciality of the French at war. A young *sous-lieutenant* entered, hurriedly saluted and, with a smile illuminating his face, declared, 'Great news, mon Colonel, we have found the weak point in the German defences. Every one is on a vineyard of inferior quality.'

We both recognized that we had reached a turning point in the battle. Said the Colonel, 'General de Montsabert must know at once, but he will give only one order, "*J'attaque*".'

Attack he did, and to such effect that in a matter of twenty-four hours the Germans were bundled out of Burgundy and the schedule of the French advance jumped boldly ahead of the Americans. None of us can forget the glorious days that followed. *Les Trois Glorieuses* are celebrated every year at Dijon and in the Côte d'Or as a feast of wine and gastronomy. It has been my pleasure and privilege to attend the sale of wine at the Hospice, the feast of the *Confrérie du Tastevin* at the château of Clos de Vougeot and the fabulous three days of the liberation of Burgundy. For a brief moment the cellar doors of the Côte d'Or opened almost of their own accord . . .

No wonder General de Montsabert's eyes sparkled as we raced up *Route Nationale* 74 in his jeep, close on the heels of his forward tanks. A blown bridge here, a demolished house there – what could these matter beside the great, overriding fact of the undamaged vineyards stretching mile after mile before us?

To our left rose the long line of the hills of the Côte; it was as if the Cotswold escarpment had been planted with vines and bathed in mellow sunshine. 'Decidedly,' said the General, 'in the matter of wine you must count me a man of the Left.'

But as, with reluctance, we left Burgundy to sweep on northwards, I sensed a change coming over the war. The exhilaration of liberation slowly faded. Our advance slowed down as we pushed towards the Vosges. There had been no swift dagger thrust into the heart of Germany to end the war in 1944. In Alsace we succeeded in reaching the Rhine at Strasbourg but the Germans clung on to some of the highest summits and to a big pocket of Alsatian soil around Colmar. Here they were under the personal command of Heinrich Himmler himself. In the north, the Allies had halted before the Siegfried Line. Ahead of us lay a December of rain, cold and snow, hiding the surprise counteroffensive of Von Rundstedt in the Ardennes. The Germans even staged a small push against us in Alsace.

It was during this winter of our discontent that I had a curious discussion in our press billets outside Strasbourg. Once again, as at Anzio, the *vin ordinaire* was in short supply and had to be augmented by purchases on the black market. We were sipping our last glass of the day around the one stove that worked and feeling a little sorry for ourselves, when someone raised the question of the stupidity of the Allies' demand for unconditional surrender. 'Europe is being handed over to the Russians and that means handed over to Communism. Why shouldn't Europe stop tearing itself to pieces and make a deal with, perhaps, a sort of Nazi régime that had rid itself of Hitler. The generals might stage a successful plot. Europe might return to the world power stage.' Yes, a deal with Germany to end the war in 1944 might make sense. 'Impossible,' said a French correspondent quietly. 'How can we talk of such a deal after we had seen Schirmeck?'

Now the name of Schirmeck will be totally unfamiliar to everyone who was not in the Alsace campaign. Yet it should be remembered for one important reason. It was the first German concentration camp we had captured. And after I had seen it I knew, sadly, that the war had to go on.

Later I became one of the very first people to enter Belsen. The world knows only too well every detail of that ghastly man-made hell. There are unhappy moments when a chance smell, encountered unexpectedly, brings it back to me in all its horrid, inhuman squalor. I shudder again at the death pits, the sound of the death rattle in the wooden huts behind the barbed wire, and at one nightmare picture which seems to me to sum up the utter unreality of Belsen and its position on the dark side of the moon. In the final few days of our advance towards Belsen, the Germans threw into it a whole series of political prisoners and their families, whom they had no time to sort out. Behind one of the huts in the women's quarters I came across an enormous pile of naked corpses. A group of little children were running around it – playing the old game of 'touch'. I turned away sick.

I felt sick at Schirmeck, too, but for a different reason. Schirmeck is a small industrial settlement slotted into a deep, wooded valley in the northern section of the Vosges. In the high hills around it there are vast, thick pine forests, and this decided the German authorities to build their concentration camp there. I doubt if the inhabitants of Schirmeck down in the valley ever knew what was actually going on in those dark woods above them. The particular horror of this camp was that we captured it intact, in full working order, with not a single prisoner, corpse or official in it. Before they retreated the guards had scrubbed out the huts; checked carefully that the death chambers were spotless and the ovens and electric fences ready to be switched on again. In the officers' quarters the tables were covered with the decorations they were already starting to prepare for Christmas. Happy letters home were on the desk: 'Father sends his greetings to Trudi and Rudi and tells them to be good and be kind to mum.' Did the writer then go down to see if the acid sprinkler in Death Chamber Two was functioning correctly before he departed? Schirmeck had been left as a macabre parody of the Sleeping Beauty's palace, built and run by men who obviously believed that what they were doing was the most reasonable, the most ordinary thing in the world. That was the peculiar horror of Schirmeck.

The old Alsatian caretaker, who the Germans had left behind, took us around. After he had shown us the special arrangements for extracting gold teeth from the corpses I felt in need of fresh air. I was standing by one of the huts, looking towards the electric fence and the guard towers. The dense pine woods were still, under a blue sky that held a touch of frost. The caretaker appeared at my elbow. 'Monsieur, the commandant told me an interesting story.'

'Tell it to me.'

'It is about a prisoner who lived in that hut. He was a Russian. Every day he was marched out for exercise and every day he noticed that a group of people he marched with were detached and sent down to the place I have just shown you. There would be smoke coming out of that chimney. His comrades never came back. He knew that he, too, would be marched down to the bottom of the camp in his turn, so he worked on a desperate plan. The Germans did not know the only important thing about him. He was a champion pole-vaulter. In his exercise period he had noticed a pole lying between his hut and the fence. Had they known about the Russian's past they would never have left it there, the commandant told me. The Germans are very thorough, monsieur.'

'So I have observed.'

'But the Russian measured the distance with his eye. Then, one evening, as they were walking back from exercise, he broke ranks, ran to the pole, grabbed it and raced straight to the electric fence. The Germans were so astonished that they couldn't react in time. The Russian cleared the fence, and before the guards could swing their machine-guns around, he had disappeared into the woods.'

'So he got away.'

'Only for three days, monsieur. They hunted him all through the woods. They used dogs. At last they brought him back here.'

'They shot him straight away?'

'Not at all. The commandant had sent a full report to Himmler who frankly couldn't believe the story. Surely, said Herr Himmler, he had invented it to cover up an administrative failure. There was only one thing to do. The commandant had the prisoner brought before him and promised him his life and a transfer to a prisoner-of-war camp if he would repeat the performance in the presence of Himmler himself. The prisoner agreed. The great day came. Half the Gestapo were there as well. The cameras and the film men were there, too, to record it. And with hope in his heart the Russian raced to the electric fence – and cleared it again! Everyone applauded. Himmler had the prisoner brought to him and clapped him on the back. They all photographed him again. Herr Himmler drove away satisfied that the commandant had told him the truth.'

'A happy ending, then?'

'Not exactly, monsieur. As soon as Herr Himmler's car had gone away down the road, the guards took the Russian and marched him not to freedom, monsieur, but to the gas chamber.'

The blue sky above the dark forests seemed cold and cruel. I knew the war had to continue.

In the spring I left the Vosges and went north to join General Montgomery's 21st Army Group. The last phase of the war was about to begin. Monty's forces were going to cross the Rhine in irresistible strength and the BBC had also assembled in strength to report the final grand assault. I met a whole series of old broadcasting friends as we joined up at the press camp. Frank Gillard was there and Chester Wilmot, the brilliant Australian who was to write the first important historical account of the final campaign in Europe. Howard Marshall lent us his magisterial voice and presence, and my old OB comrades, Stewart Macpherson and Michael Standing reappeared in my life. Richard Dimbleby had gone to report the RAF side of the assault, but Edward Ward, now Lord Bangor, came back to front-line reporting, rejoicing in his release from a German prison camp. Since the Normandy landing, the BBC had run a major programme entitled 'War Report' and our transmitting and recording facilities were now on a grand scale. And it was on a grand scale, with every reporter strategically placed at a key point of the action, that we prepared to bring to the British public the last triumphal act of the tragic drama that had begun nearly five years before. We should not be blamed if we rejoiced at that moment with Milton:

Oh, how comely it is and how reviving
To the spirits of just men long opprest,
When God into the hands of their deliverer
Puts invincible might . . .

The invincible might was there all right as I saw the vast array of tanks and guns and assault craft rumble up towards the banks of the Rhine, but the spirits of this particular just man sank a little when I found the part I had been selected to play. I was to cross in one of the leading Buffaloes of the 15th Scottish Division. Jim Mellor, my engineer for the crossing, was already installing the gear in this armoured assault craft that had tracks and armour like a tank, could swim like a duck and had a ramp which came down to allow the soldiers to pour out into the attack. We were warmly welcomed at Battalion Headquarters in a gaunt farmhouse a few miles back from the bund, the huge bank built to contain the wide river. The colonel confided an ambition to me.

'We've always had a tradition in this regiment; I think it goes back to Waterloo. We go into action to the skirl of the pipes. In the last war, they went over the top as the pipes played. This war has been different. You can't get a piper prancing about playing the bagpipes in front of a couple of Tiger tanks. But we could have a piper in the Buffalo with you, and you could actually record him piping the bra' lads into battle.'

I realized, with a slight sinking feeling, that he'd also be blowing me into the centre of the battle. I'd had luck all the way so far – Berlin air raid, assault at Anzio and the South of France – I had survived them all. Would my luck run out in the last few months of the war? I wasn't the only one who felt this way. Chester Wilmot had interviewed one of the commandos who had been assigned to cross near Wesel.

'Will you be the first over?' he asked him.

'Not if I can help it,' came the confident reply.

As the colonel finished his proposal I heard a familiar and welcome voice in the next room. It was my brother Vaughan, now a brigadier in Combined Operations. What on earth was he doing in the one spot I never expected to meet him? Apparently he was duty-bound to report on every type of maritime assault. The Rhine, in my eyes, was certainly as wide as the sea and twice as dangerous. Over a whisky after our frugal lunch, he confided to me, 'I've fixed it with the colonel. I'll be in the Buffalo alongside yours.' Then he laughed. 'The Vaughan-Thomases will lead the advance into Germany. But, for heaven's sake, don't tell mother.'

Thus it was that together we went down in the moon-suffused darkness to climb into our waiting Buffaloes. The guns thundered behind us, and ahead the night was lit by flashes and sudden flare-ups. Away to our right a great glow in the sky marked the burning town of Wesel. There followed that awful delay of waiting, when you can't think of anything except 'Let's get this over with. For heaven's sake, let's get this over with!'

At last, the signal and we moved to what seemed in the dark the mountainous wall of the bund. Up, up, then a lurch and we went down towards the Rhine. I picked up my microphone and I recorded this commentary (I note it now from the transcript):

'The driver feels for the edge of the water – we're guided up right to the very edge by a long line of small green lights that have been laid to take us off to the jumping-off ground; we've reached the water's edge and we can see the Rhine – not running bright under the moon, but running red, because right on the opposite side of the river, every single house and hay-stack you can see is burning, beaten down by the fury of our barrage. We can't tell whether there's anything coming at our boys. We hope the stuff we hear is going into Germany, the German positions; but in this thunder of the guns, and the tracers that beat all around us, it's impossible to tell which ways things are coming . . . It's going to take three minutes, and believe me every minute's going to seem a year.

'We're in – the Buffalo tips its nose and it's opened up full power. Three minutes to go and we're racing across; side by side of us goes another Buffalo. The searchlights cast a white beam, they go right across the river on one side of us, but ahead of us is only red water.'

I paused for a moment and looked across at the other Buffalo. A mass of water-splashes sprouted all around it. I

thought of my brother's request. 'Don't tell mother.' But I had
to go on telling the world. On I went.

'The driver is still fighting the current. It's running like a
millrace, carrying us down off our landing place on the other
side. Now the tracer is quiet, drowned by the revving of our
engines. But that bank is coming nearer and nearer.'

Up we went over the bund with mortars whistling around
us. We came to a burning barn. Down went the ramp. Out on
to the east bank of the Rhine leapt the gallant piper and raised
the chanter to his lips. He blew. A sad sigh came forth. He tried
again. In the middle of the battle, the burning farms, the rattle
of the machine-guns, he huffed and puffed but achieved only a
series of noises resembling orchestrated flatulence. In despair,
he cried to me, 'Ma pipes, man, they'll no' play.' A bullet had
passed through the bagpipes and punctured a hundred and
fifty years of regimental tradition. No matter. Even without
the encouragement of the pipes, the bra' lads, and the whole
army as well, were now racing into the heart of Germany. I
made haste to follow them. My last running commentary on
the war was done, but I had still to send back my despatches
on that strange, tragic final agony of Hitler's thousand-year
Reich.

I went with the advanced units through a countryside of
total defeat, where the farmhouses all had white sheets and little
groups of broken German soldiers tried to make last stands in
cities which had become bombed-out shells, where the roads
were alive with escaped Russian or Polish prisoners of war
rightfully laying their hands on any pig or chicken in sight,
where the air was alive with rumours that Hitler was dead or
planning a new last-ditch stand in the Bavarian redoubt
among the mountains of the south. For a memorable week I
travelled eastwards through the collapsing Reich with the
distinguished military commentator, Major Lewis Hastings.
He must now have been in his late fifties but his energy and
enterprise were unbounded. He had been in the thick of things
in the First World War, and had hurried back from Rhodesia
as soon as the Second had begun. He had perforce to be
content with pontificating from a BBC studio, but in the final
five minutes of the game he had succeeded at last in getting off

the sidelines. He was determined to make the most of it. I was playing for time. He felt it was time to play.

Urged on by the major, armed to the teeth, we hurtled along roads that I felt sure were strewn with mines. Nervously I pointed to tank tracks across our route. The major jumped out and felt them as if they were traces of elephant in the bush. 'Spoor's hot,' he pronounced. 'One of ours. Forward!' We were first in to many a small town, by-passed by our fast-moving tank columns. Burgomasters hastened to placate us. 'Must order them to disarm immediately,' the major told me, and issued the crisp enquiry '*Waffen?*' (weapons). Unfortunately, as he usually removed his false teeth into a little box in his pocket before going into action, the anxious civilians thought he was shouting '*Wasser!*' Our progress into the remnants of the Reich was accompanied by continuous offers of cups of cold water!

We had gone into Bremen together, a city which was a heap of rubble. The major had remembered that there was one strong point still resisting, the famous Ratskeller which was reputed to contain the largest barrel of wine in Germany. The treasure, we ascertained, had survived all the concentrated bombing of the RAF. We swept westwards and crossed the Elbe near Lüneburg. We felt almost insulted when a German plane swept down and strafed us. It must have been one of the last left in the air. We joined a British 'recce' unit to find them in a state of suppressed excitement. A message had come through that a German field marshal was waiting in a country house some miles beyond our most advanced position. He was prepared to surrender. Our hearts leapt. There was only one field marshal we could think of who would not still be with his troops at the moment. It must be Göring himself!

Hurriedly the colonel formed a flying column, with scout cars, Bren-gun carriers and a few tanks in support for the report of surrender might be false. Göring might be preparing a dramatic last stand. None of the top Nazis had yet been caught and they might all go down fighting. At midday we encircled a pleasant country house which looked strangely quiet. A trap perhaps. The tanks covered the main door, the infantry were deployed in the garden, and the young captain, the major and I crept cautiously up towards the door. The major rapped on the door which opened to reveal a frightened and very aged old lady dressed almost in Victorian costume. She waved us in, and rather shamefacedly lowering our guns we followed her along a quiet corridor. She opened the door into a big drawing room. A strange figure from another age stood before a tall chair. Nothing more unlike Göring could possibly be imagined. The old white-haired man with a white moustache who rather totteringly confronted us was dressed in full uniform of a most un-Nazified pattern – could it have been that of Kaiser William's Death's Head Hussars? The array of unfamiliar medals and orders glittered on his chest as the firelight caught them. He said not a word but looked at us almost with unseeing eyes as if we were beings from another and far from pleasant world. The old lady bowed and said, in broken English, 'I am to present der famous Feld-Marschall von Mackensen.'

Von Mackensen? Of course! Shades of the 1914–18 war! Von Mackensen, the Kaiser's favourite, the commander on the eastern front, the conqueror of Rumania! Apparently he had been brought westward from his estates in East Prussia as the Russians advanced. His relatives felt this survivor from Germany's military history should not, at all costs, be allowed to fall into Russian hands. They were surrendering him to us as a venerable old relic of a once-glorious past. Should we put him, not into a prisoner-of-war camp, but into a museum? For a moment the last representative of Williamine Germany confronted the new conquerors across the ruins of Hitler's Reich. Then we saluted. There seemed nothing else to do. The major was all for staying. 'Marvellous chance to find out what really happened when he quarrelled with Von Falkenhayn after the

The splendour of Lubeck.

capture of Bucharest.' I felt I ought to investigate more modern military matters. Away in the north Monty's advanced forces were well over the Elbe, racing towards the Baltic to seal off the Schleswig-Holstein peninsula which might provide a more convenient bunk-hole than Bavaria for the top Nazi rats. I left the Major to dwell on past imperial glories and drove off towards Lübeck.

From a distance the old Hanseatic city looked unhurt – a noble procession of Gothic spires marching across the skyline above the outlying woodlands. Inside lay the architectural mess left by long bombing raids. Yet this architectural mess was nothing to the human mess I now found scattered along the roads to the east of Lübeck. The German army that had been facing the Russians had thrown in its hand. All its soldiers wanted to do now was to let us through as quickly as possible. The men in field grey were littered all over the landscape. Army records, paper, old uniforms were everywhere. Extraordinary numbers of horses and carts cluttered up the ditches, for the German army at the end had run out of petrol. There was a mad holiday air about everyone and everything. Here was I, driving right through the German army on my own, with occasional drunks waving bottles and cheering me on eastwards. At last, just outside Wismar, I came to a group of British uniforms again. They were men of the Sixth Airborne and there, with them, were men in unfamiliar uniforms. The Russians at last. We leapt out of the jeep and joined the joyous impromptu party that was going on in the middle of the road. We slapped each other on the back, exchanged cigarettes, showed photographs of sweethearts and wives, offered hock for vodka – and all the time a group of sappers on the Russian side were busy setting up a wooden barrier. By nightfall other, more senior officials, appeared – polite but formal. The happy fraternizers disappeared eastwards never to reappear. Within twenty-four hours the wooden barrier had become the Iron Curtain.

That evening I heard that Hamburg was ours and that, next day, Monty would be accepting the surrender of all the German forces opposite him in the north at his tactical headquarters on the wide Lüneburg Heath, where the old Imperial

German army had held those peacetime manoeuvres which the Kaiser was always tactfully allowed to win. I felt that I, too, had to receive a symbolic surrender. All through the war the housewives of Britain had listened to the sneering tones of William Joyce, christened 'Lord Haw-Haw', as he gave them a continual and depressing commentary on the irresistible power of the Axis forces from Radio Hamburg. He was our Radio Enemy Number One. I decided that my last war report should come from Joyce's own microphone in Radio Hamburg.

I raced through the ruined city to find the radio station intact and Joyce's desk still littered with drafts for his final broadcast. He, himself, had fled to the north. Afterwards he surrendered and, later, was executed after a trial which raised some pretty points of international law. Perhaps, after all, he was only acting honestly according to his own strongly-held convictions. An empty gin bottle rattled in a drawer as I sat down at his desk. I had a momentary pang of sympathy for him – a man at his wits' end with his world in ruins around him. What would I have said or done in his place? Perhaps my broadcast seems slightly vindictive as I re-read it over thirty-five years later, when all the anguish, the drama, the very causes for which we fought have passed into the grey forgetfulness of history. But as I spoke, at the time, I remembered those housewives of Britain. Here is my last despatch from the battle front. The day is 4 May 1945.

'This is Germany calling. Calling for the last time from Station Hamburg, and tonight you will not hear views on the news by William Joyce, for Mr Joyce – Lord Haw-Haw to most of us in Britain – has been most unfortunately interrupted in his broadcasting career, and at present has left rather hurriedly for a vacation, an extremely short one if the Second British Army has anything to do with it, maybe to Denmark and other points north. And in his place this is the BBC calling all the long-suffering listeners in Britain who for six years have had to put up with the acid tones of Mr Joyce speaking over the same wavelength as I am using to talk to you now.

'I'm seated in front of Lord Haw-Haw's own microphone, or rather the microphone he used in the last three weeks of his

chequered career; and I wonder what Lord Haw-Haw's views
on the news are now? For Hamburg, the city he made notorious, is this evening under the control of the British Forces, and
we found a completely and utterly bomb-ruined city . . .

'Rummaging through Lord Haw-Haw's desk, we found a
revealing timetable he drew up for his work, for April 10th,
1945, and at the end of it this glorious item: "1430–1510 hr, a
pause to collect my wits." Well – he and the citizens of Hamburg have now plenty of time to collect their wits, for tonight
the sturdy soldiers of the Devons, the famous Desert Rats, are
on guard over Haw-Haw's studios, the Allied Military
Authorities are now running his programme, and instead of
"Germany Calling" the colonel in charge gives you the new
call sign of "Radio Hamburg, a station of the Allied Military
Government". And from Hamburg we take you back to
London.'

Which was exactly what I, myself, did a fortnight later. My
personal war was over.

CHAPTER SEVEN

Ends of an Era

'This is the way the war ends,' to twist T.S. Eliot's celebrated lines a little, 'not with a bang but a whimper.' At one moment you are hot in pursuit of the news. Every day brings a new sensation. Then Monty signs his name on a piece of paper in his caravan on a windy heathland near the Elbe and your whole world stops still. You have a wild party that night in the press camp, and you pace the streets of the little bombed town next morning and watch the lines of disbanded soldiers, clad in field grey, bereft of their watches and tramping listlessly away to nowhere in particular. And you wonder where you yourself are now going.

When I took stock of myself as silence fell on the western front, I detected an anxiety creeping over me, a rather unworthy anxiety I admit. I had become so used to the spectacular excitement of war that I feared the placid dullness of peace. A certain spurious glory had attached itself to BBC war correspondents. How quickly would that vanish and how painful would that process be? The war against Japan could not last long. That was one war that did end with a bang not a whimper. And the BBC's 'War Report' programme would obviously come off the air once there was no war to report. I came back to London anticipating a gloomy personal future.

Things turned out differently. For two very good reasons. First, I found an Outside Broadcasts department which had been charged with a new dynamism by its war experience, and soon new colleagues came to join us, who each brought a new approach to the business of running commentary. Audrey

Russell had a varied career before her appearance in OBs, which ranged from being one of C.B. Cochran's young ladies to journalism and war reporting. I particularly rejoiced in that advent since it freed me from a nightmare that had beset me as soon as we resumed commentaries on royal occasions – the problem of giving an accurate description of the Queen's dress.

Then there was the imposing figure of Richard Dimbleby. Richard came to his own with the development of television, but he was already acquiring that impressive manner and formidable memory which eventually made him the public voice of that first postwar period. Critics who envied his success later labelled him as pompous. They had never heard him improvising on the piano and relaxing with it in congenial company. And what a superb professional! He practically created the art of TV commentary single-handed. There came a time, many years later, when it fell to my lot to pronounce the closing words of the commentary on the memorial service to Richard at Westminster Abbey. No broadcaster had ever received such a posthumous honour before, and no one is likely to again, for no one has ever established such a grip on the general affection of the public. His voice somehow gave people assurance in an unpleasant crumbling world.

Happily all that was still a long way in the future. A third newcomer arrived to bring a gloriously buoyant personality to the Outside Broadcasting scene. Stewart Macpherson declared that when he was a war correspondent he had met an extremely gallant young Guards officer who had won the MC, but who was that rarity, a Guards officer who could talk. 'He could talk the turret off a Tiger tank if he wanted to,' declared Stew. Lobby decided we should give this talkative guardee a try and I was detailed to let him record a trial street interview. I remember listening to the candidate and thinking, 'This is the most talkative Englishman I have ever met.' Indeed he was! Within a few weeks Brian Johnston had joined the department. And within the next few months he was almost taking it over. He invented a fascinating small-scale version of cricket which we played in his office with a toy bat and a small rubber ball. This became an all-absorbing interest, and every distinguished cricketer who called at the office was swiftly initiated. I remember the Bedser brothers and Denis Compton became specially skilled performers. Denis Compton's century made in half an hour one Monday lunch time still stands as an all-time record which has not yet – to my sorrow – appeared in Wisden. Alas, there came a day when Lobby tactfully indicated that, perhaps, Outside Broadcasts had to take priority and Brian transferred himself, amongst other things, to the world of real cricket – with resounding success.

The arrival of new blood in the OB department of the BBC and all the feeling they brought of a fresh start in a rapidly changing world was the first cause of my returning optimism after my immediate end-of-war depression. The second cause was far more important. Charlotte and I decided to get married in the middle of austerity! Wartime restrictions were still in full strength. The gaunt spirit of Sir Stafford Cripps brooded over our union. There could be no question of a white wedding. Coupons were required for everything, and even with coupons there was precious little to buy. Charlotte confessed to me afterwards that her wedding costume had been skilfully reduced from an outsize garment, which was the only suitable one available in the shops. We received exactly four wedding presents, not from any lack of good will in our friends but because of the impossibility of finding anything worthwhile for sale anywhere. They responded enthusiastically, however, with money gifts and we were able to stage a delightful reception for them in Whistler's old rooms in Chelsea when we returned to London. Sherry at least was plentiful in those days at prices that seem fabulous today. Charlotte's parents made certain that austerity was banished as far as possible from the actual ceremony, and I left Engedi Chapel in Caernarfon with Charlotte on my arm in a state proper to a newly-married man – delighted daze. The organist played, with great feeling, Bach's 'Sheep may safely graze'.

The grazing pastures in London were not exactly plentiful immediately after the war. With great good luck, through friends, we eventually managed to find a rather gaunt Victorian house on a short lease in Hampstead, which we were able to possess through a mortgage for what then seemed to be the extravagant sum of £2000. Here we set up home, or more correctly, Charlotte set it up. Marriage had revealed a horrid personal truth to me – I was utterly deficient in all the practical skills which most men seem to acquire almost automatically as easily as they breathe.

We had four layers of tenants in the flats above us, whose occupants were constantly changing in those days before the Rent Acts froze everyone into bankrupting immobility. All actors full of hope or public relations experts on their way up or down, with the exceptions of the Misses MacKinnon, two spinsters of slightly uncertain age, who roosted like pigeons in the topmost flat under the eaves. They rarely appeared until the day was well aired, and I was only aware of their continued presence by the books they left down on the hall table to be collected for vicarage jumble sales.

I'm ashamed to say that I always went through the collection and abstracted the gems, after leaving a fair exchange for the vicar in their place. The Misses MacKinnons' taste had been firmly rooted in the maidenly world of 1910 with some secret thrills of the 1920s. But first they seemed to weed out the reading of their childhood. I became possessed of *Little Miss Peggy*, by Mrs Molesworth, and splendid examples of the work of Silas K. Hocking ('over a million copies of Mr Hocking's books have been sold. Silas Hocking is the prince of story-tellers' *Free Methodist*). My favourite is the splendidly titled *Dick's Fairy, A Tale of the Streets*. ('There are few if any stories better than this one.' The *Spectator*). The throw-outs then took a more spectacular turn. The works of Elinor Glyn entered my life – *Three Weeks*. I turned the pages and the words sizzled across forty years as Elinor described The Lady reclining on Paul's tiger-skin rug. 'Garbed in some strange clinging garment of heavy purple crepe, its hem embroidered with gold, one white arm resting on the beast's head . . . between her lips was a rose. . . .' How the Misses MacKinnon must have thrilled in their lonely nest up amongst the rafters as they read it. I, too, was thrilled later when I discovered that the tiger skin still exists. It has come to rest in Miskin Manor, not far from Cardiff in South Wales, for Elinor's daughter married the squire of Miskin, Sir Rhys Lloyd Williams. The next selection was devoted to the more lurid works of Mr Edgar Wallace.

Here, I think, Charlotte took fright. We had enough books invading the flat already without this new inrush from the Edwardian past. It was then that she took the bold decision to remould the flat and to turn for the reconstruction to a friend we had made after we had settled in Hampstead, the brilliant modern architect, Kenneth Capon. Kenneth was one of a group of young architects who had received their first chance after the war at the Festival of Britain on the South Bank in 1951. In the group was Michael Ventris, the brilliant decipherer of the Minoan script of Linear B, who was sadly killed in a motor accident not long after he had announced his triumph of archaeological deduction. Architects' Co-operative.Partnership converted me to the new architecture.

Charlotte went into serious conferences with Kenneth and the members of the partnership who, between them, produced an ingenious composition of lowered ceilings, skilfully placed platforms, new room-space and surprising vistas in which it became a perpetual delight to live. Michael Ventris contributed the oblong fireplace set in the wall, Kenneth suggested the patterning of the terrazzo on the patio to echo the lino tiles of the kitchen and hall, which gave a feeling almost of a colonnade running out into the green of the garden. We had a blackboard inset over the swinging door of the living room on which we could make coloured chalk drawings which could be changed at will. Usually we made copies of the palaeolithic wall paintings of animals from the Lascaux caves. They seemed in keeping with the new Stone Age which was beginning outside. There were still shortages in some areas, so Charlotte calmly sat down and crocheted a large and splendid circular mat, sixteen feet in diameter, out of agricultural twine, which fitted perfectly on the pine floor of the living room. Her masterpiece stood immediately inside the entrance hall. She had long cherished a fondness for those *fin-de-siècle* bead curtains that flourish in France. They were impossible to buy in London at that time, so with a stroke of genius, she simply threaded sticks of macaroni and coloured beads on to long strings and, lo and behold, we had a perfect French-style bead curtain – for the time being, at any rate. Luckily we were able to replace it with the real thing before the mice of Hampstead heard about it.

Our flat was a resounding success. We even rated an article in *House and Garden* and – final accolade – in the *Architectural Review* as well. We must have been among the first postwar people to convert rooms in a Victorian house to the dreams of Gropius and 'Corb'. Someone else approved of it wholeheartedly – my three-year-old son, David. I can see him now, sturdy and golden-haired, followed by Siani, the cat, walking hand in hand with Mr Beaney, the foreman, to inspect the exciting new cupboards and stairs that were starting to appear in all parts of his once-familiar home. Most exciting of all, the new plan meant that he would have a room to himself. I found it fascinating to watch David growing up. This was difficult at first, for in his first year we had an extremely competent but extremely strict nanny – not merely strict but ferocious where fathers were concerned. She regarded them as incompetent bunglers unfit to hold such a fragile masterpiece as a baby in their clumsy arms. My first contacts with my son were regulated by a stopwatch. But nanny departed and David started to speak at what seemed to me a miraculously early age. We had now acquired an au-pair girl with the difficult name of Lossnitzer. There came a morning when David, aged eighteen months, looked at her and said, 'Hullo, Lossnitzer' with a perfect German accent. Clearly I had a linguistic genius on my hands. A child who could pronounce Lossnitzer at eighteen months had boundless possibilities.

That evening I began the usual father's game of planning our son's career before it had even started. Perhaps he had inherited his grandfather's mathematical ability. These things always skip a generation, I said to myself. In that case, he was on his way to becoming a great scientist. I could see Charlotte and me sitting in the theatre at Stockholm as he went up to receive the Nobel prize. Or perhaps his astonishing precocity of speech marked him out for a dazzling career at the Bar. I pictured the moment when he first made the headlines with a brilliant oration for the defence. I calculated I would just about last long enough to be present in court to hear him. On one thing I was determined – he would never enter the world of the artist, which had brought unhappiness to my father, or the world of radio and television, which had brought uncertainty to me.

David grew up, of course, exactly as I had done – with no reference at all to the course dreamed up for him by his father. He went happily through school and university, and is now busy carving out a successful career for himself – as a scriptwriter and director in films! I am surprised but pleased.

I have one regret when I look back to that time when Charlotte had given up her important job as joint secretary to a Cabinet subcommittee to create our avant-garde home and David had arrived to give it a new dimension. I always seemed to be racing off to do commentaries in some distant corner of Britain.

> Driving down the Motor Way.
> In the track of dying day,
> As the lances of my light
> Drive a tunnel through the night,
> Every sign they touch shall be
> A witness to my constancy.
>
> Dual carriage-way ahead
> Leads me to your double-bed,
> Where all the traffic-lights are seen
> Set at a soft, permissive green,
> And launch me on a flying start
> Down the bright clearway of your heart.
>
> Oh, make me, as I end my ride,
> A loving lay-by at your side,
> Where you shall feel, as I arrive,
> My amorous automatic drive.
> U-turn – then I'll turn till I rest
> On the soft verges of your breast.

No time for further rest! The royal tours had now begun, which were to become an important contribution to Britain's slow and sometimes painful adjustment to the realities of the postwar world. We tend to be somewhat cavalier in our attitude to Royalty these days. We count the cost of the upkeep of the institution with parsimonious care. Voices are raised which question the whole concept of monarchy in the eighties. Changes occur inevitably, but in the immediate postwar world, the monarchy stood for something of enormous value which no other organization could represent – that strange feeling of continuity with a past of splendour and power which had brought us through the war. Winston Churchill might have done it but the election had removed him hurriedly from the official scene. Clement Attlee was a formidable prime minister who ran his cabinet with ruthless efficiency, but that strange, undefinable personal magic which it became fashionable to call charisma eluded him. Royalty alone filled the bill.

I felt this repeatedly as Outside Broadcasts covered a whole series of royal events in the forties and early fifties. I was the commentator inside the Abbey for the wedding of the Queen and the Duke of Edinburgh, and I had the uneasy feeling that the whole country was listening eagerly to my words. Austerity was still the watchword but everyone demanded that the old royal splendours should be revived for that day. People needed colour, pageantry, romance, and we set out to give it to them in full measure.

I nearly came to grief in my eagerness. Frank Anderson, our experienced administrator in OBs, together with R.H. Wood, our engineer, had managed to persuade the Abbey authorities to give us a splendid commentary position in the organ loft itself, with a perfect view down the aisle to the west door and then up to the area known as the theatre, before the altar. On this slightly raised platform before the high reredos bedecked with glittering gold and silver plate and guarded by the soaring thirteenth-century Gothic arches, most of the great royal ceremonies take place before an audience representing the ancient power and glory of the realm. Because of this prominent position, with the choir before me and the organist close at hand, I had to stay in semi-darkness in my commentary box and the vital order of ceremony, on which I had to work, was placed on a small shelf under a tiny hooded light.

All went well. The wedding procession moved with pomp and dignity from the west door and I gave a hurried glance at the order of ceremony to check the exact point at which I would cue over to the archbishop as he came forward on the theatre to greet the bride. To my horror, it had fallen off the shelf into the darkness of the floor. John Ellison, my second, was desperately on his knees feeling around for it. I bobbed up and down to join him, while desperately keeping the commentary going. If all the words spoken in that box had been recorded, the nation would have had a shock and the Monarchy would have fallen, 'Slowly, with quiet dignity . . . (For God's sake John, find it) . . . the bride's procession moves now under the noble Gothic arch of the organ loft . . . (John, John, what the hell are you up to?) . . . and enters the choir, filled with the high dignitaries of state in their robes and orders . . . (Hurry, for heaven's sake, the damned archbish. is coming forward. I've had it, if he opens his mouth) . . .' At that moment, John found the vital document. He slid it under the hooded light, and I cued over in the nick of time. But I'm told that the audible sigh of relief I gave made listeners in Australia think that the archbishop had fainted!

Today, would anyone worry about a commentator's slip in a royal broadcast; or in any broadcast for that matter? Thirty-odd years ago, the establishment still had an appearance of power, whatever might have been working steadily below the surface to undermine it. When Royalty first went on tour, it carried a special aura with it. Even Stewart Macpherson felt it, in spite of the detached transatlantic view he brought to the British social scene. In those days, the royal staff who were to travel on the tour usually invited the accompanying broadcasters and court correspondents to a small party before the departure day. As we walked up the stairway in that last refuge of elegant, impeccable good manners, Buckingham Palace, Macpherson exclaimed to me in triumph, 'Jeez, Colonel, if the boys in Winnipeg could only see me now!'

When the 'boys' in Australia or Nigeria or Jamaica got their first glimpse of Royalty they, too, were impressed. Those early tours were much slower, more elaborate, more carefully arranged with an eye on protocol, than the fast, flying in-and-out-in-a-few-days dashes which seem to be the pattern of royal visits today. Perhaps the slow, measured approach at long intervals might still be more effective. I am not a keen

Architecture in Perth.

supporter of the back-slapping, Scandinavian bicycling type of monarchy. I hanker after a little ritualistic dignity, although maybe the time has long gone by for this. I wonder, for example, how a repetition of the royal tour of 1954 would go down in the anti-Pommie oriented Australia of today.

In that high summer of the first visit of a Crowned Head of the Commonwealth to Her Dominion of Australia, the Aussies still relished a little glamour. Official Australia, at any rate, still claimed to value the British connection. There was a stir of consternation when the liner *Gothic*, the royal yacht for the occasion, came slowly past Sydney Heads into the wide waters of the harbour crowded with welcoming craft of every description, and the Australian commentation picked up his microphone and cried to an astonished nation, 'Ladies and gentlemen. At last the great moment we have waited for so long has arrived. Here comes the Royal Clot Yothic.' From the word go, in spite of all the veneer of splendid ceremony, the official receptions and the grand parades, the true delightfully refreshing and irreverent spirit of plebeian, democratic Australia kept creeping in.

There is the story of the Queen and the Duke arriving at a little town in the outback where the local radio station had got the mayor himself to do the commentary. The royal car appeared in the distance, moving towards the special dais before the town hall through a forest of waving flags. The mayor warmed to his work. 'The royal party are coming towards us, and in a moment or two they'll be stepping up onto that lovely, special Axminster carpet on the dais that we've brought all the way from Sydney for the occasion. Now, I don't mind admitting that it's cost the Council a pretty penny, and so, in persuance of our party's policy of keeping down the rates, as soon as the lovely royal couple have stepped on it – we're going to raffle it. There are pretty girls moving around the crowd at this moment with the tickets, and as you buy them I call for three cheers now for the Queen and the Duke.'

The mayor had not realized, however, that the royal car was fitted with a discreet radio set which had received the mayoral commentary. As the Duke mounted the steps onto the dais, he felt in his pocket, produced a shilling and said to the mayor, 'Will you get me a couple of tickets.' The shaken mayor obliged. As he said afterwards, he had no idea that austerity had hit Buckingham Palace so hard.

I was lucky. I was able to fly ahead repeatedly before the royal party and see an Australia that hadn't brushed itself up for the occasion. I liked everything about it – from the strange, brightly painted country south of Alice Springs to the legendary, never-never land around the Gulf of Carpentaria. No one had suggested to me before that the Australian landscape was full of a strange, silvery beauty or had prepared me for my

Kangaroos
disturbed at
Broken Hill.

first collision with the Australian sense of humour. I had to go up to Port Darwin to record a special loyal message from this remarkable outpost of Australian culture. Darwin, at this time, had not been wrecked by that tragic hurricane. It was still a place where all the houses were built on stilts to avoid the white ants. I assembled three of the leading citizens to interview. I began with an ex-mayor. 'Tell me,' I said rather floridly, 'what's to see and do in your fair city.' He looked me squarely in the eye. 'Mr Thomas,' he said, there's damn all to see and the only thing to do is to get to hell out of it.' Hurriedly I snatched the microphone away from him and tried my luck with my next interviewee, a leading cattle proprietor. 'We could do with all the meat you can send us in Britain today,' I said. Again a slow grin and the swift punch line. 'We'd send you plenty, Mr Thomas, if it wasn't for those bastards of civil servants down there in Canberra, who don't know a cow's ass from a cricket bat!' My last interviewee was a crocodile hunter. I banked everything on him for the loyal message. 'You are a romantic figure to us at home. Tell us about your job. What's the best part of a crocodile and how much will you get for it?' 'Mr Thomas,' came the immortal reply, 'it's just like the women here in Port Darwin. The best part's the belly and you can have it for three bob.'

There are not many better ways of putting down a pompous Pommie! Australia kept it up to the end of the tour. The *Gothic* sailed from Fremantle Harbour carrying the royal party towards Ceylon. I took part, with my ABC colleagues, in the farewell commentary. We sang 'Auld Lang Syne' and the bands played 'Will ye no come back again'. The *Gothic* began to move slowly away from the pier as we cued back to the studio. Then came a race against time to load the heavy BBC equipment on to the *Orontes* in another part of the harbour. Audrey Russell was already on board and the liner was straining at the leash to catch the same tide as the *Gothic*.

We reached the quayside in record time, and looked around for the wharfies who were to hump the gear on board. There was a line of them leaning against a wall carrying an inscription, which was an unsolicited testimonial to the virtues of Prime Minister Robert Menzies, 'To Hell with Pig Iron Bob'.

A sudden fear overwhelmed me. I had struck one of those remarkable intervals laid down by the law, in which the wharfies take a rest from their labours; 'Smoko', 'Cardo', and a host of others besides. The Australian wharfie has got the port authorities sewn up in a way that would make even a Liverpool docker gasp. Legend maintains that the wharfies of Port Darwin refused to unload a cargo of lavatory seats for the uranium mine of Rum Jungle until they were paid 'embarrassment money'. I turned to the chief wharfie. 'Excuse me, can you tell me who is going to load this gear?' He slowly removed the cigarette from his lips, paused, looked me up and down, then uttered one pregnant word, 'Yew.'

It is one of the pleasant ironies of history that, during the same period in which I was reporting, and as I have just admitted enjoying the royal tours which were designed to unite and reanimate the Empire, the politicians were planning to give it away with both hands. To people of my generation, brought up in the 1920s, the Empire had been the solid background to our whole way of life. The pictures that hung in the

Wharfies discussing their woes
outside their spiritual home.
Freemantle.

classrooms at Terrace Road School showed Wolfe scaling the Heights of Abraham and Gordon gallantly confronting the dervish spears at Khartoum. We had been to the Empire Exhibition at Wembley, and listened to the King-Emperor sending his husky-voiced message to the Empire at Christmas-tide. We turned the pages of our atlas and agreed with G.K. Chesterton:

> Half the world's red, and the rest of it's grey.
> And that is the meaning of Empire Day.

In the progressive thirties we read shock-haired Kingsley Mar-tin in the *New Statesman*, and admitted that perhaps the Raj was not quite the brightest jewel in the imperial crown. Mahatma Gandhi was a saint, and something should be done to give Congress real power. There was Burma, too, waiting in the wings, and some of those West African colonies were making remarkable progress. No doubt the Empire would be turning gently into the Commonwealth; but, somehow, at the back of our minds, we went on thinking of the Empire as still there, still, in some indefinable way, British.

Then from 1947, on through the fifties, the dismemberment gathered speed until it became a headlong rush. Giving away power willingly is a difficult technique. Until we began it, no one had voluntarily divested themselves of their imperial pos-sessions. France followed suit, a little reluctantly; the Por-tuguese were compelled to; Russia has not the slightest inten-tion of ever giving up an inch of soil conquered by the Tzars. But we developed an almost standardized ritual for the pro-cess. In Kenya, Ghana, Nigeria, Jamaica, in a whole atlasful of places, I found the same formula. The Parliamentary Delega-tion arrived to present a replica of the Mace. The Colonial Secretary – usually Mr James Griffiths – made the hopeful speech about the bright future of the new member of the Commonwealth family. The selected Royal Personage flew in to be saluted by the Guard of Honour, and all was set for the flag-lowering and raising ceremony at midnight. The com-mentator (Godfrey Talbot, Raymond Baxter, Audrey Russell, myself – take your choice) took up his microphone at the stroke of twelve. 'So the Union Jack comes slowly down in the bright pool of light before the Parliament House, and now, to the cheers of the vast crowd that has gathered in the darkness, the brave new flag of . . . (quick glance at the programme to make certain we had got the right country) . . . flies proudly at the masthead bearing with it the hopes of a new nation.'

Not everyone welcomed the transformation. In Ghana, two old Coasters sat alone in the Accra Club, watching Prime Minister Nkruma being carried shoulder-high out of Parliament to greet his delirious supporters who were dancing with delight under the spotlights. One turned to the other and remarked sadly, 'Well, I suppose, after this, we'll have to clean our own teeth tomorrow morning.'

The culture clash could start within days. The University of Ghana was still organized on firm western lines and the build-

ings formed a series of Oxford-college-type quadrangles. The dons assembled in mortarboards and gowns and the principal cultivated an atmosphere of high endeavour in the style of Balliol. Into this curious grove of Academe came the flamboyant figure of the great Louis Armstrong, invited by Prime Minister Nkruma to be one of the chief guests at the celebrations. The principal took Satchmo on a tour of the buildings. He struggled to make conversation across a vast cultural gulf.

'Tell me, Mr Armstrong, do you find people who appreciate – er – your sort of music in a place like this?'

'Sure,' said Mr Armstrong. 'Der's cats everywhere!'

The puzzled principal led his visitor onwards to the common room where a distinguished group of professors had assembled to meet him, clad in their academic robes.

GOD'S HELP TAILORS

OLOYI ADALIWYO OKUMO BLESSED OREANS RENOVATORS.

On the way to the Beauty Contest.

'These, Mr Armstrong, are the Fellows.'

It was the turn of Satchmo to look puzzled, until at last he broke into a broad grin. 'Hiya, fellers!'

At the same time, another cultural misunderstanding was taking place in the Community Centre at Accra. New nations tend to equip themselves as soon as possible with magical symbols of power – especially airlines and steelworks. But these take a little time to acquire. Ghana made a flying start by staging the first beauty competition ever held in West Africa. My sympathy was completely with the organizers, for a beauty competition is a fantastic western ritual whose rules are very difficult to explain to the average westerner, let alone to the inhabitants of Accra. So it was not surprising that there were some unusual moments when the entrants arrived at the Community Centre in a bus marked 'Mass Education'. There had been six hundred applicants and now here were the finalists, competing for a free trip to London and the battle for the title of Miss World. Other countries in Africa had their eyes on the title, however. The local press that very morning had warned Ghana of the dangers of competition, 'Six Dakar Cuties Couched by French Experts for World Honour'.

When we arrived, the Community Centre was besieged by

amorous wolves who kept up a running fire of comment as the ladies debussed.

'Ah, man, man, that's a Jaguar girl.'

'What you think this girl.'

'At all.'

'She drink Kellie-wellie?'

'Eh, master, I beg of you.'

My friendly Ghanaian guide explained, as we were ushered into the reserved seats, 'Now, do not expect to see what you see in Europe or UK. These ladies will be well clothed. Miss Northern Territory and Miss Trans-Volta will not be very lively; it is only Miss Western Territory who will do that. She had danced much High Life – this dance is very suggestive without meaning anything. But she has lived a carefree life. Maybe the judges do not like this.'

The privileged guests – black, white, Indian and Lebanese – were no sooner seated than there was a roar like a dam bursting; the wolves were storming the hall. A fierce struggle broke out at the back, chairs cracked and fists flashed. 'Ah,' said my friend, 'it is only the power of love.'

Then the contestants came on the stage, and once again the hall fairly rocked with a roar from the audience. Each young girl came shyly up to the microphone, against the backdrop inscribed Mass Education, and made a little speech to the assembled public. Miss NT was clad in a splendidly voluminous gown which was at the opposite pole from a western beauty queen's traditional bikini. Her actual figure remained a mystery. Said my guide, 'How difficult it will be to decide on what we are to judge. Are we to cheer for our traditional type of beauty where we are demanding a nice lady with much comfortable fat, or for your new western type where everything is displayed, but is very thin? I am thinking it will be the African beauty we will be preferring here, but maybe we should send you Miss Accra, who is a real Jaguar girl and has no fat.'

Miss NT was extremely traditional. She murmured into the mike, 'My name is Monica. I am seventeen years old and I am still at school. When I grow older I will be an infant teacher, for I love little children. I have four brothers and a sister at home just like me.'

How I wish I could hear a speech like that from one of those Mecca beauties! Then came the sensation, Miss Trans-Volta, Togoland. She had everything that the Ghanaian wolves demanded – a delicious coffee-coloured skin, ample areas of satiny flesh and a smile like a row of pearls dropped in a cup of chocolate. She started, 'My name is . . .'

But it didn't really matter what her name was; for the moment she had scooped the kitty.

Miss Eastern Region, with the attractive first name of Comfort, tried to recapture interest with a quick potted biography, 'I am a seamstress and I live with my mother, for my father has died. I have been taught by the Scottish missionaries.' All in vain. No one could believe that the worthy missionaries could have taught Miss Comfort what girls learn easily in Togoland.

Miss Accra had plastered her hair into snake-coils and shot

Medusa-like glances at her rivals. Miss Western Region did her best, while cooing softly, 'I live alone with my father,' to fulfil expectations as a carefree girl. Her supporters, for the moment, seemed to win the noise competition and chaos filled the hall. A neutral Lebanese tried to suggest a compromise between African and Western standards of beauty. 'Why not judge on the proportions of the Venus de Milo?' There was a storm of protest. 'That lady is not in this competition.' Miss Upper Volta, Togoland, rolled her generously proportioned figure, and swept everything before her and the prize was awarded to Ghana's very own *boule de suif*. And quite right, too!

Or was it going to be so right after all? The gaiety, delights and splendours of so many of the freedom celebrations were followed by anguish, distress, even civil war. There were exceptions of course. but often it seemed that freedom never came for free. There was a price to be paid for it. The pattern had been set by the first, the biggest, the most spectacular of all the imperial giveaways – the handover of power in India and Pakistan. I was lucky enough to be chosen as a member of the biggest BBC team to leave these shores since the days of 'War Report'. Perhaps there was some similarity between the two events.

I think I owed my position to the influence of one of the most creative administrators ever produced by the old BBC in its days of exclusive sound. Laurence Gilliam was a man of big presence, curling hair, ruddy-featured and with an infectious laugh. Unconsciously you automatically divide people you meet into those to whom you have to give vitality and inspiration and those who give it to you. Laurence was a man of that second class – a life enhancer. 'Features' were peculiarly a BBC creation. They combined the authenticity of good radio talk with the impact of radio drama. The feature writer dealt with reality. He used all the radio tricks, especially the new techniques of recording, to make his subject come alive. It was an art form that came with sound and went, alas, when sound passed its heyday, but not before Laurence had attracted to it a whole series of distinguished poets, literary men, historians and novelists. In Laurence's house in Highgate, as he generously poured out the wine and prepared his famous *moules marinières*, you would meet poets like D.G. Bridson, Laurie Lee, Louis MacNeice, Terence Tiller, W.R. Rodgers, Henry Reed and Patrick Dickinson. Great talkers like Compton Mackenzie and Moray Maclaren. Stephen Potter would look in and I once took Dylan Thomas home sober from Highgate – a rare event, but then Laurence was busy persuading him to write *Under Milk Wood*. For the Indian operation, Laurence had invited Louis MacNeice to see the event with a poet's eye, and the gloriously vital Jack Dylan, with his boundless energy and squeaky voice, to shape a series of feature programmes which would include recorded material by me. I tend, therefore, to see the handover of power in a series of sharply contrasting feature-type flashbacks.

My first scene took place a few days after we arrived. Lord Louis Mountbatten had invited the BBC team to the last great reception he would hold as Viceroy of India. We clad ourselves in sharkskin jackets with black cummerbunds and climbed with Gordon Mosley, the BBC representative in India, into the special Rolls-Royce, driven by a magnificently bearded and turbaned Sikh chauffeur. Our car passed the Red Fort and on through the swarming crowded streets of old Delhi out onto the wide tree-lined boulevards and vast ceremonial avenues of that New Delhi created by Sir Edwin Lutyens to mirror the imperial dreams of Lord Curzon. 'Make the central avenue wide enough for the Viceroy to ride down on an elephant, with half the Indian army', seems to have been Sir Edwin's brief. He obliged by creating a super-Wembley in the sun. Our car drew up at the foot of the vast flight of steps that led up to the pillared Viceregal Lodge. Lutyens had planned them for a moment of drama. At the top of the flight beyond the pillars and visible from below was a vast dome, illuminated from above, and in the pool of bright light stood Lord Louis with Lady Edwina at his side. He was in the full dress of a Viceroy, in silken breeches with stars and orders glistening and the Garter collar golden around his neck. Lady Edwina wore her jewellery with a queen's authority and grace. The red robes cascaded from their shoulders exactly as pictured for the annual portrait in the summer exhibition of the Royal Academy. Here was absolute power splendidly personified – for the last time. As we mounted the stairway lined with Bengal Lancers I felt we should have done the last flight on our knees. We bowed deeply and passed on into the reception rooms.

Here the cast of the drama were all assembled – maharajahs bedecked with pearls, soldiers in full-dress uniform covered with medals, higher civil servants in white tie and tails, and the ribbons of the orders granted by custom to administrators. Congressmen in their statutory Kádar cloth caps, and in the centre Pandit Nehru, handsome and already marked with that authority he would assume in two days time. An orchestra played discreetly in the background. There were handshakes for those who were touchable: smiles, and hands placed together as you said 'Namaste' for those who were not. Over all rose a general buzz of animated conversation. In India as in Wales, talk is expected and respected.

I walked out into the gardens with a distinguished politician who would undoubtedly be a man of power in the new government. There was a cool tinkle of water falling in the Mogul gardens and the stars were very bright and near in the clear night sky. 'Tell me,' I said, 'what are your hopes for the new India.' He gave me a quiet smile, paused and then said, 'Sometimes I hope that from the pitiless blue sky there will fall on my unhappy country a remorseless shower of contraceptives.' The sound of the orchestra came to us over the general hum of conversation in the distance. They were playing an arrangement of Amy Woodforde Finden's 'Indian Love Lyrics'.

A quick change of scene. Two days later at midnight on 15 August, at the precise time chosen by the astrologers, the new government is proclaimed in the great circular Assembly Hall. I stand on the balcony and look out from the hall to the crowd outside. A great roar of approval laps around the building as Pandit Nehru comes forward and for the first and only time in my life I hear the sound a million people can make. Lutyens had planned for the future after all. He had provided room for them all in his great avenue – room for them to salute the end of Curzon's Raj. It was two in the morning before we got back to our hotel through the crowd that patted us on the back, cheered us, almost lifted us off our feet. A message awaited me. It said, 'Lahore in flames. Massacres. You are booked on the 9.30 plane.'

Now come the worst scenes in the 'feature'. The Punjab has exploded. Moslem against Hindu, Sikh against Moslem. The Hindu quarters in Lahore and Amritsar are being burnt and looted. The Sikhs are being killed in the Canal Colonies. I have become the chief corpse counter, driving every morning down the Grand Trunk Road where no boundary has yet been set up between India and Pakistan, and where General 'Dagger' Rees and his border force are desperately trying to keep order. He has given guards of Gurkhas for the long unhappy hordes of Moslems who are marching on foot out of the India which no longer wants them towards a Pakistan which is not yet organized to receive them. Old men, women and children have to camp on the roadside at night huddled together not so much for warmth as from fear of the Sikh armed bands who hover around like wolves ready to cut down all they can.

I come across the first day's contingent staggering on through the dust, two to three thousand of them with thirty miles still to go to safety. There will be twenty more similar bands on the move up every section of the Grand Trunk Road this day. They are the lucky ones. In the abandoned camping place, which is an obscene litter of abandoned bedding and dirty rags, I come across an old man leaning helplessly against a tree. The vultures are waiting; still at a respectful distance, but soon they will close in. I cannot stand it. I lift the old man on my jeep and turn around to Lahore. I drive to the hospital but they are overwhelmed with similar old men and women. 'No point in taking him in,' they say, 'next time bring us one with a chance.' As they lift him out of the jeep, I see they are right. He was gone and the cloth-covered copy of the Koran, which was the only thing he held in his hand when I found him, lies at his feet. I pick it up and it is still on my library shelves at Fishguard.

Next day I drive to Beas Junction. This siding on the line from Delhi to Lahore has acquired a sinister reputation. The long trains loaded with Moslem refugees are halted here while the engines take on water. The Sikhs arrive, armed with sinister curved kirpons. They go ruthlessly through the trains, which then move on through the heat to Lahore, each carrying two thousand dead. Some unhappy corpses have been left behind between the platforms, where the pi-dogs are starting to worry them. A distinguished American photographer has arrived as I shoo the dogs away. 'Leave those doggies alone,' she shouts, camera to eye. 'They are better than my Calcutta vultures. This will make *Life* as sure as hell.'

Callous? Not really. She is there to show the public what is happening. A professional must do the job, even when the world is falling around her. The same feeling overwhelmed the Anglo-Indian in charge of the marshalling yards at Lahore. I call on him on the way back from Beas. Six trains, all corpse-laden, have come in during the day. He looks at the rows of bodies drawn up along the lines and utters the despairing cry of an honest man who sees his whole world of decent routine in ruins. 'Oh, Sir, it is hardly worth issuing tickets any more.'

The scene shifted again. With infinite relief I found myself back in Delhi. I felt the need to cleanse my mind. Gordon Mosley advised me, 'Why don't you attend one of Gandhiji's prayer meetings? Anyone can go.' It was, indeed, an astonishing fact that the spiritual leader of India, the inspirer of its march to freedom, the idol of the toiling millions, should come out at a set time every morning and sit quietly on a lawn in New Delhi and simply pray in public, while anyone who cared to could sit down with him and join in. Only in India could it have happened. How easy it was to assassinate him. It was almost as if he was offering himself as a sacrifice.

The frail, dark figure appeared from Birla House and, leaning on one of his lady disciples, moved slowly through the quiet seated crowd on the lawn to a carpet placed near a symbolic spinning wheel. He was clad in his famous dhoti. He wore dark sunglasses and his strange, emaciated dark body and spidery legs and arms seemed to carry all the suffering of the world. From where I sat I could not hear the words he spoke. They were in Hindi and his voice was a mere whisper. Yet, somehow, I felt the strange compelling power of the man. This was how the early saints of Christendom, the ascetics, the dwellers in the wilderness, the lonely Celtic hermits exercised their spell. I was profoundly glad I had come.

The civil servant who had brought me looked around at the millionaire Birla's house, and the wide-spreading well-kept lawns. 'Ah yes,' he whispered. 'It takes a lot of money to keep Gandhiji in the poverty to which he is accustomed. . . .'

'Always end a feature with a punch line,' advised Laurence Gilliam. 'Give them a final image they won't forget. Don't worry if it's obvious. Say something that will stick.' The same applies to a television programme. I found my punch line for India and Pakistan by going up to the hills, to a little settlement called Nathia Galli behind Abbottabad. It wasn't a fashionable hill station – just a little collection of pleasant bungalows amongst the pines, high enough to be cool in the summer. I was taking breakfast on the balcony with an old Indian hand, who had just retired from government service. 'Will you come back to Britain now?' He shook his head. 'No, my father was here before me and his father before him. This is where I belong. India, now Pakistan, what does it matter? The people are still the same. I like them. They like me.'

We talked about the way history would judge the Raj which we had just watched being finally wound up, all its splendours put away for keeps in the historians' dusty files. 'Well,' he said, 'we made mistakes like everyone else. We were pretty ruthless, too. But in the end, I will say this for us. We meant well. We really meant well.'

A quiet servant entered, bowed and said. 'Sahib, you told me to tell you when it was there. Sahib, it is there now.'

We went out on the balcony and my friend pointed north. At first I could not see what he was pointing at. The morning mists still swirled among the pines below us, blotting out the deep trench of the Indus valley. 'No, higher, higher, still.' Then suddenly I saw it, far far higher than I ever expected a mountain summit to be. Before me was the vast shining wall of Nanga Parbat, over 26,000 feet high. It was far away to the north but for an hour in the morning it deigned to appear in all its glory, its glaciers plunging down in thrilling icy cascades, its ridges and pinnacles infinitely high and remote. I looked at it with a deep feeling of almost religious awe. I had got the right end to my feature on the handover of power. Nanga Parbat put us all in our proper place.

But as I entered my fifties, I began to wonder what was my proper place in the world of television and radio. I had discovered enough about myself, and the BBC had discovered enough about me, to realize that administration was not my forte. I have a naturally untidy mind – excellent for quiz programmes but useless for office routine. I left the staff of the BBC and became a freelance. I retained the happiest relations with the corporation, while I ventured off into new worlds. The corporation's exclusivity had been broken with the advent of Independent Television, and perhaps, in the long run, this was a good thing. It put the BBC on its mettle and it entered a

new, vigorous, even daringly modern period under Sir Hugh
Carleton-Greene. I enjoyed my contacts with the stimulating
minds of Donald Baverstock and Antony Jay. Here were men
who were standing the old accepted rules of television on their
heads and making them work.

I wrote books, enjoyed myself on lecture tours, and even ran
a private closed-circuit television company. I had a fruitful
freelance fifties, but I was early determined on one thing. I was
never going to toddle towards my sixties playing out time. The
word retirement would never enter my vocabulary. If I
couldn't go on meeting exciting people I would cease to be
exciting to myself, leave alone being exciting to others. People,
after all, are the real business of radio and television. I have
been lucky in the people I have succeeded in recording, but oh
how I wish I had managed to pin down some of the more
elusive specimens for my collection. Somehow it was always
the most interesting who succeeded in wriggling out of my
collector's net. I have a choice anthology of The Ones That
Got Away!

CHAPTER EIGHT

The Ones That Got Away

One of the minor casualties of the war was the gentlemanly interview. In the early days of radio the embarrassing question was studiously avoided. The interviewer would begin with the polite formula, 'I am sure listeners would be interested to know, Mr X . . .' and continue with, 'And perhaps you might care to tell us something about. . .?' The interviewee would be encouraged with helpful interjections of 'Ah, yes' or 'Most interesting', and the happy, innocuous encounter would end with a polite epilogue of mutual thanks. The only danger came when the microphone was taken outside the safety of the studio. In those days of live broadcasting, the unexpected reply, like the bomber according to Mr Baldwin, 'was bound to get through'.

There was the celebrated tour of a farm in Kent where the new system of mechanical milking had been installed. The commentator described the modern marvel of the machines quietly milking a long row of contented cows, but at the end of the row was a single cow still being milked by hand by Old George, the cowman. 'Ah, tell me,' said the commentator in his blandest manner. 'Why isn't this cow attached to the machine?'

Old George looked up in surprise, 'Yer couldn't do that. This be old Daisy. Her be a wrinkly-titted old sod!'

After that there was no alternative but the hurried cue, 'Back to the studio.'

After the war, such anxieties over the rough reply began to seem slightly old-fashioned. By the sixties, the barriers were down, especially where politicians were concerned – and why not? Politicians are used to the roughhouse of the hustings and violent debates on the floor of the House. They have no right to protest, as some of them do, about unfair questions. Television has given an added zest to the political interview. In the hands of a master like Robin Day, it is 'sport to see the engineer, hoist on his own petard'.

The tough interview was already well established on American television. In that strange world of perpetual chat shows interspersed with adverts, the interviewer has always been king. His assistants daily scour the social landscape to feed the insatiable demands of the four-hour-long Al Kitzblitzer Show. The 'personality' who quizzes you in front of the camera has no time to waste in studying his victim in depth. He takes a quick glance at his hand-out and plunges in. 'Proud to have you on Station ZQDJ, Mr Von Thoma. Now-er, Yes – tell us something about yourself.'

When Miss Wales came to New York on a promotion tour from the Tourist Board she appeared at the studio in national costume – shawl, red flannel skirt and tall black hat. The announcer was nonplussed. 'Gee lady,' he gasped, 'what do you represent?'

'I represent Wales.'

'Well, in that case, where's your harpoon?'

I also met my match in Los Angeles. I had just landed after being the guest of SAS on the opening flight of their new service from Copenhagen over the Pole to California. The local Al Kitzblitzer put me briskly through my paces, but halfway through my eloquent description of the Greenland icecap he remembered his duty to his sponsors, makers of deodorants. 'Cold, eh, Mr Van Thoma, I bet it was. But don't forget folks' – and here his face filled the screen as he got in the message – 'It may be December outside, but it's always August under your armpits!' There are better aspects of American TV. The men who interview presidents, politicians and the pompous great have a true cutting edge, but the chat show always runs on the edge of banality on both sides of the Atlantic.

Let me admit that I am a coaxer not a cutter when it comes to interviews. I like to talk things over first and create an atmosphere of mutual trust. A little too cosy, perhaps, but I have never been in the damaging revelations business. This may account for the fact that the interviewees I remember most vividly are the ones who got away. Perhaps Sir Thomas Beecham had the right idea, after all. He regarded the microphone as a regrettable nuisance when it came to real talk, a view reinforced by a certain incident in the early days of interview recording. He had invited the BBC to his flat where he was already entertaining a charming lady to Pol Roger '08 and elegant conversation. He talked and the lady attacked the champagne with more gusto than wisdom. It eventually became clear from her gentle snoring that she had been overcome by the splendour of the occasion. Sir Thomas talked on into the microphone, giving no sign that he noticed a somewhat *pizzicato* accompaniment. The lady slid gently on to the floor, Sir Thomas gave a sign to his butler, the admirable and imperturbable White. White murmured, 'Shall I replace the lady now, sir, or will you wait?' Sir Thomas continues his measured and eloquent discourse. He concluded, bowed to the lady on the floor, then to the BBC engineers and retired quietly and gracefully.

Next day the BBC was surprised to receive postcards from certain music lovers who declared that they had naturally been delighted with what Sir Thomas had said, but even more delighted to discover a facet of Sir Thomas's character that they had not suspected – namely, that he was a keen dog lover. How charming it had been, while Sir Thomas had been talking about Sibelius, to hear the friendly and highly intelligent snuffling of his dear little pet in the background!

But I discovered Sir Thomas's real feelings when I, too, went to record him with Anna Instone in Paris on the occasion of his eightieth birthday. We had armed ourselves with a bottle of champagne and a box of his favourite Monte Cristo cigars. He received us with all his old-world formal politeness, clad in a silk dressing gown and in dazzling form as he spoke into the microphone I held out for him. He poured out wit and epigrams with reckless generosity. His revelations about his contemporaries became more and more indiscreet. Of a certain most distinguished English composer he declared, 'He wrote his symphonies with all the wild abandon of an unmarried organist waiting for retirement in one of our damper cathedrals.' I knew I had a first-class scoop on my hands – until I happened to glance down at my machine.

The tape had stuck. Not a word had been recorded!

I turned anxiously to explain to Sir Thomas. He was chuckling to himself with the greatest good humour. 'My dear fellow,' he said, 'I saw that your wretched contraption had stuck from the moment I began to talk, so I knew that I could really let myself go. Remember all the best talk is never on but *off* the record.' Then he turned to the embarrassed French engineer, 'Young man, cease caressing your churlish contraption and apply yourself to the excellent wine of your country.'

In a slightly less Edwardian manner, the late Brendan Behan also demonstrated his distrust of the radio interview as a revelation of character. I had gone down to record him in the top flat of a house in the middle of Blackheath, which we entered by means of the fire escape. Brendan was in full blast on the telephone. From the right-hand side he looked like a reincarnation of Michael Collins, from the left like Nero after a thick night out at the Colosseum. If you lay on the carpet and looked up over his ample tummy, you saw a Falstaff who had learned Gaelic. He was bellowing expletives down the telephone to his correspondent at the far end. He held the phone with disgust at arm's length, while a disembodied voice floated through the room, 'But may I say, Mr Behan, in the matter of royalties we will be most happy to meet you in every possible way, and we propose . . .'

'Ah, b—— you,' bellowed Mr Behan, still holding the receiver as if it were a cat about to be sick in the drawing room. 'What will you have, boys? Powers?' He poured out two stiff tots with his free hand and drowned one of them at a gulp.

'By God, I'm bloody well destroyed. Bloody awful . . . No, not you, you bastard,' – this to the far-distant gentleman on the telephone who kept on murmuring to himself as the instrument lay on the table, 'I'm sure you'll find us, may I say, Mr Behan, not ungenerous in the matter of payment, provided we might discuss the right format . . .' 'Ah, hell,' said Mr

Behan and banged down the phone, 'I'm destroyed utterly I tell you. Let's go out for a drink.'

'You must do your interview first about the state of the drama.'

'It's the state of the dramatist you've got to bother with now.'

'What do you think of Mr John Osborne?'

'Him, an angry young man! He's about as angry as Mrs Ruddy Dale. You haven't got a real theatre; a nation of fifty millions and you can't support Joan Littlewood. Now we in Ireland can support a national theatre and send the actors to the sea for their holidays.'

'You don't like the English?'

'Switch that bloody thing off. Sure I like the English, but you know bloody what? It wouldn't be commercially viable for me to admit it.'

And he burst into song. ' 'Twas the night the Holy Picture fell . . .' He stopped after the first verse and announced, 'There's a grand pub down in the village and they're waiting for me now.' There seemed no point in continuing to try to record for the moment, and soon the recording car deposited us at the pub. Brendan flung open the door. A row of assorted ladies, mainly a choice collection of old dearies obviously devoted to gin or Guinness, cheered his arrival with delight. 'Darlings,' he shouted, 'your troubles are over. Here's the man from the BBC who's rolling in money. He's a real bloody Croesus. Set 'em up, Joe.' And he, himself, swept everyone aside to lean against the bar and burst again into song:

Ah, it was the tyrant Gladstone, and he said unto himself,
I never will rest aisy 'til Parnell is on the shelf

It was a different way of dodging an interview from the mischievous Edwardian evasive tactics of Sir Thomas Beecham's, but it was equally effective.

Perhaps my most successful interview dodger – if I dare use such a vulgar word about him – was Sir Max Beerbohm. Not long after the end of the war, Sir Max had resumed his residence in his Italian villa at Rapallo, and I happened also to be in Italy with a BBC recording car for a programme on a return journey to the Anzio beachhead. Talks Department wanted to record Sir Max reading some of his delightful essays, but the producer also cherished another hope. He asked me, 'Could you also persuade him to give you an interview?' 'Don't rush him. Feel your way gently. I'm sure you understand how tactfully you'll have to approach him. Good luck!' I should have realized, before I started, that Sir Max had already gently withdrawn from all such vulgarities as newspaper or radio interviews. He had retired to his Italian hide-out. He had stopped the clock on some golden Edwardian afternoon, when the fashionable world was still elegant and exclusive and small enough to be encompassed in drawings of fragile, venomous brilliance.

I approached Rapallo with some apprehension. Italy had just been through the tribulations of an election, and we had to race up from Rome overnight to keep the appointment. As our car lights swung around one of the numerous suicidal corners of the Rapallo road, they illuminated a vast blank wall plastered with political slogans – *Viva CD, Viva Garibaldi, Viva Il Papa Re*. At the foot stood a little, middle-aged, moustachioed gentleman busy filling in the one vacant space with another slogan. He had just finished it when our headlights caught him and he scuttled away into the safety of the night. He had written in flaming, defiant red paint a clarion call to the downtrodden Italian middle classes — *Viva Amore* – long live love!

We took this as a good omen as we brushed ourselves up prior to calling at the villa, for I felt sartorially inadequate in my austerity suit. Max seemed to have lived his life in such a perpetually well-dressed atmosphere that it seemed indecent to present myself at his door in a garb whose outlines had been dictated by Sir Stafford Cripps.

But it was also a desperate adventure to reach his door at all. His house, the Villa Chiara, stood on a steep hillside which gave a glorious view over the blue sea and the whole sweep of the coastline of the Italian Riviera. When Max and his wife first saw it just before the First World War, it must have seemed the perfect place for the man who proposed to opt out from the growing vulgarity of the petrol-soaked twentieth century. I could see the couple arriving in a slow-moving cab from Rapallo and deciding that the little villa on its terrace, with its vines, its small garden and summerhouse perched up on the hill was the predestined and charming cell for these most elegant of hermits. What Max and Lady Beerbohm never realized was the danger implicit in their hermitage's proximity to the main trunk road from Genoa to the south. The Via Aurelia runs almost underneath the front windows. All may have been peaceful in 1910, but by 1947 the motor lorries had arrived, driven by Italians who treated the Via Aurelia as if it were the Indianapolis circuit. They thundered around Max's corner in a continual imitation of the chariot race in *Ben Hur.* We parked by the gate and squeezed the BBC recording car against the wall, in imminent fear of being crushed by the next ten-wheeled monster.

We walked up the stone steps and rang the bell, standing under a strangely shaped lamp which had been designed by Gordon Craig. Everything that surrounded Max seemed to link him irretrievably to his era. Even the big pine trees across the road leant – according to Max – 'backwards like Swinburne when he was talking to you, don't you know'. When we were shown into the tiny library I got a strange feeling of stepping back, myself, into some spring evening just past the turn of the century, when portly King Edward was entertaining Mrs Keppel to dinner with Sir Ernest Cassel; when Mr Balfour was uncoiling his willowy length from the Front Bench of the House of Commons to give a look of infinite understanding, and distaste, at Mr Bonar Law; and when Max himself in spats, top hat and an exquisitely cut overcoat complete with astrakhan collar, was carefully putting on his gloves, prior to taking the last hansom to the St James Theatre, where he would review – writing with a silver dagger – the latest dramatic offering of Mr Jerome Klapa Jerome, the *Passing of the Third Floor Back.* 'A savoury *oeuvre*,' according to Max, which proved that 'twaddle and vulgarity would always have the upper hand.'

The books, the pictures, the furniture, everything dated from the days before the First World War. Max had deliberately stopped his clock. In his seventies he went on living as if

King Edward VII was still on the throne. He entered the
library as we were looking at his drawing of the ageing Carlyle
striding unhappily along Chelsea Embankment. The first thing
I noticed about Max was the elegance of his clothes, the
negation of everything about which the long-winded Carlyle
pontificated in his unread *Sartor Resartus*. 'I, too, failed to
read through those uncouth, repetitive sentences,' said Max. 'I
shall never understand how a man could write 622 pages on
the philosophy of clothes and yet refuse to go to a good tailor.'

Max's English was as elegantly and carefully dressed as his
person. His sentences could never be as slovenly as Carlyle's.
You felt that his adjectives were wearing spats, every noun he
used had a crease put on it, every verb was chosen to avoid
vulgar excitement. His precise, beautifully modulated voice
gave a remote quality to everything he said. It was as if I were
listening to the voice of someone who had returned from a
journey into outer space and was mildly astonished to find that
the world was still going on.

This precision of speech fascinated me. When I first joined
the BBC precise utterance was at a discount. The advent of the
microphone was held to have revived easy, natural talk after
many years of the dominance of the written and printed word.
As each carefully written script arrived the devoted producers
in the Talks Department struggled to make it natural. Many a
man fashioned a high reputation for himself by the expert way
he was able to insert an 'er' or 'of course' or 'as you know' into
an intractable slab of statesman's prose.

Max would have none of this. 'To "er" may be human,' he
said to me, 'but to continue "er-er-ing" is hardly divine.' His
voice had the quality of a beautifully played flute, every brea-
thing pause carefully calculated, every hesitation used as a trill
to embellish a particular word. 'The theatre?'

'No, I have not, as it were, frequented the *coulisses* for some
years. The last time I went to the London Theatre there was a
play being staged by a man who . . .' – slight pause and
disarming smile – 'yes, who smoked a pipe. It was hardly a
play, it was a sermon. Now the one thing I will not suffer in a
theatre is a preacher in full flight, especially if he preaches . . .'
– again a gentle smile of resignation – 'with a northern accent.'

'What about G.B.S.?' I interrupted slyly.

'Ah, he never preached. He simply talked to you on the stage as he talked to you in private. And I do not think he expected you to believe a word he said. Not so this other dramatist. His play had the title, if I remember correctly, *I Have Been Here Before*. I retired after the interval, merely remarking to the manager as I left, "and you will not see me here again,"'

Max spoke about G.B.S., and indeed about Arthur Balfour, Oscar Wilde, Rufus Isaacs and a host of other people who flourished until 1914, as if they were still alive. After 1914, the curtain came down. But he talked of the Edwardians with such a sense of immediacy that I kept glancing uneasily around the tiny room in case, at any moment, Henry James might ooze his bulk into the chair opposite and start a splendidly interminable monologue. Max was going to record his essay on Hall Caine, but clearly we could not set up our microphones in the library. The lorries outside would have shaken the recording to pieces. Max never seemed to hear them. It was as if he had sealed off his ears as well as his mind from this vulgar twentieth century, but our engineer was only too sensitive to the noise!

We adjourned to the little summerhouse at the top of the garden. Here we placed Max in his easy chair with a hot-water bottle in his lap, a vast array of travelling rugs around his legs and a reading desk before him, supporting a beautifully written manuscript. He sipped glass of the local white wine and prepared to read the opening sentences.

A volley of shots erupted from over the wall outside. I rushed out into the lane, among the olive trees that overlooked the top wall of Max's garden. A splendidly equipped hunter stood before me, a *cacciatore*, complete with feathers in his hat, leggings, gun under his arm and game basket slung over his shoulder. He was prowling through the gardens shooting at every tiny tom-tit in the district. It was as if the shooting season had opened in Tooting instead of on the Scottish moors.

'Silence,' I commanded, 'a great English writer is recording a masterpiece.'

'A masterpiece? Ah, I understand. It is that pleasant old

gentleman who dresses in the style of D'Annunzio and who seldom comes out. We know him well here, but, pardon me, we did not know he was a writer. Is he a novelist, perhaps, or a screen scenario creator?'

'England's greatest,' I said.

'In that case I will go and shoot over Signor Benoni's garden. They say the larks are bolder over there.'

I may have committed a crime against wildlife, but I was giving life, for posterity, to a piece of prose on which Max had worked for a year, a carefully wrought verbal jewel. The words flowed easily, eloquently, musically. He talked of his first meeting with that humourless best seller, Hall Caine. Hall Caine is forgotten now, but as Max rolled the names of his novels appreciatively over the tongue – *The Deemster, The Christian, The Eternal City* – I could see Hall Caine before me, bearded, gloomy, tweedy – and a whole procession of late Victorians followed. 'Balfour was the only man I knew who did not seem to have a backbone . . .

'Asquith never drank seriously, don't you know; no man who could write those neat, precise letters of his – and he wrote constantly all through the day – could ever be regarded as a wine-bibber."Squiffy", indeed! Why, all his Cabinet were afraid of him until Lloyd George came into prominence. These two men were made to secretly despise each other . . . Kipling! I never thought of him as a writer but rather as a photographer.

'Hall Caine was not in this class, but he had a presence, undeniably a presence. It was expected of successful men in those days. They had to dress the part. So Hall Caine wrapped himself in a cloak – was it, perhaps, a memory of Tennyson – now *he* was distinctly a "cloaky" person.'

We could have gone on recording for hour after enchanting hour but the age of irreverence came roaring in. We could not cut out the sounds of the Via Aurelia. The crash of the lorries changing gear seemed to bring the postwar world roaring through Max's front door. They flattened his fragile defences at six-minute intervals. Insolently their engines proclaimed that there was now no escape. The man who opts out will be pursued by the mechanized furies to the loneliest ends of the earth. They were also the perfect sound-screen behind which Sir Max could hide without offence. Did he know this all along?

Or was the fault mine? I had committed the cardinal sin of an interviewer. I had been so delighted by our *rencontre*, as Max described it, that I had forgotten the practical purpose of our meeting. In the most subtle and polite way Sir Max Beerbohm had gracefully withdrawn from the interviewer's trap. In these less leisurely days an interviewer has to be more insistent and perhaps better briefed and prepared than we were. Michael Parkinson rightly goes into action after thorough research on his subject. David Dimbleby never lets any evasive reply go unnoticed, Robin Day makes 'flaying alive a pleasure for the victim'. They are all modern masters of the strange art of the interview. For an art it is, which cannot be practised without some special gift in the practitioner. He may have mastered all the rules. He may have done his homework, he may avoid all the platitudinous openings, he may be prompt in his questioning but if he cannot somehow instantaneously create an atmosphere of confidence between himself and his interviewee he is doomed. There have been great masters of the microphone and the camera who never mastered this elusive art of the interview. The classic example is the late Gilbert Harding.

Gilbert was one of the first television personalities – one of those men for whom the media was specially created, and whose qualities could only be displayed live in front of camera. I knew him in the early days of his association with the BBC when everyone recognized that he had something but no one was quite certain what it was. Clearly here was a man with a compelling voice and a magnificent command of the language, but he was obviously a deeply unhappy man, a frustrated homosexual in a then non-permissive society, a Catholic convert tormented by his failure to live up to the precepts of his new religion. No stranger figure ever became a popular idol. With his bristling moustache, staring eyes and booming voice he erupted on the screen in a way that sent a delighted shudder through his audience safe in their suburban villas or terraced houses. Secretly they wished they were capable of such outbursts themselves. The legends about his spectacular rudeness grew with the telling. There was the story of the farewell dinner given to him in Canada after he had ended his stint as a BBC representative after the war.

The usual complimentary speeches were made and Gilbert rose to reply. 'It is with regret that I now prepare to leave this Colony of Canada.' There were faint murmurs of protest at the word colony but Gilbert ignored them. 'And may I say, as I leave,' he continued, 'that I deeply appreciate the kindness I have received in the Colony of Canada.' The murmurs rose in volume, 'No Colony! Dominion! Dominion!' Gilbert continued with magisterial indifference. 'And I shall always retain the happiest memories of my sojourn in this Colony of Canada.' The hall erupted in thunderous indignation: 'Withdraw. Withdraw! Dominion! Dominion!' Gilbert waited until the uproar had subsided and then looked out over the still-furious guests. 'You are right, Dominion. Had you been a Colony you would at once have been better governed – and better mannered!' Canada had been treated to a Harding's farewell.

The United States fared no better at his hands. He was on the train from Canada to New York just after the war when controls were still strict. At the border he was handed one of those endless immigration forms which Americans then delighted to inflict on their visitors. Gilbert filled in the form with mounting revulsion. 'Can you read? Can you write? Can you speak English? Are you Caucasian?' At the end was the question, 'Is it your intention to subvert the government of the United States?' Gilbert seized his pen and wrote in large letters, 'Sole purpose of visit!'

He was out on the cold platform at Buffalo in a matter of minutes.

Of course he made enemies, but they never had the chance of seeing the real man behind the TV façade – the Gilbert Harding who rushed to send flowers or an apologetic letter to the latest victim of his outbursts; who was secretly ashamed of his meretricious success; who honoured and patronized rising young painters and writers; who was passionately determined to maintain the standards of spoken English. A sad, strangely attractive, surprising man – but most emphatically no interviewer. An interview with Gilbert was hardly a meeting. It was a spectacular collision.

He willingly admitted his total lack of that ingratiating charm which is an important weapon in the interviewer's armoury, and summed it up in a memorable reply to Mae West's P R officer. In one of the many attempts made by the BBC to fit Gilbert into the structure of the corporation, just after the war, it occurred to some bright boy in Talks that the master of insult might yet be a good link man in a chat show. 'In Town Tonight' was still running, but the producer soon found that it was easier to stop the roar of London's traffic than to control the bellows of rage of his interlocutor. The programme was still being originated deep underground in the wartime studio created by the BBC in the Monseignor Cinema at Marble Arch. Gilbert's most important interviewee was Mae West, and the rehearsal – to say the least – was not exactly a success. Mae retired to her dressing room to read a selected passage from the Bible, while her PR man trotted around to give a pep talk to Gilbert. It started with a slap on the back. Gilbert winced, but the breezy American gave him the works. 'Gee, that was great, Gil, yeah, really great, but can I just make one suggestion. Could you just sound, you know, a little more kinda interested. After all, Mae is still a vurry, vurry attractive woman. Couldn't you sound, when you are talking to her, kinda sexy?'

Gilbert slowly rose from his chair. In a voice of thunder he replied, 'If, as you suggest, I had the capacity of conveying in my voice the power of overwhelming sexual attraction, I would not now be interviewing a has-been female in this dismal basement!'

There was no more to be said. The PR man muttered, 'Yeah, yeah, I see Gil!' and hurriedly backed away. 'Gil' went on to different and perhaps higher things.

While Gilbert was suffering that particular torment reserved for those who know they have failed on radio or television, I, too, was working my way towards the failure in interviewing I most regret in my years in the Outside Broadcasts department of the BBC. The failure may have been preordained, for I was attempting not merely the impossible but the invisible as well. When O Bs began again after the war, Lobby, once again the head of the department, applied his ingenious mind to the problem of finding new fields for the microphone to conquer. Sport and processions and public events were all very well, but why not try our hand at the occult? Let the listeners judge for themselves whether the claims of the psychic research investigators were true or not. Why not broadcast a poltergeist? Marvellous broadcasting material on the face of it, with objects flying about all over the room, mysterious crashes, unexplained sudden collapses of furniture, paintings falling off the walls, a whole gamut of sensational sounds – if only they were genuine! Or at least had the benefit of the doubt. Lobby looked at me thoughtfully. Was I the right man to investigate the project? I was a Celt and Celts are popularly and erroneously supposed to possess a peculiar affinity with the mystic world, but I was also a Welsh agnostic. Perhaps I possessed the right combination of sympathetic curiosity and gentle doubt. Lobby took the plunge and invited me to investigate the numerous cases of guaranteed poltergeist phenomena that now poured into the department. Indeed I became so involved that every time a book fell off the shelves or a file slipped off my table I became convinced that I had a resident poltergeist in the office, maybe hanging around in the hope of obtaining a lucrative BBC contract.

Thus it was that I met the late Harry Price, the most famous psychic investigator of his day, and for three months I found myself moving in the strange world of ESP (extra-sensory perception), apports (any stones or objects that suddenly shot across rooms) and revenants. At my side stood the irrepressibly enthusiastic Harry, always ready to drag me around that dangerous corner that divides reality from the dream world. Indeed I am still not certain if he, himself, knew in which world he was living. You may not have been convinced by everything he said, but it was impossible not to enjoy the way he said it.

He was, indeed, an old hand at the investigation business. He had made his name in Edwardian days as the terror of fake mediums. In between the wars he had become the owner of the

most haunted house in Europe and books on the strange
goings-on in Borley Rectory poured from his pen. This grim
Victorian house stood isolated in the dampest part of the Essex
marshes. It was once the residence of the aptly named
Reverend Bull and the psychic phenomena were always on
tap, according to the fans, from mysterious bell-ringings to the
resident ghost of a White Nun. The house had burnt down but
not for a moment did the spirits desert their favourite site in
Britain. Harry invited me down to see and hear for myself. In
the sinister dusk, with a cold wind sighing in from the wide,
level marshlands, we walked among the ruins. Suddenly a dark
object rose in front of me, seemed to pause for a moment in
mid-air and then fell at my feet. Harry shouted, 'Did you see
that? You're lucky. On your first visit too! You've seen an
instance of spontaneous levitation.' The object was nothing
more romantic than an old brick, and it had certainly shot
into the air. But where exactly was Harry in the semi-
darkness? Oh, unworthy doubt, for I immediately featured
in Harry's next book; true only in a footnote but there
I stand as an unimpeachable witness to the Case of the
Levitated Brick.

Of course, it is easy to be sceptical writing all this down in
broad daylight in my comfortable study in my house in Fishguard with everything normal around me, but it is another
matter when you are out on the Essex marshes with a cold
wind blowing and a firm believer at your elbow. I was mal-
leable material in the skilful hands of Harry Price. Let me
admit straight away that I enjoyed being moulded. The telephone would ring and the persuasive voice would begin, 'My
dear chap, are you free tonight? Good. Meet me at the Reform
Club at six o'clock. This time I've got an absolute winner.' At
the Reform Harry would be sitting waiting at the fire, in the
vast hall that had seen the dramatic return of Phileas Fogg
after his adventurous journey *Around the World in Eighty
Days*. Harry was ready to propose an even more adventurous
journey – to 127 Inkerman Street, South Streatham. 'Remarkable phenomena. Pools of cold air moving across the hall.
Apports flying up the stairs. But first, a glass of port. The club
still has some worthwhile vintages!' My nerves would tingle as

he talked. This was how Sherlock Holmes lured Dr Watson
from his moribund practice to high adventure in Tooting Bec
and Upper Norwood. Harry, too, had Sherlock's gift of making drab, commonplace suburbia a magic, slightly sinister
world where anything could happen. How could bombed, still
semi-darkened London seem dull when, at any time, the presents from Blackpool on the mantelpiece of 'Torestin' in Glen-
dale Garden Suburb could leap in the air or all the doors of 91
Windsor Terrace, Mitcham, silently open together on a still,
windless night? With eager anticipation I would help Harry to
collect the worn gladstone bags that carried a choice collection of flashbulbs, litmus papers, thermometers and all the
investigative paraphernalia that had pursued the ghosts of
Britain for the last forty years. We climbed in the B B C car and
set off through the quiet streets like Holmes and Watson in
their hansom. This time we would surely find the poltergeist
waiting to broadcast.

Somehow or other, he always seemed to elude me. Witnes-
ses would be waiting at the scene to reassure me that the
phenomena had indeed occurred on that very spot, and there
always seemed to be a tall, gaunt, cadaverous retired Church
of England clergyman among them. But usually the poltergeist
never joined the party at the right time. I felt I might be a sort
of psychic repellent.

At last, there came a moment when everything seemed to be
set fair. The telephone rang and once again I heard that
persuasive voice, 'My dear fellow, believe me, I think I've got
exactly what you require. No suburban villa this time. We will
be dining with an ex-proconsul, and the evidence of the manifestation is' – and Harry rolled the word on his tongue with
relish – 'impeccable.'

That evening did see us, indeed, dining in a noble house in
the Home Counties. As Holmes might have remarked, 'My
dear Watson, we are moving in exalted circles.' Over a delightful meal, our distinguished host explained the problem. 'It is a
question of our local vicar. The poor man is deeply distressed,
for he is convinced that he is being haunted, even persecuted,
by some sort of manifestation, some type of what I believe you
call – er – a poltergeist. I have done my best to help him. I've

had the bishop down, and we've even had an exorcism, but to no avail. You, Mr Price, must be our last resort.'

'What form do these manifestations take?' Harry enquired.

'They are, I admit, extremely unsual – not to say, embarrassing. I am sure it will be better if our incumbent explains them to you personally.' Then he added, 'In this house we usually have the vicar in with the port.'

The port was excellent – Taylor's '27 – mellow and untroubled. Not so the poor vicar. He was clearly a man with a problem which he longed to discuss with someone sympathetic. He was unmarried and obviously had few people to whom he could turn. We arranged to spend the night at the vicarage, said goodnight to our host and walked with the vicar down the drive to his house which, in classical fashion, overlooked the churchyard.

Edgar Allan Poe would have been proud of the setting. Owls hooted, clouds scurried over the moon as we walked among the graves and under the yew trees towards the light over the doorway of the eighteenth-century vicarage. 'And now, my dear sir,' Harry began in his reassuring manner, rather like a genial doctor asking his patient for his symptoms, 'tell us exactly what is happening to you.'

The vicar glanced back at me as we walked. I was carrying the gladstone bags. The owls hooted and our feet rustled among the fallen autumn leaves. 'My dear, sir,' said Harry, 'you can speak freely in front of Mr Vaughan-Thomas. He's my trusted assistant, a most experienced man.'

'Well then,' said the vicar, 'the manifestations seem to occur in the evening around the the time I am preparing to go to bed'.

'Ah, yes,' Harry agreed, 'typical of poltergeist phenomena. Typical.'

'I become aware of a sort of column of cold air approaching me.'

'Yes, indeed. A typical poltergeist phenomenon.'

'It seems almost to encircle me.'

'Typical, typical,' said Harry.

'Then as I kneel down to say my prayers . . . I find it a little difficult to explain.'

'Speak freely, my dear sir, speak freely.'

'Well, then . . . I feel I am being violently interfered with . . . from behind!'

'Ah, yes,' said Harry, 'typical polter . . .' and then he stopped dead in his tracks. Typical indeed! Far, far from it. We were in the presence of the first queer poltergeist in the history of psychic research.

We had no option. We must obviously pursue the inquiry to the bitter end. We entered the haunted rectory. We sat up our usual research paraphernalia of thermometers, tripwires and the rest around the vicar's bed and arranged for him to thump with his stick on the floor as soon as he felt the presence of the poltergeist.

We retired to keep watch in the room next to the vicar's. It was furnished with an enormous four-poster, a sort of rival to the Great Bed of Ware, and a choice view over the owl-haunted churchyard. Harry suggested that he take first watch, while I would take over at one o'clock. I composed myself to sleep . . . Suddenly I woke. The sun was streaming in through the window, and there lay Harry, snoring gently, fast asleep! I shook him hurriedly. He leapt off the bed. 'By heaven, the vicar!' We rushed into the next bedroom, falling over the tripwire on the way. The vicar was sitting up in bed. He regarded us reproachfully. 'I gave you the signal,' he said, 'but no one came.' Then he added more in sorrow than in anger. 'The manifestation occurred three times during the night.'

We had no option but to pack our gladstone bags and retreat. I had found a poltergeist but could not dare put him on the air. This was the non-permissive world of the immediate postwar period. I could not be the pioneer of gay lib in the realm of the occult. Project Poltergeist was abandoned. I admit I missed those adventurous journeys into the unknown with Harry Price. I still regret the moment he faded from my life. Or did he? As I write this, I have a distinct feeling that the air is suddenly getting colder around my desk. Did that picture move? Was that a tap on my shoulder? Do I hear a husky, fascinating voice now whispering to me from the shades, 'At last, my dear fellow, I can give you positive proof.' I dare not look around. I will bring this chapter hurriedly to a close.

Envoi

Back to the Beginnings

'The only reason a man should attempt an autobiography – or, as I prefer to call it – a short account of his life,' said my old Oxford tutor C.T. Atkinson, 'is to trace the steps by which he became the fool he is now. He should put in all the embarrassing slips in life, the hesitations, the false starts. Cromwell as usual was right when he told Lely, "Paint me, warts and all." And when he's finished, his friends may chuckle or curse, the public might be amused, but he, at least, will have come to know the truth about himself.'

'And at what point in his career should he lay down his pen?' I asked anxiously, for at the age of twenty I was already planning a daringly frank and modern *Apologia pro Vita Sua*.

'At fifty,' said Atters firmly. 'If a man doesn't know himself at fifty, he never will.'

Pincher, the portly Sealyham, growled his approval. I think that Atters had just been reading Margot Asquith's memoirs, and as a violent anti-feminist he was not in the best of tempers. But he had a point. After your fiftieth year the world can change around you, but for better or for worse you, yourself, cannot change. There you are, warts and all, for the rest of your life. When I get up to shave in the morning and marvel at the grey-haired, weatherbeaten and lined reflection that stares back at me through the lather, I always have the same thought. Can this really belong to that Welsh Candide I contemplated as I turned over the photographs of my Oxford days?

As a historian I am automatically drawn to dividing my life into ten- or fifteen-year periods. My prehistory began at

Swansea, my Bronze Age continued at Oxford. No question but that my Iron Age took me to my depression days in the Rhondda Valley. My Classical Age saw me in the Imperial Rome of the early BBC. My Dark Ages came with the war. My Middle Ages – well, they came naturally in my own middle age. By the time I was into my fifties, I felt I was in need of a Renaissance. If I could no longer change in myself, at least I could change my surroundings before I fossilized in the attitudes I had been slowly forming over the last twenty years.

The unlikely Erasmus who inspired me to try a new departure at the age of fifty-eight was John Morgan, the distinguished journalist and TV reporter. John also comes from Swansea and its Grammar School but from a younger generation than myself. He reminded me that I once addressed the assembled school in my war correspondent's uniform on my return from the bombing raid over Berlin. 'You looked heroic,' he told me, 'a man capable of anything. Let me now launch you on a more daring raid than your foray over Germany.' He pointed out that in 1967 the TV franchises granted by the Independent Television Authority were coming up for renewal. Why shouldn't we try to form a consortium which would apply for the franchise for Wales and the West. The proposal had one irresistible attraction for me. If we won, it would involve me returning to live in Wales.

Now I am not a fanatical nationalist, a man who believes that there is some special virtue in belonging to a particular race or country. I will admit (to my fellow Welshmen and not, of course, to anyone else) that we Welsh may have our faults and that some of the attributes on which we pride ourselves may not be unique to Wales. In our more expansive moments we see ourselves as naturally witty, articulate and imaginative. We inhabit a world of poetic fantasy denied to the solid, hard-headed English. We are gifted singers and delightful lovers. Fiery and impetuous and Fluellens to a man!

A day spent bargaining with Anglesey farmers at a cattle mart or listening to the debates in the Dyfed County Council will give you a slightly different picture. No matter. All nations need their illusions. I have never ceased to cherish mine. I pictured my return to Wales as a personal Renaissance, a renewal, a start of a new chapter in my life. There came a memorable moment when our consortium of Welsh and West Country applicants (and the inside history of our formation is a story I must relate one day) was invited to send a small delegation to the Independent Broadcasting Authority's headquarters in Knightsbridge one Sunday, to hear the Authority's verdict. Four of us had breakfast secretly with our chairman, Lord Harlech, in the Hyde Park Hotel and slipped quietly through a back door of the ITA building to the back lift up to the eighth floor. The air was full of rumours. The press were watching like hawks. We waited in an alcove to be summoned to the presence of Lord Hill, then the ITA chairman. Along the corridor, accompanied by an embarrassed looking, still busily explaining official, came the unmistakable figure of the late Lord Thompson, his thick glasses twinkling angrily like an old-fashioned army heliograph signalling a Pathan attack on the North-West Frontier. Clearly unpleasant changes had been made in Scotland. What was to be the fate of Wales and the West?

We were ushered into the Chairman's sanctum. We sat before his desk as if we were a group of newly appointed prefects confronting their headmaster. Lord Hill relishes a little drama, especially if he is the centre of it. He looked us up and down, and then said, 'I have invited you here to announce the Authority's decision in the matter of the contracts. After careful consideration, the Authority has decided to offer the franchise for Wales and the West' – and here Lord Hill made a carefully calculated pause – 'to the Harlech Consortium' – I gave a sudden gasp of delight – 'under the following stringent conditions,' Lord Hill continued blandly, looking hard at me. But no conditions can be too stringent to people who are being offered a TV franchise. We agreed to them all. As the interview ended, Lord Hill gave us a warning that the full press treatment was about to descend upon us. 'Do not, therefore, return to that indiscreet caravanserai where you had breakfast.' I have never returned there since!

Instead I returned to Wales to begin the most recent chapter in my life – a chapter which I am happy to feel is still not completed and of which I am continually postponing the final line. I had planned to spend five years as Programme Director in Cardiff and then to retire gracefully. Five eventful and tumultuous years they proved to be, with enough problems to turn anyone's hair white overnight. How could we introduce more programmes in the Welsh language without infuriating our English-speaking listeners? How could we change from black-and-white to colour without bankrupting the company? How could we better the coverage of TV in lonely, narrow Welsh valleys? Complex administrative problems, and as my far more competent colleagues will readily agree, I am not the world's most gifted administrator. Why, then, have I stayed happily on in Wales with the word 'retirement' continually receding towards an ever more distant horizon – or so I hope? The answer, I tell myself secretly, is that at long last in my life, I have found a Cause.

In the Wales of my youth, The Cause was usually a modest chapel founded by a small group who felt so deeply about salvation or conversion, or any one of the thousands of complex subjects that bewilder the outsider as he contemplates theology, that they had to build their own small tabernacle in the heart of the secular wilderness. My own Cause is perhaps less exalted but I have started to devote myself to it with increasing determination as my time slips remorselessly by. I have become a strong defender of the Welsh countryside – and indeed of the whole countryside of Britain.

When I returned to Wales, I found myself, to an ever increasing degree, being drawn back into the general life of the country. I enjoyed a hurried plunge in the Welsh arts world. I served on the Welsh Arts Council, I became a director of the Welsh National Opera Company. I was President of the Contemporary Arts Society. I became a patron of the Great Little Trains of Wales. I was Chairman of the Council for the Protection of Rural Wales. I was even invited to become a member of the Gorsedd and to join the bards in their white robes as they assemble around the stones of the Gorsedd circle during the week of the National Eisteddfod. I felt a slight twinge of conscience about this because, in my irreverent youth, I had concocted a light-hearted poem about the Eisteddfod, in which I imagined Alexander Pope returning (probably with the help of Harry Price) to cast a puzzled eye over the festival. It was a long, long poem – we Welsh don't mind length in poetry – and ended in a finale in which the Adjudicator, carried away by the splendour of Welsh choral singing, took upon himself the task of picturing the Wales to come:

'All hail,' he cries, 'Ye more than heavenly choirs!
Your music fills me with prophetic fires,
I see a vision of the Promised Land,
Wales of the Future, jet-propelled and planned.
A super-streamlined Principality,
Ruled by Big Business, Science and TUC,
See Snowdon's Sacred Heart is blasted wide,
While pipe-lines like spaghetti strew her side,
See night-clubs double Aberdaron's charms,
And Coleg Harlech safe in Butlin's arms.
Flame-throwers and tanks on Berwyn's heights shall roam.
All Pembrokeshire one glorious aerodrome!
The Church replaced by cinema and bank!
Capel Bethesda run by Arthur Rank!
See Jazz go up, Canu Penillion down,
See Saunders Lewis pensioned by the crown!
The last Welsh-speaker parcelled and addressed
To the St Fagan's Home of Cultural Rest!

As I walked with my fellow-initiate, Alun Williams of the BBC, towards the Archdruid waiting in the splendour of his golden Celtic decorations at the Logan Stone, I couldn't help thinking of my Popian vision of the Wales to which I was now so happily reuniting myself. How much of the prophecy had been fulfilled? Luckily a lot of it – like most forecasts – was very wide of the mark, but enough of the lines were a little too close to fulfilment for my liking. The flame-throwers and tanks may not possess the wilder uplands, but the forestry certainly does. Is the landscape of Wales destined to become a collection of pretty postcard peeps between pine trees? Does it matter if it does?

I feel that it matters profoundly. If you destroy the countryside of Wales you destroy the nation itself. I walk again on the great uplifted ridge of the Carmarthenshire Van, where I first had my vision of the glory of the Welsh landscape, and fear that in my own time I may see the motorways, the caravan parks, the industrial estates, the housing developments, the quarries and the pylons creep up almost to the foot of those nobly layered Old Red Sandstone cliffs that encircle the dark waters of Llyn-y-Van Fach. Not if I can help it, I vow.

So, as I pass into my seventies, I still tramp through the valleys and hills broadcasting as I go. I plan my yearly television series to take the camera into parts of the country which are not usually visited by the tourists. I like to feel that I am passing on a message to my fellow Welshmen. 'Look on this carefully. If you let it be destroyed, you will, whether you realize it or not, be living in a poorer, meaner, less worthwhile world.'

Sometimes a rage seizes me as I see the spoilers at work, and I call for a new Ice Age:

> Lord, let Thy glaciers come again,
> Out from Snowdonia's fastness flow
> Thy rivers of avenging ice.
> Remote, remorseless, cold and slow.
> To pile, in one supreme moraine,
> Our godless Cities of the Plain.
>
> In snow-numbed silence let them move
> Through Birmingham and Coventry,
> Down every foul arterial road,
> To sweep into the cleansing sea
> Pylon and pump and caravan,
> The muck that marks the Common Man.
>
> One rocky ark of refuge leave
> Above the icy winding sheet
> Where, huddled in their rusting cars,
> The shivering last survivors meet,
> There, Lord, if so Thy Mercy please –
> Leave them one space – to use their knees!

But then I remember that some of the doughtiest defenders of the landscape of Wales have come from the huge industrial centres like Birmingham or Coventry. I hurry to give them hope and encouragement in a vision of a world where the glaciers of development have melted. We start again with a clean sheet:

At last, the warm reviving Spring
Shall make the prisoned waters run,
And over Earth's returning green
The trees cast shadows in the sun,
Till, through a soft, caressive rain,
A man-free Eden blooms again.

No changing gears disturb the peace
Where, clear of oil, the waters lie,
And sweet the untransistored birds
Shall sing beneath a jet-free sky.
The whole bright world will bathe anew
In crystal, non-detergent dew.

Oh, might we enter, hand in hand.
New Adam and his fairer Eve,
Whom no forbidden fruit could tempt
Or serpent stupidly deceive;
For who would dare confess the crime
Of Eden lost a second time?

I re-read that last page and a doubt creeps in. Here am I,
brought up as an agnostic, immediately starting to yield to the
one temptation that besets all Welshmen who talk. I am
starting to preach. I have even written two hymns. I am almost
about to launch into the *hwyl* – that mesmeric chant of the old
artists of the Welsh pulpit whose voices rose higher and higher
as they approached the climax of the sermon, and the congre-
gation rallied with encouraging Amens. One of my uncles used
to carry a tuning fork to chapel, and as the minister rocked the
roof with the splendour of his eloquence, uncle would strike
the tuning fork and cry out in admiration, 'Top C! Top C! Well
done, Williams bach!'

No, I must cut out the *hwyl*, for the only way we can save
the Welsh landscape – and the English, Scottish and Irish
landscape too – is by endless cunning. The price of beauty is
eternal vigilance. We will win the battle if we can convince the
spoilers that development need not involve destruction and
that care for a landscape actually pays. To be commercially
minded need not mean being bloody-minded.

In the early days of television, just after the war, I interviewed the great Frank Lloyd Wright, the pioneer of modern
architecture, the revered prophet of generations of young

aspirants to be the heirs of Bramante, Wren and Adams, the man whose revolutionary hotel in Tokyo was the only one to survive the Great Earthquake of 1921. He had been invited to receive an honorary degree from the University of Wales in a ceremony at Bangor. Wright was intensely proud of his family connection with Wales and had named three of his houses after the ancient Welsh poet, Taliesin. Television had limitations in those days. The nearest point to which we could bring a mobile studio and transmitter was Rhyl. We invited Wright to join us at Rhyl and booked the man who had propelled American architecture into the Twentieth century to stay at that masterpiece of early Edwardian fretwork, the Queen's Hotel.

Frank Lloyd Wright must have been well over eighty at the time, a thin upright figure with a face of leathery parchment, like one of those Middle West farmers Gar Wood delighted to paint. He gave the impression of immense wisdom in reserve. He was accompanied by a delicious secretary in her twenties. Before the camera he appeared extremely fragile. Viewers would amost expect him to pass away in front of them. I resolved to lead him on quickly to the heritage he would leave behind him, and after a discussion about his ideals and the principles on which he had based his lifework, I introduced the subject of his legacy to posterity.

'Have you got any young disciples,' I asked, 'to whom – how shall I put it? – you are going to hand over the torch?'

He gave me a slightly old-fashioned look, but went on. 'Yes, sir. I'm glad to say that I have a group of splendid young men working with me, and we have a great number of exciting projects in hand – the new centre at Baton Rouge, the extension to the Guggenheim Museum, the Mile High Project. And if the Lord spares me . . .' (here I looked suitably reverent) . . . if the Lord spares me, as I devoutly hope He will,' (a slight pause from the Master and then the pay-off line) 'I reckon we'll clean up a cool three million.'

No, I have never had the chance of cleaning up anything in the world of high finance, and quite frankly I've never tried and could not care. I have enough to allow me to live as most sensible men would wish to live, in a house overlooking the sea at Fishguard. It was built by Sir Evan Jones, the friend of Lloyd

George, who constructed the Fishguard breakwater at the end of a long and successful career as a great contractor for big-scale engineering around the Empire. 'Pentower' is the direct antithesis of our avant-garde flat in Hampstead. There are Art Nouveau decorations everywhere, delicious curlicues on the fireplaces, teak panelling in the dining room. The entrance hall, with flights of stairs starting off in all directions, is the perfect setting for one of those Aldwych farces in which Tom Walls and Ralph Lynn hopped in and out of the wrong bedrooms, while Robertson Hare lost his trousers at regular intervals to the perpetual cry of 'Oh, calamity'. Upstairs, there is a small suite which, we flatter ourselves, was used by Lloyd George himself – but exactly for what, history does not relate! It all reminds me that, by birth, I am an Edwardian. I have settled back into my own period.

The garden overlooks the sea. Charlotte finds the sea wind and the rocky, salted soil somewhat unkind to a keen gardener, but I selfishly rejoice in the view out over the old harbour, the eighteenth-century fort on the point and the great hull of Dinas Head rising above the gorse-clad hills. The pointed cone of Carn Ingli makes an elegant climax to the landscape to the north. The Irish boats round the breakwater and the gulls wheel in a white cloud around them. All except Nelson, the bold seagull who has adopted us, and arrives promptly at five o'clock to tap on the window with his beak until I come out to feed him by hand with the scraps we have saved from lunch. I have never seen plumage of such pristine whiteness.

On a writing day I put my pen down at five o'clock and turn to the piano in the corner of my studio. It is the Broadwood which belonged to my father and on which he composed his music. My pianistic powers are limited and critics tell me that my interpretation of the Chopin preludes sounds best from the garden through two closed doors. I don't mind. Music means most to me when it flows out from under my own fingers.

Thursday, in Fishguard, is Market Day. Fishguard people, in the Pembrokeshire dialect, call it '*Shwd 'da chi heddi, heddi*' – or in English, market day is a 'how are you today' day. I walk along the little Regency street of Tower Hill, past my local,

View from "Pentower"

The Globe, to the square where The Royal Oak still proudly shows the room in which the French signed the treaty of surrender after the last invasion of Britain in 1797. All the way I hear the greeting. '*Shwd 'da chi heddi*, Mr Thomas.' Yes, I'm sure I now belong.

So here I've settled in my house above the sea, looking down on the 'heron-priested shore'. From it, I still make my happy forays back into the big world. For if – as that cunning old guide I met so long ago in Naples maintained – life is like the Solfatara, I think that, at long last, I have discovered how to pass over the more dangerous parts in safety. I get ready for fifteen more years of adventure. I pour out a glass of Cockburn's '55 from the cellar and drink to the future in the traditional Welsh toast, '*Pob llwyddiant i'r Achos*' – all success to the Cause! But what cause, only a Welshman can tell you!